TIME
TO WAKE UP
My Love

DO NOT SPEAK
UNLESS IT IMPROVES SILENCE

ELISHA ROSE

Elisha Rose
Time to Wake Up My Love

Copyright © 2025 by Elisha Rose
First Edition

Paperback ISBN 978-1-7388850-5-3
Hardcover ISBN 978-1-7388850-3-9
Ebook ISBN 978-1-7388850-4-6

All rights reserved under International and Pan-American Copyright Conventions. Manufactured in Canada.

No part of this publication may be reproduced, stored in, or introduced into a retrieval system, transmitted in any form or by any means (electronic, mechanical, photocopying, recording, or otherwise), and/or otherwise used in any manner for purposes of training artificial intelligence technologies to generate text, including, without limitation, technologies that are capable of generating works in the same style or genre as this publication, without the prior written permission of the publisher.

This book is sold subject to the condition that it shall not, by way of trade or otherwise, be lent, resold, hired out, or otherwise circulated without the publisher's prior written consent in any form of binding, cover, or condition other than that in which it was published.

Book Design | Petya Tsankova
Editor | Alison Whyte
Publishing Management | TSPA The Self Publishing Agency, Inc.

I dedicate this book to all the unspeakable mistakes.

As I lay down on the grass,
It makes me feel like an hourglass,
In the end I feel a little doubt,
I feel my time is going to run out.
—Hailey Rose

CONTENTS

AUTHOR'S NOTE	1
PROLOGUE	3

PART I *Time*

1. The Dwelling Place	7
2. A Boy I See	19
3. Moments of Wallowing	31
4. Not Smart Enough	41
5. Feeling Forever Less	55
6. The Building with a "t"	65
7. Daughter of a King	77

PART II *Wake*

8. Green Eyes	89
9. The Truth According to…	103
10. Wanna See a Big Dick?!	127
11. Grief Is for the Living	145
12. A Monster Calls	157
13. End of the Season	173
14. I Am Worthy 101	185

PART III *Love*

15. A Barbie Girl	199
16. Rose-Coloured Glasses	213
17. Most Much More	225
18. Dragons and Red Coats	241
19. I and the Father	255
20. Long Haul	267
21. Don't Run Away, Walk ON!	277
EPILOGUE	289
ACKNOWLEDGEMENTS	293

The two most powerful forces are patience and time

AUTHOR'S NOTE

My truth is all I have. My truth is my freedom.

I wrote this book to clear the record so I can live my life with transparency and move forward with authenticity and integrity. I share my truth to bring an end to the silent shame I have long felt and in hopes of helping others understand their own trauma.

I made a choice and took the chance to end the silence because I want to inspire others to be authentic. Healing will always bring discomfort, but refusing to heal is worse for everyone. When you avoid the hard work of recovery, everyone around you suffers. I am an addict who is still in recovery, and this is my story from the beginning.

This story includes descriptions of emotional, physical, psychological, and sexual abuse. It is sometimes graphic and may be triggering for readers. If you are a survivor of violence, addiction, or intergenerational trauma and feel triggered, please be gentle with yourself.

This book is not fictionalized, and I took great care to be as accurate as possible, using my own journals as a guide with respect to timelines, dialogues, and settings. Some names, distinguishing features, and locations have been changed to help protect the privacy of certain individuals.

*Knowing who you are is hard,
so give yourself a fucking break*

PROLOGUE

I am breathing in the fresh air, smelling the scent of straw, and feeling the moisture of the dew. The sun rises, and bright orange and pink colours reach across the horizon. I watch as the shadows slowly fade across the earthly shapes: snow-covered mountains in the distance surrounding a lake—its reflection a faultless portrayal.

Eyes are upon me, a deer in the distant meadow. Sitting on top of a haybale, I watch her gaze at me.

Coffee? I smell coffee!

The smell of coffee pulls me away from the beauty of my dream. I am barely awake and still laying motionless.

I hear the lightest sound of footsteps and the creak of the door as it opens. My head is turned to my left, my arms under the covers. I hear and feel a light breath of wind that sends shivers down my neck. A hand reaches for my face and strokes back into my hairline. The bed shifts as his weight pulls me into his touch. As he bends down towards me, his lips sweep across my neck, then to my eyes and finally they tickle my cheekbone. I smile, feeling so adored by his touch. His lips move, hanging tenderly above my ear as he whispers, "It's time to wake up, my love."

I open my eyes to a dark room, a dark space, and a dark reality. I roll over to the other side. I close my eyes again praying for the dream of light to come back, for him to come back. Who was he? The voice was unfamiliar. Those words echo louder as I try to keep my eyes shut. "Time to wake up, my love." I start crying, wishing I was dead, hoping to disappear into dust. I crave his warmth, but I don't understand it. How can I dream of someone I have never seen?

I am pulled out of my depressive state by the feeling of hair against my chest. I push it away with my hand. Her pearl-like skin glows in the moonlight, each freckle a silhouette on her tiny button nose, her forehead, and her cheeks. Her face presses into my chest while her arms squeeze her teddy bear tight. I feel so heavy, as if someone has put a stack of bricks on me. I move my leg to feel another foot twice the size of mine. I can't move my arm as another weighs it down. A loud, deep sound comes from behind my neck. I dare not move. Is this another dream within a dream moment? Or am I going insane? As I question my state of mind, wondering if I've finally gone batshit crazy, my daughter turns over, pushing her little butt into my abdomen. I feel the vibration of air come out her ass cheeks.

FRAAP!

Then there is a series of little puffs, accelerating, as the last of her fart escapes.

THPPTPHPHPHHPH.

"Hailey! Are you fucking kidding me!?" my son yells from the other side of the bed, angry at this rude awakening.

I start giggling as I catch a slight smile creep across her face.

Nope! I was definitely *not* dreaming.

PART I

Time
Being nice is a choice—so is being a jerk

What if I took all the responsibility?
Then would I be loved?

The Dwelling Place
1. *Tacheeda Lakes, 1994*

I have sand everywhere. Dad lets us play naked in the cut banks. My little brother has sand rings around his mouth and eyes. I am brushing off my sister—she has gotten sand in her eyes. I look up and, in the distance, I see my mother. She is pacing back and forth at our campsite.

"She doesn't look happy, Joe!" my uncle says, turning to look at my father.

My father doesn't say a word, but I hear the boat motor rev up.

The look on my mother's face says it all.

I remember her words from that morning's conversation: *Please, Joe. I have a gig tonight and need you here by 3:00 pm.*

"Where have you *been?!*" my mother shouts.

I take both my brother and sister by the hand while my dad and uncle bring up the boat. My mother is still yelling at my dad, waving her arms like a bird and losing her shit. I have a bad feeling, so I decide to hide my siblings in a nearby bush.

"Stay here!" I tell them firmly.

My dad still hasn't said a word to my mother. She is directly behind him, still yelling while my uncle walks on ahead of him. I start walking up to the picnic table, and that's when I hear it.

WAP!

I freeze. It sounded like a gunshot, but deeper.

My mother comes from a family of six. She is the youngest, born and raised in Prince George, BC. I may be biased, but I think my mother is stunning and out of all her siblings, her beauty glows the brightest. She has long, dirty blonde, curly hair, bright blue eyes, and a smile that can melt your soul. But for all her beauty, it's her character and talent that make the biggest impression. She grew up learning the guitar, singing, and writing songs. Her handwriting alone would make you jealous; she has such incredible penmanship that it made forging notes in high school impossible for me. She used to sing and dance in beauty pageants, designing and making her own clothes in her spare time. My mother is a hippie. She loves her weed, too. She brags she doesn't smoke cigarettes anymore to my father, yet she smokes her weed on a daily basis. She is funny that way and quick with her sense of wit.

Her mother was a stay-at-home mom to her, her siblings, and any neighbourhood children that needed her. My grandmother was a hard-working woman. Mondays still bring on my mother's fondest memory of her mother: the smell of freshly baked bread, over a dozen loafs, and homemade cinnamon buns every week. My grandmother's loving touch shone through her baking—it brought everyone home. The only time she ever got angry was when she caught someone cheating at cards. She would never play with them again, ever! Otherwise, I never heard her raise her voice, but she was always honest with her words. If someone wasn't her cup of tea, she would simply whisper, "I don't much care for her."

She taught me how to take care of people, but she also taught me to be true to myself. And best of all, she taught me to have a sense of humour. I remember our last conversation before she passed away on January 2, 2016. She looked at me and said, "I just want my girl to be happy!" I didn't fully understand her soft words at the time, but I dwell on them now. As I contemplated them at her bedside that day, she said softly, "And your sister is my favourite granddaughter." Ha!

My mother's father was a taxi driver; he was well-known in his community and people respected him. He was a natural entertainer. He loved to shoot pool, sing, and play guitar. My grandfather taught my mother everything he knew about music, and my mother passed all this on to me. I don't play guitar, but I can sing. I'd say my voice is ok, but my daughter says it sounds like an angel from heaven. My grandfather was a good father and husband. Every Valentine's Day, he would buy his wife a single orchid. He was a kind and loving grandfather, always making his grandkids laugh. I remember him pulling out his false teeth and making zombie noises while chasing us around the house. He adored my sister, my brother, and me. As a child I didn't know him very well or even see him all that often, but I do remember that he often looked tired. He always seemed so very tired. I know now that he struggled with addiction.

My grandfather was an alcoholic.

"When you're raised by an alcoholic, you either become one or you abstain from it." These were my mother's painful words as she witnessed the acts of cruelty this disease inflicted on her life. She herself wasn't corrupted by the disease, but she lost a sister to it.

I only ever saw my grandfather cry once. He had suffered a major heart attack and was never able to fully recover from it. Within two years, his body slowly started to fail him. I was in his room at the hospital, swinging my feet as I perched on a chair by his bedside. I was looking out the window and singing. I was singing a song I didn't fully know the lyrics to, but I'd heard my mother sing this song so often, part of it was embedded in my memory.

"But you lied to me, set my heart free.

I love you. I will always love you."

I heard my mother say, as she entered the room, "Dad? Is everything ok?"

I stopped singing and looked at my grandfather; his eyes, full of tears, stared back deeply into mine. My mother moved towards him, but he held his hand up to her. Without looking away from me, he said, "Sing, my angel." Then he wrapped his arms around my mother and cried while I sang.

My grandfather passed away on January 25, 1996. At that time, I was just ten years old, and I didn't know that my grandfather had written that song for my grandmother. He titled it, "Garden of Roses." She was his darling, his soulmate, and the love of his life.

I still sing that song to this day and often to my daughter. I find it magical that my favourite flowers are *roses*, and I am covered in a *garden* of them all over my body. I can feel my grandparents all over me—their love, their creativity, and their authenticity. I truly believe that we are a product of our ancestors and that a part of them lives on in us. That part? Their soul. It's why we look or act a certain way, and it's why a family member says, "You're just like your mother!" I remember asking my grandfather, "Grandpa, what is your favourite colour?"

"Purple," he replied.

Purple! It's my favourite colour, too.

My father comes from a family of five. He was the youngest boy, born and raised in Prince George, BC. My father got himself into everything as a young man. Drugs, drinking, girls, and lots of fighting. Most of my father's best friends were guys he fought. He was mean and foolish, surrounding himself with bad influences. My father is very rough around the edges, yet with a slightly higher pitched voice than his father. He has dark brown hair, a strong nose, and a square jaw line. His eyes are blue, but darker than my mother's. They are compelling but also terrifying sometimes. My father can do anything, a jack of all trades. He trained as a mechanic, but he also worked as a welder, a plumber, and an electrician. Above all, he followed God.

His mother, "Oma" as we grandchildren all called her, was German, and she fled through Poland during World War II, eventually coming to Canada. My Oma was remarkably disciplined and brought order and structure to the home. At the same time, through her soft direction, she *loved* a lot and *forgave* even more. Her dedication to her faith led her in everything she did.

I was my parents' first child, and apparently, I was not an easy baby. My mother would give in to my every demand. Any time I woke up in the middle of the night, she would make me a bottle of milk and come to soothe me and quiet my crying. Until one final night, my Oma stood outside my bedroom door and refused to move! My father had to hold my mother as she became hysterical, hearing me scream louder and louder for her. My mother begged my Oma to let her see me, but my Oma stood guard outside my door all night. After hours of crying, I soothed myself and went back to sleep. It was a long night for my mother, my father, and me.

The next morning, my mother woke up early and raced to my room with my father by her side, but I was not there. They found me in the kitchen in my Oma's arms, a big smile on my face as my Oma covered me in kisses. The smell of homemade porridge and coffee filled the room. My eyes were blotchy from crying most of the night, but my mother saw the love I was given—more love than ever.

I never cried at night again after that.

My Oma taught me how to love, how to cook, how to serve others, and most of all, how to persevere. When I was younger, she gave me structure in my studies. She would sit with me for hours and make me read out loud. She would make me start from the beginning if I didn't pause where I was supposed to, or if I tried to add a word that wasn't actually written. My Oma, in my eyes, was fearless and stunning. My father worshipped her too. He melted around her.

My Oma died of cancer in 1996. She was only sixty-two. I remember it like it was yesterday. I was ten years old, coming home from school, when I saw my father walking from the hayfield by our house. I could see the look of pain in his eyes. As my father placed his hands on my shoulders, he got down on his knees, and his eyes filled with tears. With his touch I knew, I knew my Oma had gone to heaven.

My father's father worked for the railroad as a conductor. Out of all my grandparents, he was the scariest. I was terrified of this man. His voice alone was like thunder and his temper made you run out of the room. As a child, I could never find the courage to look into my grandfather's eyes.

He made an issue out of everything and if you didn't see it his way, you got his temper. In some cases, he'd hit us. My grandfather was an abusive man and an alcoholic. Hitting was his way of discipline. He lacked order in his own life and became uncontrollable. My father told me that, as a child, he never once fought with his father. But when he was sixteen years old, and on the cusp of becoming a young man, he challenged his father for the first time to protect his mother. My grandfather was angry and was beating her. My father stood between his dad and his mother, using his body to protect her.

In tears, he held up a single hand and said, "*Stop!* Please Dad, Stop!"

When I asked my father why he had never fought back before, he answered, "I respected my father."

"Weren't you scared of your father?" I asked.

"I was terrified of him, but I respected him because he taught me how to be a man," he said. "Yes, he had his flaws, he wasn't perfect, but he loved me."

Then he told me how his father used to call him Joey—a nickname he adored. "Come here, Joey!" he'd say, beckoning with his hand. My father would grab a pillow and place it on his father's legs and lay his head there while my grandfather stroked his hair.

I don't have many memories of my grandfather. To me, he was a hard man with a really deep, scary voice. I didn't like being in the same room with him. I felt he was indifferent towards girls. He preferred boys.

My father took my siblings and me to Vancouver to visit him once. We were all walking along a path in a park and my brother, who was three at the time, spotted the biggest black slug he'd ever seen. He loved little critters; they were his friends. He'd collect them and then my mother would find dried up worms in his pockets because he'd forgotten about them. He loved to throw snails at my sister and me. He thought bugs were the coolest things—they were all precious to him.

When he saw this huge slug, my brother raced over to pet it, but just before his little hand could touch this beautiful creature, my grandfather's big boot stomped on it, and green slime oozed out from under it. My brother screamed in horror and started wailing. My grandfather didn't understand what had just happened. He reached out to take my brother's hand, but he pushed it away and ran into my father's arms. I watched intently as my father tried to explain to his father what he had just done.

"Dad! Dad, you don't understand. They are his buddies," my dad pleaded.

My grandfather looked at my father as if he had three heads. He could not see it his way. As my dad wiped my brother's tears away, he started laughing at his father's destructive behaviour, traumatizing his grandson over a little critter. My grandfather tried several times to get close to my brother after that, but my brother wouldn't have it. He called him a monster.

It wasn't until years later that my grandfather was finally forgiven. He was visiting for Christmas and had bought my brother a make-your-own-critter kit with molds, plastic, and glue. Finally, my brother could *make* his little buddies. Worms, beetles, snails, and even a big slug. Like my dad said, he wasn't perfect, but he loved people in his own way. My grandfather's lesson to me was that even a monster can love.

When my grandfather died at the age of seventy-one in 2005, his one wish was to be buried with my Oma. My grandparents had separated many years before. My grandfather united with another woman but never remarried. My Oma remained alone and dedicated her life to her grandchildren. On his deathbed, however, my grandfather expressed a lot of fear and regret. He left everything to his common law partner, but he requested that his remains be interred with my Oma.

My mother met my father at a house party completely by accident. She went to the party with another guy who turned out to be creepy as fuck, so she used my father as an escape. With no warning, she pulled him in and laid a big fat kiss on him! Trust me, he didn't mind. In September 1986, they had their first child, a little girl. My mother stole my name from my aunt. I was only six months old when my mother got pregnant again. My sister was born in December 1987. Then in September 1989, after my mother had prayed for a son, my baby brother came along.

We were each other's world. Growing up in the country gave us a sense of belonging as we played in the hayfields and created our own adventures. We were taught to work hard, to be disciplined, and above all, to love one another.

I watch in horror as my mother's legs go up and over the table. Her body flops down on the other side of it, and she lays there whimpering. Still frozen in place, I look at my father. His hand is still, and his eyes are on mine. I dare not move. I don't recognize him as my father. He is like some green-eyed monster. Green? But his eyes are blue? He leaves her there and continues his task. I feel safe to move and slowly make my way to my mother. Her long, blonde, curly hair covers her face. I can hear her breathing and her cries. I gently touch her hair, but she slaps my hand away.

"Mom, it's me, Elisha," I tell her.

"Where are your brother and sister?" she asks. I point to the spot where I have hidden them. I look back at her. Her bright blue eyes are on me, and blood seeps from her nose and lip as she slowly sits up. I stare at her. It is the first time I have ever seen her like this, the first time I have ever seen my father hit my mother.

A short time after that, my mother separated from my father. All four of us drove away in a police car that day, escaping another episode of abuse. I remember staring out the back window, my father nowhere in sight.

We moved downtown, close to my grandpa's favourite pub, which was called First Liter. I called our new home "the shacks." There were what seemed like a never-ending series of apartments, row upon row, and we were in number 18. I hated my mother for taking us into the city. It was not my home. I wanted to live with Dad in the country where I could stare out my window at the stars. Instead, I looked out the window and saw buildings, all with the same beige siding. In front of me was the street. I wasn't used to seeing so many people; some were walking really slowly, but most of them sat down wherever they wanted. I thought they must be really tired like my dad after he got home from work. Other people on the street looked like my dad covered in dirt and grease. I assumed they were all mechanics like he was.

I had never seen so much garbage. It was everywhere, and the city smelled of rotten eggs and baby puke. I hated it. I remembered the smell of flowers, of clean air that you could taste something sweet from, and I could feel the tears run down my cheek. I stared at the number 18 of our new home: a home without my father. I overheard Mom talking to Grandma saying he wasn't allowed to visit, something about a "restraining order." I had no idea what that meant other than we could only see Dad once a week. I was very angry at my mother for taking me away from my father.

I hated my new school and the girls. They all looked at me differently, told me I had weird clothes and that I smelled funny.

That part didn't bother me, but the way they talked? The bad words? My dad would have bent me over his knee and spanked my ass for saying those bad words. But my dad wasn't there. I missed him and my old school in the country so much. But then I had an idea. I decided to learn some of those bad words I was hearing from the older boys.

"Fuck!" My first swear word.

"Fuck, Fuck, Fuck!" I repeated it while spinning faster and faster on the merry-go-round. I really liked that bad word. I could say that bad word because my father wasn't there.

After school I always had to go find my sister so we could walk home together. She was easy to find in her pretty dresses and pigtails. I hated dresses and stuff in my hair. I preferred boy clothes. They were way more comfortable, and I could run super fast in those boy clothes.

One day, my sister's eyes were red and puffy. As I got closer, I could see she was crying; she had tears in her eyes. She was holding her teacher's hand. Then I saw blood coming from my sister's wrist. The teacher was making her bleed. Her nails were in my sister's skin, squeezing her hand so hard, my sister's skin turned red. I don't know what my sister did to deserve this, but I guess the teacher was disciplining her for something. I lost control and threw myself at her teacher. I started screaming, pulling at her hair, and scratching her face with my hands. I felt something pulling at me, but I dug my grip into the teacher's neck as hard as I could.

The next thing I knew, my sister and I were waiting in the office for my mother. She was still crying.

"Let me see," I said, reaching for her hands.

I took her tiny wrist in my hands and started kissing her bleeding wounds with my lips. I used my shirt to wipe her tears and then used the dampness from her tears to clean her arm. I missed my father. He wasn't there to protect us. I felt responsible for my sister, but I also felt abandoned by him. Didn't my father love me enough to keep his anger in check? What if I took all the responsibility? Then would I be loved?

Someone
I can call mine

A Boy I See
2. *Sisto Road, 1991*

I look outside my bedroom window and see nothing. A layer of white fog covers over my backyard and trees. I have to get up for school. I look over at my younger sister who is sleeping peacefully. I hear footsteps and rush back under my covers and pretend to sleep. *I love this part.* His cold, hard, calloused hands brush my hair away from my face. He lays his hand on my cheek. The cold on my face feels like icicles. The next thing I feel on my cheek is as rough as sandpaper.

"Time to get up, sweetie!" my father says while petting my hair with his cold hand and squishing his spikey whiskers into my cheek. He showers me with kisses before he leaves for work. I climb down from my high bunk bed and go in the kitchen to look at the stove clock. The clock says six-one-five, and I have to leave when the clock says seven-zero-zero. That is what Dad says.

I hear his service truck start pulling away and race to the window. I place my index finger on the window and hold it in place. He does the same to his truck window as he pulls out of the driveway. I stand there for a while, thinking of the story my mother told me from when I was a toddler. Anytime I heard my father leave, I would go to the window and point at him. Before he would leave, he would place his index finger up against the window, mirroring mine. It became a ritual that I decided to continue.

I can't wait until tomorrow when Dad is home. No work on the weekends! I make my way to the kitchen and pour myself a big bowl of Captain Crunch cereal—my favourite. I'm sitting at the kitchen table and swinging my feet back and forth as I count the number of yellow items my mother has in her kitchen. Everything is bright yellow and has the words "no name" written on it. I lose count after twenty. I finish my bowl of Captain Crunch and throw my dish and spoon in the sink that is still filled with cold and greasy water from last night's dishes. I go to the fridge and grab the yellow "no name" package of bologna and the "mouse turd." I start giggling inside thinking of the nickname I have given the mustard; I am sure it's the funniest thing ever.

"Hey Dad, can you pass the mouse turd?" I say, thinking about how my dad would laugh, but my mother? Not so much. She had zero tolerance for goofing around at the table. Sometimes she would get so mad at Dad for goofing off she would slam her plate down and stomp out of the kitchen saying bad words under her breath. If my mom wasn't home for dinner one night, out for a girl's night, Dad would mimic her. He'd act just like her, throwing his hands up, waving back and forth stomping around the house. My sister, brother, and I would laugh hysterically. My sister laughed so hard once, milk came out of her nose.

I am supposed to make a bologna sandwich for lunch. I grab the bread, the cutting board, and a knife. I place my slices of bread side by side and squirt the "mouse turd" on both sides of bread. I don't like the way my mother makes my sandwiches; she only puts a little mustard, and it dries up into the bread by the time you eat it. I like *a lot* of mouse turd. I look around me before

I slice two big pieces of bologna. (I am only allowed one.) I slap my bologna and mouse turd sandwich together and pat it like a baby's butt. Before I place it in a sandwich baggy, I take a big bite out of it—to mark my territory so everyone knows it's my damn sandwich.

I head to the closet and roll my eyes at the sight of all the matching outfits my sister and I have to wear.

"So much pink, barf!" I mutter. I hate my clothes, and I hate dressing like a girl. I want to be a boy so badly.

I find a white, long-sleeve turtleneck, a pair of black sweatpants, and a couple of mismatched socks—one blue and the other white. I brush my hair and teeth and tie my hair into a ponytail. I do want to be a boy, but I still love my long blonde hair. I make my bed quietly and then find my backpack. Staring at the damn thing, I give it the stink eye and say, "Chicken fart nuggets!" My mother doesn't understand how much I *hate* pink. And look at all the girly crap on it: glitter, sparkles, some fuzzy crap, and all *pink*.

Why me? Why can't she just doll up my sister more? *My sister* actually likes this stuff. Why can't she leave me alone in the boys' department with the water guns, slime balls, and cool clothing. I hate my life. I turn my head away from this abomination to look at the clock: six-five-one. Turkey biscuits! I have got to go. I put on my jacket and boots and grab the pink, girly, fart, eyesore and throw it over my shoulder.

I can barely see, the fog is so bad and have to walk what seems like a lifetime to get to my bus stop. As I turn the corner, I hear the cars on the highway and know I'm close. They are already standing there, the three bigger boys and a girl. I go to my usual spot, standing a little farther away from where they are all waiting. Looking down at my feet, I start kicking a couple of rocks. Minding my own business and humming to myself, I suddenly hear something behind me. I turn to look, but nothing is there. I can still hear something, it's getting closer and louder, but I can't see anything. Confused, I start to turn back around to face the highway and bus stop. My heart jumps as I see a dark figure is standing in front of me.

I grew up being the boy I wanted to see. I loved playing with my homemade wooden sling shot, shooting squirrels, and scaring the birds away. My mother was always yelling after me as I disappeared into the woods, leaving behind my sister and her Barbie dolls. I loved playing with Lego and racing cars with my little brother, but he was too young to come with me on my adventures. I would steal one of my dad's work shirts and a pair of black sweatpants, rolling them up as they were always too long for my little legs. Before I left, I would make my sister help duct tape my boobs together—another girly trait I hated. I was not looking forward to "becoming a woman," as my mother would put it. I dreaded the day I would bleed out of my furry beaver. Gross.

Often, I would pretend I was lost and become a hunter, looking for animal tracks and scat, covering my face with mud to camouflage myself from predators. I loved climbing trees and always went up as far as I could. Sometimes, the trees would be so close together, I could go to the edge and tie the branches together, making a little hammock. I would just lay there and breathe in the fresh air and enjoy the view of Pilot Mountain with its endless trees, lined up, row upon row, all different shades of green. The only girly thing I allowed myself to keep was my voice. I loved singing more than anything in the world. It brought me joy when I was sad and comfort when I was alone. The most beautiful thing to me was singing myself to sleep. I remember one day just about to drift off as I sang "Amazing Grace" up high in my tree hammock.

"Elisha!"

I ignored my mother and kept singing.

"ELISHA!"

I continued to sing louder.

"ELISHAAA! Do not make me get your father!"

"Goddammit!" I yelled out loud, and then remembered I am not supposed to take the Lord's name in vain. *Shit!* "I'm coming!" I shouted in a snarky tone. *Please forgive me, Lord*, I silently prayed, looking up to the sky. I climbed down, taking my sweet time. Eventually, I reached the ground, where my golden retriever, Douglee, was waiting, wagging his tail and ready to lead the way. I walked as slowly as possible, finally coming out of the woods into the clearing and my backyard. There, standing in the grass in front of our woodshed, my father waited. I immediately slowed down even more, looking down at my feet.

"Hustle!" his deep voice barked. I started running until I was standing right in front of him. "Look at me!" I slowly looked up from my feet to meet his eyes. I noticed they weren't green and felt my heartrate go down just a little. "Did you hear your mother?" my father asked.

I wanted to lie so badly, but I knew he was a smart man. I also knew that lying guaranteed an ass whooping.

"Yes," was all I could say, as softly as possible.

"Then why didn't you answer her the first time?" His eyes stared, and a frown appeared on his forehead.

"I…I wanted to finish my song, and she was interrupting me," I stammered.

All of a sudden, his whole body shifted and relaxed. His eyes softened slightly. "Elisha, you come when your mother calls the first time." I looked down.

"Pardon me!?" he yelled.

"Yes, Dad!" I replied.

He motioned for me to come with him and get washed up for dinner. I started walking beside him and placed my little hand in his. I dared not look at him just yet.

"What song were you singing?" he inquired.

"'Amazing Grace.' I heard it in church last Sunday," I said with a smile as I looked up at him. He shot me a look, and I saw a smile meet mine. If I mentioned God, church, or my singing, my father melted every time.

Later that evening, the house was finally quiet, and I slowly made my way to the kitchen. The clock said one-one-two. It was dark, but the moon was so bright, it lit the pathway into the woods. Douglee was waiting for me; he knew it was time. It was so hot that day, and I was sweating climbing out of the kitchen window. I waited until my feet touched the woodshed below. I made it look like the window was closed but left it cracked open slightly. I climbed out onto the right side of the shed where I knew an old fridge was leaning against the side. I used it like a step and then jumped down to the earth. *Thump!* My body hit the ground hard. I got up and I ran as fast as I could to my teepee fort.

I hung my nightie and put on some old pants, a hoodie, and boots. Douglee was whining for me to hurry up. Together, we raced to the hayfields behind our property—they went on forever. I looked for a bale in the centre of the field, trying to pick one with the best view. I climbed up the scratchy hay and started peeling off my clothes until I was buckass naked. I laid my clothes out on the rough hay in a shape that matched my body so I could use them like a blanket and then flopped down. I turned onto my back, placing my hands behind my head, and opened my legs so that I could feel the wind blow against my beaver. It felt so good.

Stars. What a wonder they were to me. I didn't believe in God just because my dad told me to. To me, I knew God was real because of the stars in the sky. Who else could create a billion tiny balls of light that shine brighter than diamonds and stick them all onto a big, dark blue carpet? I also did not understand who this Jesus character was, only that he really loved me and that he died on a big tree shaped like a "t." I could stare at the stars for hours and hours, tracing my fingers along the shapes and patterns. I remembered asking my father what they were called.

"Constellations," he told me, but I could never pronounce words well, so I just mumbled my way through it. I was more interested in discovering The Big Dipper, The Little Dipper, and Orion's Belt, but I would easily get lost on my mission every time a shooting star would zing by. This was an opportunity to make a wish! I always asked for the same three things.

Wish number one: "Please make me beautiful when I grow up, with really long hair."

At that age, I had no friends in school. Everyone made fun of my clothes and told me I was ugly, but then I gave them the ultimate opportunity to tease me about my hair. It wasn't my fault; I loved brushing my hair, but one day, I used my mother's round brush because I couldn't find mine. It got stuck right at the top of my head. I didn't want her to get mad at me, so I cut the brush out with some scissors. I remember screaming and crying all at once, watching my beautiful, blonde hair fall to the floor. I looked like a freak. The top was so short, the hairdresser shaved the back of my neck to leave some length on top. I was an ugly mushroom! My neck was like the stem. Every time I saw a mushroom in the woods, I was reminded of our resemblance—we were practically related! I would stomp on their heads, squishing them into the ground as hard as I could. I blamed my mother. Why did she leave such a dangerous thing in the house? Smiling up at the stars, I remembered how I took care of it.

"You ready to go?" my father asked. We were going to the dump and in my hands, I held the evil brush. It had taken its last strand of hair. My dad watched as I threw it in the big, yellow bin.

"There! It won't ever hurt another girl's hair again," I proclaimed, feeling justified in my mission.

"What did you just throw in there?" he asked.

I looked up at him, straight in his eyes, and shouted, "That evil hairbrush made me look like an abomination—a freak!" I lifted my arms up and pointed to my mushroom cut. My father could not stop laughing, hands down on his knees, howling over my indignation. I didn't think it was funny. This stupid brush took away my favourite thing in the whole world: my long, golden hair. (I hate the movie *Tangled* by the way. It was good up until the man the woman loves cuts off all her very long hair. I would have let him *die*. This movie traumatized me as a grown ass adult.) My dad fell onto his knees in front of me. My frown softened as he cupped my face with his hands, trying to hold in his laughter, taking in the sight of my hair.

"Dad, it's not even the worst part. Because of my hair, Mom keeps putting me in dresses. *Pink* dresses, Dad!" Tears were forming pools in my eyes. He looked away from me, but I saw his shoulders moving quickly up and down. I didn't know it then, but he was laughing even harder but trying to hide it from me. Once he had regained his composure, he turned to face me with a softer and higher pitched voice than normal, trying to keep his words steady. "Not a word to your mother," he promised.

It became an inside joke between the two of us. We'd catch each other's eye and try to keep from laughing whenever my mother would go on a tirade. "Where is my round brush?" she'd ask, as she stomped around the house, looking everywhere for it.

Another shooting star zoomed by.

Wish number two: "I want a best friend who is a boy, someone just like my dad, but someone I can call mine—a boy I can kiss."

As the sky carpet shifted, turning from dark to light blue, the sun began to rise. I thought about my third wish: "I want to become something extraordinary." I didn't realize it at the time, but that third wish was a lot more important than long hair and boys. I know I stole it from the movie *Pocahontas*, but I loved that movie. And I loved her. She was free, happy, and had all the courage in the world to change the way people saw her.

She also had very long hair.

It's one of the boys.

"Why are you standing here?" he barks.

I say nothing, my eyes as big as coconuts. None of these boys has ever talked to me before. I hear the other boys start laughing.

"Are you fucking dumb? I asked you a question."

He's said a very bad word. It's all I can think of. I hear the bus screech, and the other kids call after him. He grabs me hard by my coat near my throat and pulls me up so close I can smell his breath, my tiptoes barely touching the ground. Then he throws me to the ground before running for the bus. My face is in the gravel and my cold hands are exposed. The fog covers my remains and the bus leaves as I lie on the firm earth. I am crying as I slowly lift my head. The tears sting my scratched-up cheek as I finally understand the noise I had heard in the fog were the older boy's footsteps.

Now it's Monday morning and my father is telling me if I hurry, he will give me a ride to the bus stop as he is running late. I am so excited because I love my father's service truck—he works on big metal stuff. Forgetting my annoyance at all the pink stuff, I run around as fast as I can getting myself ready before jumping in his nice, warm truck. I scoot right beside him as he wraps his arm around me.

As he turns the corner towards the highway, I see the same boy and the others waiting at the bus stop. Suddenly, the events of last Friday come flooding back to me. I never told my mother what happened. I didn't even go home because I didn't want to get in trouble. I ended up staying in the bushes all day playing house and eating my lunch until the bus came back. That's when I knew it was time to start walking home.

As I remember what happened, I start to shake. Before I know it, I'm crying. My dad puts the truck in park around the same spot I usually stand.

"Elisha? What is wrong?" he asks in the softest way.

I just keep crying harder and harder. It's like I can't breathe. Finally, my father grabs me by the shoulders, hard, just like the boy did, and I wail in pain.

"*Please*, Daddy! Please don't make me go to school!"

Now he is in shock, totally confused. He holds my gaze as he lightens his grip on me.

"Elisha, tell me what happened right now!"

I love my father, but I know that when his voice changes like that, there is no escaping. I must obey. So, I tell him everything. He cuts me off the minute I mention the boy grabbing me. I can see his eyes start to change colour to green. He is mad! He tells me to point to the boy who touched me. Then he leaps out of the truck and comes to my door. He opens the door and grabs my hand firmly and leads me towards the group.

"Which one of you touched my little girl?" he yells, pointing his index finger at them. None of the boys says a word. "You see her?!" he asks, holding my hand up in his. His voice is like thunder. All I can do is stare at the ground.

"If you ever touch my little girl again, I will kick the living shit out of each one of your fathers, and then I will come and kick the living fuck out of you!"

I look up at my father. His breath is fast and short. He bends down towards me and looks me straight in the eye before kissing my forehead and cheek. He wipes away my tears and says one word, only one:

"Go!"

I go to stand right at the bus stop and suddenly the girl is all nice and talking a lot to me, promising to stand up for me too if the other boys are being dicks. I have no idea what that word means but she uses it a lot. They make fun of me for wearing boy clothes, but they never touch me again. Not once. I think to myself, *my father keeps me safe and loves me so much he was going to kick those boys' butts to protect me. He is my best friend and hero. I will never have worry about another boy hurting me again.*

Helping people in a way that preserves their dignity

Moments of Wallowing
3. *Edgewood School, 1996*

I am playing on the playground at lunch time; I manage to climb up the monkey bars so I can get a view of the entire school grounds and keep an eye on where my sister and brother are. I am always on the look out for their safety. I can see my sister playing on the swings and my brother is on the spinner. He is hanging on the round handlebars and running as fast as he can, spinning round and round. Sometimes, he spins so fast, he flies off into the sand. I quickly adjust my feet and start to climb down. Once I reach the bottom, I decide to join my brother. Just as I look up, I see this dark-haired girl grab my brother and throw him off the spinner and face first into the dirt. My brother's tear-stained face is covered in sand.

In the fall of 2003, I was a senior in high school, finally the oldest amongst the grades. I had a few crushes during my years in school, but only one stood out. That "one" was two grades younger and a boy I could not be bothered with dating. Every girl he was with was cuter than the last, and I knew I stood no chance of winning his heart.

It was also my last year playing basketball, and I promised myself I would make it a great final year. I trained physically all summer long, but more importantly, I trained emotionally. I loved playing the game, but I struggled with my relationships with the coaches. They were awful men: arrogant, chauvinistic, and entitled pricks. Fucking cocksuckers, to sum it up. They had made the previous year hell for me, and, at one point, I was determined to quit. One coach would humiliate me, yelling, "Throw the fucking ball!" The other coach would make me feel inferior, pointing out my lack of knowledge for the game and telling me, "You are not smart enough."

The yelling stopped me from taking in the information. The lack of support made me afraid to make mistakes. I was forever questioning myself and doubting my skills. I could not understand why the one coach made it his mission to verbally attack me multiple times in a practice. Everyone would pause what they were doing, stare, and watch the show. His abusive words and yelling crippled me. He loved the other girls on the team, favouring them, but he dismissed me.

I wanted to quit but struggled with making the decision. Finally, one day I said to my father, "'I cannot do this anymore, Dad! I have given them my best." I tried to convince myself to give it up, but my eyes filled with tears at the idea that I would not be playing next year, my last year in high school.

My father knew about my issues with the coaches, but he also knew how much I loved the game. He had seen the endless tears and had watched me struggle for months. I had told my father everything, and he always gave me comfort, but not this time.

"Grow up, Elisha!' he said firmly. His voice was not compassionate; it was hard. "Don't tell me you're doing your best because if that was the truth, then you wouldn't be quitting."

I was in shock. Where the fuck was my father's soft, tender, and loving heart? He left me sitting there while he continued his chores around the house. I sat there for a long time. After the shock wore off, I got angry. I realized my father was treating me just like those cocksucker coaches!

What the fucking, fuck, fuck!? I thought to myself. *He fucking knows everything about the awful cruelty of these men. If I don't quit and leave, it will ruin me. My mental health can't handle going through this shit again.*

I started angry crying, which is never a good sign. I grabbed the axe beside me and started swinging it into a log. I lost control and channeled all of my pain into tearing apart this log. I eventually winded myself and started to hyperventilate, falling over on my side in the fetal position. I panicked over the idea that my father might think I am a failure. His words: "Grow up, Elisha!" repeated over and over in my mind. The coaches' words echoed in the background: "Seriously, what in the hell are you doing? Are you ever going to make a pass? Can you use your head?"

I laid there crying until there was nothing left to cry about. In a daze, a memory from when I was younger and still going to church came to me. A woman who led the Bible study said, "Not all suffering is beneficial, but it can be. Through great suffering we receive joy if we find our purpose in it."

What is my purpose? I wondered.

My father's words came back to me: "the best" and "the truth."

The truth was my father said what he had to because it *was* the truth. I needed to grow up! I realized that if I allowed anyone to take away my happiness, then I would not be giving my best.

I realized that I had allowed these coaches to rob me of my joy, in both the game and in my identity. I had been suffering for so long for no reason!

I sat up and looked around for my father. Not seeing him, I stood up and started searching for him. Eventually, I found him in the shed crying.

"Dad? Are you ok?" I asked, as tears formed in my eyes.

"I've been sitting here watching you and it was the hardest thing I have ever had to do,' he replied. "But I couldn't be the one to pick you up this time. It had to be you."

Both of us cried together and, embracing one another, we walked out of the shed hand in hand with smiles on our faces.

"So, what are you going to do?" my father asked.

"My best, Dad. Because not giving my best will keep me up at night."

I can make my dad laugh really hard sometimes. That day, I got one of those laughs and with it, a big hug. With tears in his eyes, he told me, "I am so proud of you!"

All summer long, I trained my heart, mind, and body. I ran the cut banks every day and sprinted in between telephone poles. I went for long walks in the hayfields by my house, praying for guidance. I wanted to learn to love these coaches, even if I didn't like them very much. I was ready!

In my senior year of basketball, I was flawless: strong and determined to play my game. It wasn't about winning for me; it was about how I played. I made a goal for each game and achieved it. When the coach yelled at me, I lifted my head up instead of hanging it down. I taught myself to smile. I took in the information but cancelled the *noise*. That was all it was, annoying noise from a five-foot, six-inch-tall yammering pelican. I asked one of my teammates to work with me on our own plays as we were always paired together on the court. She was my post, and I was her guard. We flowed perfectly on the court together.

At a tournament that she got MVP for, I was giving her my congratulations along with the know-it-all coach. "I only got this award because of you and your help," she told me as she gave me the award, *right in front of that cocksucker coach*, the same coach who told me I wasn't smart enough. I took it and tearfully thanked her before turning to look the coach directly in the eye and show him the biggest smile I could muster.

Within two months of the beginning of the season, the little pelican coach had a major heart attack and was no longer able to coach. We all signed cards for him, wishing him well; honestly, deep down, I felt sympathy for the man. With my change in attitude, I guess I realized he wasn't all bad. I decided to make him a card just from me to tell him that I thought he was a good man, that he had taught me a lot about the game, and that I was praying for his recovery and well-being. While it was true that his short temper and harsh words had caused me great suffering, it had also helped me to develop some resilience—not just in my game, but in my character as well. Frankly, I was grateful. I may not have liked him or thought he was a good coach, but I learned to appreciate what he had taught me.

A couple of weeks later, he came in for a surprise visit at the end of one of our practices. Most of the team ran to greet him. They were all hugging him, showering him with affection, but I just couldn't. I was still terrified of the man, and while I had developed some respect for him, I still didn't like him. I knew my mother was waiting for me, so I just gave him a smile and a nod as I headed for the exit. Just before I went outside, I heard my name.

"Elisha! Do you have a second?"

I wanted to play dumb and pretend I didn't hear anything.

I looked behind me and there he was walking towards me. The alarm bells were going off in my head. I was alone with this man. No one else was around, and that has never happened before. I wanted to run screaming out the door at full speed, straight to my mommy. But instead, I turned around to face him. My heart was pounding so hard it felt like I was going to have a heart attack. He was standing awkwardly in front of me. I was waiting for words to come out but there was nothing, so I threw out an icebreaker.

"You wanted to see me, Coach?" I asked.

Still, he said nothing. He wouldn't even look at me.

"I hope you are well. I have been praying for you," I said. At hearing that, he looked up at me, and I saw the tears forming in his eyes.

"Elisha, thank you so much for your card!" he said finally.

He pulled me in for an embrace, and I carefully reached my arms around him. He held onto me for quite sometime. The rest of the team was approaching, and he let go very slowly. The tears were now on his cheeks. He looked at me for what I believe was the first time. I smiled instinctively. In my heart, I knew that was his apology.

After that, he would sometimes come to practices and one-on-one coach me from the sidelines. He'd wave his hand at me and give me instructions, but he never yelled at me again.

I remained a disappointment to the other coach, and the team, when I made the hard decision not to participate in provincials. I had always dreamed of becoming an RCMP officer and had learned about an opportunity to earn extra credits towards graduation while learning about the police force. I decided I had played my game, and I was done. It was time to move on.

The decision was also partly financial. Ours was a single

income home, and my father had enough on his plate just trying to provide three teenagers with the basics. Basketball was an extra, and I did not want to take away from my siblings or be more of a burden to my father because of the sport. Between food, transportation, and hotels, the cost of travelling for tournaments really added up. My teammates would tease me for packing an extra bag for food, but I was trying to stretch the little bit of money my dad could spare me by avoiding eating out. I never told my dad that the money he gave me wasn't enough, because I knew he was doing everything he could for me.

I remember one time we were all at a Red Robin restaurant in Abbotsford, BC early in the season for a tournament. I decided everything on the menu was too expensive, so I had planned to eat back at the hotel. I had brought sandwiches, apples, granola, and snacks to cover me for the trip. Suddenly, the server was handing out milkshakes to everyone. When mine arrived, I panicked, telling the server I hadn't ordered one and I couldn't pay for it. She smiled and told me it was already paid for. It turned out that the father of one of the other girls had ordered a round for everyone. As the rest of the team began placing their food orders, I sat silently, sipping on my milkshake. The girl's father came over to me and said quietly, "Sweetie, order anything you would like." I looked at him nervously. "I will pay for it!" he assured me as he handed me the menu. I pushed the menu right into my face to hide my tears. The best news was the fries were all-you-can-eat.

After that, anytime we travelled, he always made sure I had enough to eat and drink. He knew I was embarrassed, so he would disguise it by buying the team something, purposefully over-ordering, so there was always extra for me. I have never forgotten his kindness and vowed one day to repay him, somehow.

Now, I play baseball with his stepdaughter, his wife, and him.

I wasn't able to pay him back until August 2022 when his stepdaughter got married. Instead of becoming an RCMP officer, I became a professional hair stylist, and at that point, I had ten years of experience. I volunteered my services and made sure to spoil the bride, her mother, and the whole bridal party with hairstyles. I focused on getting everything perfect, and I gave them the same tender care and attention that he had given me all those years ago. On the surface it was for the bride, but deep down, it was all for him. I wanted to give him back the consideration he had given me. He had helped me through what could have been an embarrassing situation in a way that never made me feel ashamed of my circumstances. In that way, he taught me a valuable lesson: the importance of helping people who have less than you, but in a way that preserves their dignity.

I feel like my head is going to explode. Like a rocket, I dart full speed ahead for this girl. Sprinting past my brother, I push her as hard as I can into the poll that holds the spinner. She hits the poll headfirst and collapses. I approach her and see it's Sara Thompson, a seventh grader. This girl is two grades older than me, and I've just started something. *Shit! This isn't good*, I think to myself. I think about running away before she can get up and realize who hit her. But then I decide she needs to know that she can never touch my family! With one hand, I grab a handful of her hair and pull her neck back. With the other hand, I scoop up some sand and stuff it in her mouth and rub it into her eyes and face until she's covered in it. Now her tears fall. I pull her close to me to say something in her ear. "If you *ever* touch my brother again, I will kick the living shit out of your brother and sister!"

My sister, who witnesses this entire incident comes over and, without saying a word, starts helping our brother. I see her eyes look past me to Sara who is still crying and trying to spit out the sand. I know my sister wants to help her—she's always been the compassionate one. But then her eyes turn to me, and I know she doesn't try to help because she's afraid of me.

Sara never ratted me out. She also never looked at me or went near my siblings again.

A reflection of good character

Not Smart Enough
4. *Nukko Lake Elementary School, 1998*

"Aww man. It's another one of those fancy women coming to test me," I mumble under my breath. I hate being singled out in front of the class and the other kids. I've been in a separate and smaller class since grade three. I really want more than anything to be normal and blend in. I had begged to be put in the regular class with everyone else so I would no longer be called "stupid." I wanted to have actual friends and stop being told to go to "dumb dumb class." No one wanted to be friends with a dumbass.

"Elisha! Time for you to go…," Mrs. Sanderson starts before getting interrupted by one of the students who shouts, "Dumb dumb class!" The whole grade seven class bursts out in laughter. I hang my head down as I slowly push myself away from my desk, my eyes never leaving the floor. Walking out of the classroom, I hear them whispering.

"She is so stupid."

"Stupid."

"Stupid!"

I close the door behind me quietly as the tears tickle down my face. All I can think of is how much I *hate* my grade seven teacher, Mrs. Sanderson. She is so mean to me and is making my last year in elementary school hell. I had tried everything to please her, even requesting extra work to prove I was capable. Her response? "No! You're not smart enough." When I raise my hand in class to get some help understanding something, she just smirks and says, "Maybe it's time for you to go to your special class." She seems to enjoy humiliating me, so I have just stopped raising my hand.

I am convinced Mrs. Sanderson has stolen the money I raised for charity, going door-to-door in my neighbourhood in the winter, getting people to place orders. I know I gave her the envelope with the order forms and the money my neighbours paid in advance, but now her assistant is telling me the money isn't in the envelope. There was two hundred and sixty dollars in that envelope, and I know in my gut that my teacher took it.

At lunch time, I decide to hide in the coat closet when everyone leaves, including Mrs. Sanderson. When everyone is gone, I tiptoe to her desk. My heart is racing, and I can't keep my breathing under control. I open the bottom left drawer where I know she always puts her purse. There, I find her burgundy wallet and unzip the top. Sure enough, there's the money. I start counting. (All those lessons with the special education math teacher Mr. Watch were paying off. I was great at counting money! He used fake money to help me understand.) I am almost done counting the twenty-dollar bills when I hear the door open.

"What are you doing?!" roars Mrs. Sanderson.

I jump but still hold onto the money in my hands. A man walks in the room to join Mrs. Sanderson. It's Mr. Baker, the principal.

I am dyslexic, which means I struggle finding, relating, and connecting the sound of a word with the letters used to create the word itself. I struggle with sentence structure. This is why I failed grade twelve English, and why I struggled with my education in general. When I was in high school, I had never heard of this disability. The form of dyslexia I struggle with is called dyseidesia. Dyseidesia makes word recognition and spelling difficult, making it hard to understand written words. I literally cannot sound out a word to save my life, but that is all I heard throughout elementary school and at home when I asked how to spell something. "Sound it out!" they all would bark. Spelling? Forget it! In my world, correct spelling doesn't happen unless I have a relationship with spell check and a professional editor.

I didn't fall in love with reading until my late twenties. The first book set I picked up was the *Twilight* series. I am the world's slowest reader, but I realized as an adult, I can read at my own pace. I don't have to keep up with anyone anymore, which is a good thing because my memory is shit. I usually have to reread a sentence or sometimes an entire page over and over to grasp the storyline or understand the sentence. Still, I love reading now that I can take my time with it.

As a child in school, my dyslexia caused issues beyond reading. I struggled with math, too. You would think numbers would have been easier, but what about math problems? I didn't know where to start with putting together or pulling apart a sentence and now I needed to know how to do that *and* solve a math equation at the same time? It was hopeless.

So many times, I would sit in class trying to dissect the notes given for the day and then struggle later when I tried to apply them to my homework. It was so hard, sometimes I would just shut down. I would spend hours at the kitchen table, trying my best, but I just could not understand the words in the math problems so I could find the answers in numbers. My father tried to help me, but his way didn't work for me. In the end, I had to figure it out on my own.

By the time I got to high school, I had developed my own methods. I began counting using my fingers, wrote endless sticky notes to help with memorization, and talked out loud to myself, giving myself directions to complete my work. It was a struggle, and I was always planning every single step of my life instead of enjoying the moment. Control was everything, and overwhelming stress paralyzed me when I tried to control the things that were out of my control like the time allotted for tests or my math teacher's instructional style that I would never understand.

It would take an average student an hour, sometimes half an hour, for homework. Not Elisha! Three hours per subject, and that's with four subjects in a semester. I didn't even consider the idea of college or university once I found out how much reading, essay writing, and time management was needed. I spent most of my high school years in assisted learning classes, which were boring and awful. I was a student who cared about my education, but I felt the other students treated the class as a bird course: something kids called a class you fly through without trying. The teachers in this program babysat you, and I hated being told what to do. I didn't need a fucking babysitter. I could never escape this feeling of not being enough. All I wanted was to be treated fairly and given the chance to prove what I knew I could do with my education.

As my grade ten year was ending, I was given that chance. I was placed into an essentials grade eight, nine, and ten math class. Essentials math was easier than the regular principals math and was for students who struggled. It used to be that you could graduate and go to college with math essentials, but they were changing the prerequisite requirements. The school board decided the essentials math class satisfied the requirements to graduate from high school, but a student would still have to pass grade eleven principals math if they wanted to get into college or university. And if they wanted to take regular math after graduating, they'd have to pay for it.

I didn't like that at all. I knew post-secondary education was unlikely for me, but I still wanted to feel it was a possibility. Besides, why would I pay for something later that is free now? There was a solution, but the road was long and hard. I would have to retake grade ten principals math in grade eleven with all the grade ten students. Then, in grade twelve, I'd have to take grade eleven principals math so I could graduate with my options open after high school.

I told my father the game plan and asked for his support and blessing, which he gave me without hesitation. The next day in my assisted learning class, I was filling out my course sheet for the next year's classes. A teacher walked over and hovered over my shoulder, looking at my selection: Math 10 Principals, English 11, Chemistry 11, and Fine Arts 11.

"You are not smart enough for chemistry," she remarked. "Chemistry is a very hard class; you need to select something more fitting, so the teacher has more time for the other students."

My head was down again while the other students stared and giggled; more water escaped from my tear ducts. This story was all too familiar to me. However, this time I made my choice. I ignored the teacher and stuck with my choices.

I fell in love with chemistry, but I also fell in love with the teacher who changed my entire perspective on learning and what I deserved for my education. Mr. Wool was my grade eleven and twelve chemistry teacher. He was a very tall man with dark brown hair and a gap between his two front teeth. I thought he was hilarious, always making sarcastic remarks to the time-waster teens in class.

"Did you just call me a loser, Mr. Wool?" a kid would ask.

"Well, if the shoes fits…," Mr. Wool would respond.

This was always followed by a roar of laughter. He was an expert at using humour to put certain teens, with their lame excuses and lack of respect, in their place. He never put up with bullying. That was totally forbidden for Mr. Wool. When a kid referred to me as "fucking stupid" once in class, Mr. Wool yelled at the kid and kicked him right out of his class without a second thought.

I loved his smile. I swear, it could raise a person from the dead. My favourite part though was his teaching style. His lessons always had a road map. Everything was explained, clear as day, and he'd even allow the students to vote for the test days. If he saw you squinting or looking confused while he was explaining the lesson on the overhead projector, he would stop and, without pointing you out or calling on you, he'd explain the concept another way until he saw your eyes light up with understanding (and your furrowed brow relax in relief).

Chemistry had math and letters in the formulas and equations, but Mr. Wool figured out how to explain it to me. He made literal road maps for me to explain the concepts. We'd move together through the maps, stopping off at "mole ville" and "particle ville." He even got me to understand the periodic table! I was taking math in the same semester, and I got a better mark because I was doing so well in chemistry. But when I received my first report card, I got a C in chemistry. My fears about not being smart enough bubbled up to the surface again. But then I noticed Mr. Wool gave me an O for outstanding work habits—the highest letter grade. I decided this must be a mistake, and I stayed after class to inquire about it.

"Mr. Wool, I have a question concerning my report card. I noticed you gave me an O for work habits, but I only have a C letter grade in your class." He was smiling as he always did and sitting in front of his computer. He turned away from his screen and looked me in the eye.

"So?" he replied.

I continued, "I don't understand. I have Bs in all my other classes G ("good") work habit grades, but in your class…," I continued.

He interrupted me gently. "Elisha, you are in class doing your best. You're willing to learn. You stay in class every lunch period to ask me questions. You are a great student and very intelligent."

I started to tear up. I had never had a teacher, or anyone for that matter, tell me I was a great student or smart before. (I had to look up the word intelligent in the dictionary after our meeting). He watched me hastily wipe away my tears and turned back to face his computer screen.

"From what I can see you are getting ninety percent on all your assignments, quizzes, tests, and practical lab work, but your answers to the lab follow-up questions are dropping your mark," he pointed out.

This was a lightbulb moment. First, I never understood the breakdown of the grading. Second, I now knew what the problem was with my mark. My lab partner and I would do the lab together, but it was her suggestion that we split up the follow-up questions. I did the odd ones, and her the even. When we got our lab questions, back all her answers were wrong. I had just learned that the lab questions accounted for forty percent of our overall grade!

"The work habit grade I have given you is a reflection of your good character, which I find absolutely outstanding," Mr. Wool said.

That changed the game in my education, and I marched into every one of my classes demanding an O from all my teachers, citing Mr. Wool's explanation: that I always try my hardest in every class, and it's a "reflection of my good character."

I took my good character and dropped my lab partner the following day. I am not a heartless bitch, but it was time to drop dead weight. Months later, as another semester came to an end, I was in line to grab my report card. I told the secretary my last name and she found my report card. Then she grabbed this big, blue ink pad and a stamp before making a big *stomp* sound on the right side of my report. Then she handed it to me. I froze in place as I saw a set of words I never thought possible, words I was told for years were impossible. Bright blue, they stuck out as if they were three dimensional: *HONOUR ROLL.*

The secretary was saying something to me, but I was in a trance and could not make out the words. "Excuse me?" I asked. Then there was another voice from behind me.

"Elisha, you need to move out of the line," another student told me. The same assisted learning teacher I had the previous year, who had sneered at my course selections, caught my attention and pulled me out of the line.

"Elisha, is everything alright?!" she inquired in an unusually soft tone, which annoyed me immediately. I ignored her entirely and continued to stare at my letter grades. Three A's, one B, and four O's, plus my highest mark: chemistry 94%! I started smiling and tears of joy were rolling down my cheeks at this point. This piece of paper proved I was enough, and I was indeed so very smart. My first thought: *Fuck all the teachers, counsellors, coaches, and anyone who ever held me back.* My second: *Mr. Wool!* I turned on my heel to run towards my chemistry teacher to tell him the news.

"Elisha, you're being very rude and impolite!" the assisted learning teacher snapped. I turned back to face her. This was my time, and I wasn't going to let her take it from me again.

"Maybe it's a fucking hint! I have nothing to say to you," I replied, looking her in the eyes.

"Excuse me! I do not like your tone nor your choice of words." She moved closer to me with her fiery, copper-red hair, but this was a fight I was prepared for.

"I choose my words carefully. You should do the same!" I said thrusting my report card in her face. "You told me I wasn't smart enough. You humiliated me in class!" My voice cracked as I realized how I'd been lied to for so long, how those lies had impacted my education, how badly they'd hurt me. I wanted her to understand the deep pain she'd caused, the open wound she'd created. And I wanted her to know that I would never accept being told that I was "not smart enough" ever again. Students walking by us in the hall stopped and stared, witnessing my exchange of words with this teacher. Finally, I said to her, "I am enough now, and I always was."

On my way to chemistry class, report card in hand, I had the biggest grin as I pictured that horrible teacher's face after I gave her a piece of my mind. I walked into Mr. Wool's class, and he greeted me with the warmest smile, the gap between his two front teeth as prominent as ever. I rushed towards him to give him the news and to express my gratitude. He had changed everything for me. Most importantly, he had changed the way I saw myself.

I am sitting in the principal's office when I hear a deep voice emerge from behind the closed door. My heart rate shoots up. It's my father. He is the scariest person alive. *What is he going to do to me?* I wonder as the tears fall. The door opens, and I jump in my seat at the sound. My eyes stare blankly at my white shoelaces as I dare not look up or move. I am as perfectly still as a statue, but I know my father is next to me. The smell of tobacco, aftershave, and burnt oil emanates from him. I sit in silence as I hear words being exchanged between the principal and my teacher. Those voices don't grab my attention, and my father doesn't say a word the entire time until he suddenly breaks the silence.

"Sit up straight!" my father demands. I immediately pull myself together. "Look at me," he says with a firm voice. I do exactly what my father asks without looking at my teacher or principal. Starting slowly from his work boots, which are covered in dirt and grease, up to his working hands, scarred and dirty from the years of pulling wrenches. Then I take in his faded blue coveralls with the white nametag above the left pocket and finally, his bright blue eyes that meet mine and look into my soul. We stay there a few seconds saying so much with our eyes, soul to soul, until I see a slight smirk across his face, which softens my eyes and slows my heart back to a normal beat. That smirk tells me he isn't angry, not one bit. Without asking me a word, he turns to the teacher and principal.

"The other night my daughter needed my help counting the money she raised for this charity for school. We together counted two hundred and sixty dollars."

There was something powerful when my father spoke. Everyone in the room would freeze. His voice would vibrate and dominate the surroundings unless there was an idiot like my teacher Mrs. Sanderson in the room. She tries to cut off my father.

"I am not finished!" he declares, his voice dropping an octave lower as he raises one hand while giving her a sharp, direct stare. "Elisha, who did you give the money to when you got to school?" he asks me.

A person should always give my father a direct, no bullshit answer. Don't dance around and waste his time. The more you do that, the more he can see right through you and your lack of respect. It makes you look more guilty. You don't need an explanation for the truth.

He still has his eyes on my teacher, and I have my eyes on him. In a tone that is sharp and straight to the point, I reply, "Mrs. Sanderson."

"Mmmmm!" is all my father says. The longest pause follows. Now Mr. Baker tries to intervene. Once again, my father holds up his hand. "I am *not* finished!" he barks. "Elisha! You owe Mrs. Sanderson an apology," he says without looking at me. Shifting in my seat and taking my gaze from my father to my teacher, I apologize.

"I am sorry Mrs. Sanderson for searching through your wallet. It was wrong of me, and I won't do it again." I look away and sit back in my seat.

"Sit up!" my father demands again from me, as imposing as ever. The principal and teacher lean forward, looking for more, but I refuse to give anything else. I know the truth, and I'm not the only one in the room who does. My father looks at both the teacher and the principal.

"Why am I here?" he asks them.

Both the teacher and principal are shocked by my father's question. They don't know how to answer him.

"Mr. Rose, your daughter was caught stealing from Mrs. Sanderson…" My father immediately cuts off the principal.

"My daughter is not a thief, and she is not a liar. I will ask you again, why am I here?!" Now my father is annoyed. There is no going back as the next step will be anger. I see the signs emerging. Veins in his hands start to pop out, his voice is deeper than ever, and there is a sharpness in his eyes.

"Mr. Rose, we need to address the matter of your daughter…"

My father slams his fist down hard on the principal's desk. Both he and Mrs. Sanderson jump back in shock. I look at my dad, seeing the snarl, the green eyes, and his tense body. *This isn't good*, I think to myself. I wish my teacher would be honest about taking the money; everything would be a lot easier. My only concern is my father doing something he will regret because when he gets angry, bad things always happen. He loses control, and there is nothing to stop him. I know what I have to do. I carefully stand up and place my little hand on his huge fist that is still sitting on my principal's desk.

"Dad, it's time to go," I say so gently it's almost a whisper. He isn't looking at me, and I know I need to see his eyes in order to pull him away. "Father, be still," I say softly but firmly. Now I have his eyes. With his eyes on me, I move my lips into a slight smirk. I feel his hand release into mine, and as he stands, he doesn't let go. We leave the office quietly, hand in hand. Once we reach his work truck, he opens the door for me, helps me inside, and closes the door. He climbs in on the other side and starts the engine.

As the diesel engine roars to life, he lights up a cigarette. I watch him breathe in the smoke. Deep and long, he inhales into his lunges and exhales the light blue poison. Not a word comes from me. He has to break the silence. He puts the truck into gear, and we begin to leave the school. Nothing is said for thirty minutes. The drive home is peaceful, with all its scenery of golden hayfields, tall, green trees, and bright blue sky. Before I blink, we are in our driveway. I climb out and head for the door to the house.

"Elisha!" my father calls out.

"Yes, Dad?" I turn to look at him.

"Thank you so much." His voice breaks mid-reply as tears start to roll down his cheeks. I go to him and reach my arms around his waist.

"Thank you for believing me," I tell him. My father's cold hands reach down to cup my face as he leans in to kiss me on the cheek. I tell him I love him and make him laugh as I skip my way inside.

"You owe me one, Dad!"

*We are told
to love our enemies*

Feeling Forever Less

5. *"The Stacks" Apartment 18, 1994*

I wake up to the sound of loud music coming from downstairs. I sit up in my twin bed and look over at my sister to see if she has woken up too. I move slowly out of bed and go to her. I gather the covers and place her giraffe in her arms, wrapping them both up together. My feet are feeling ticklish from the vibrations of the music coming from underneath the floor.

    I make my way to the door and open it quietly in case my mother hears. I hear voices; some are talking, others are laughing. My mother's voice stands out the most; she is always so loud. I am worried that the party might have woken up my little brother. I creep into the hallway, making my way to his room across the hall. As I enter his room, I see a dark figure hovering over his bed.

    "Daddy!" I shout. I haven't seen my dad in months, and I miss him terribly. The man moves towards me, and I am so excited; I'm ready to jump into his arms and smell his sweet, spicy scent of aftershave. Suddenly, the man emerges from the darkness before me.

    He is *not* my father.

It was the summer of 2006. I was nineteen and relishing the sight of the moonlight shining down on my naked body. I loved swimming naked under the stars, especially the silence and the feeling of peace. I felt as though nothing in the world mattered.

I had just had sex for the first time with a boy I'd been dating for almost two years. We decided to go camping at Crystal Lake, a forty-five-minute drive north of Prince George. I had not allowed anyone to touch me until this moment. The truth was, I was getting bored of the relationship, and I felt guilty as he was still very much engaged. I figured I'd finally give in and spice things up a little.

In the end, it didn't last and within five months I had ended the union. He took it hard. Well, I hurt him something awful by cheating on him with the same man I eventually had children with and married.

The children's father and I were together just shy of eight years and married for two before we got divorced. It was no surprise. I was too immature and selfish to share my life with someone else. I felt the biggest form of abuse in my marriage was neglect. I was unable to truly love myself and was therefore unable to love anyone else. I couldn't love him because I simply didn't know how to trust him. He was emotionally unavailable, and I needed that connection to feel loved. I broke his heart. The best thing we did was create two little humans: a son, a mini version of him and a daughter, who is most definitely a mini me.

He remarried and continued to add to his family. I, on the other hand, became an intoxicated whore. Fuck was I a slut! But the power it held? To be carefree and unattached? I felt like a god.

After my marriage failed, I dove into dick headfirst and thought of nothing else in the world I created. It was raining dicks. Morning, noon, and night.

Dick, dick, dick—like the sound of consistent rain drops.

I was sexy, unique, and flawless. I manipulated and used men to get what I wanted, how I wanted it, and how often. I was in charge and in control. I very seriously thought of becoming an escort to make some money for my talent in the bedroom. Why not? I was a professional. I learned to fuck properly and became an expert at giving pleasure. I was extraordinary, and my pussy was like cocaine to an addict—a gateway to desire. I was no vanilla flavour, stuck up, skinny bitch either. I had love handles and an apple booty!

Anytime I would see these beautiful, younger, and skinnier fidget bitches roll up, and I could feel my self confidence start to wane, my first thoughts were *I can fuck and suck better than YOU!* This was my addiction: sex. And I used it as a tool to abuse men.

I was an empty vessel in search of something. What was it that I was searching for? I didn't know, but I created a path of destruction to find it. I mastered gaslighting and other forms of manipulation to seduce men. Translation: I was a narcissist.

Lying was my favourite form of abuse to inflict on my victims, the one-night stands, or the "fuck 'n chuck" types as I used to call them. I became a compulsive liar to get what I wanted: some dick and to get laid. I would lie about the most trivial things, just to get the attention I wanted. I lied about how often I worked out, the number of people I knew, the fancy makeup brands I wore, that my eye colour was natural (I was wearing contacts), the cost of my clothes…you name it, I lied about it. I now realize that the things I lied about don't matter really, but at the time, they did matter. And the lying spread to beyond my sexual conquests. I took advantage of my parents many times financially, lying that the money was for rent and food when I was in school for cosmetology. Nope! I needed that money for my fake eyelashes and shopping sprees so I could win attention from men.

To snare a man I wanted, who was either a bad boy with a big stick, an honest man who had money, or a man I had simply always fantasized about being with, manipulation was the name of the game. For a short time, I made these men believe I wanted to build a life with them. Once I had my claws buried deep within them and was in complete control, I would carefully construct false narratives and use gaslighting to weaken them. If that didn't sway them, my magic vagina was a great back-up.

The most twisted and demented tactic I used on these men was to garner their sympathy in the wake of the death of my former partner, someone I'd been with for a decade. When he passed, I felt untethered, and a state of emptiness consumed me. That experience was legitimately traumatic. So traumatic in fact that it formed the subject matter for my first book, *I Am Worthy*. While my pain in the aftermath of his death was genuine, my use of it to lure men in to fill the void was not.

I used all three tools—lying, my magic vagina, and my "grieving widow" persona—to fuel my sex addiction. I was so disgusting and still struggle with forgiving myself. Don't get me wrong, I don't feel bad for taking advantage of these men. Fuck them! They knew what they were doing: they were taking advantage of a widow. But I should have treated *myself* better. The cost on my poor soul was high.

In September 2021, I went to see a therapist who specialized in trauma and addictions. In my first session, she told me, "The question you need to ask yourself is, 'Why do you hate men?'"

"That's a little harsh!" I replied. "If I truly hated them, then why fuck the shit out of them?" I asked, with a giggle. The therapist smiled at my reply and responded with conviction.

"Because it gives you a false sense of power and control over them."

I looked down in shame and started to cry. She had hit a nerve. I realized she was right. I was looking for power and control over these men. I was holding them accountable for the suffering I had endured at the hands of other men since I was a child. It started with having to witness my father's physical abuse of my mother, but there were other incidents. The first time my innocence was taken was in apartment 18, when that stinky man put his hands on my genitals. Then there was the male babysitter who was supposed to be like family but asked me to stroke his cock. Another time, a neighbourhood boy pulled me under his bed covers and forced me to get undressed. There was my high school boyfriend who locked me in a bathroom when I was drunk so he could try to take advantage of me. Later, a police officer tried every trick in the book to get me to agree to be his mistress while his cop wife stayed at home raising their twin baby boys. Even my first love, a drunk and an addict, stole my dignity by ridiculing me and screwing his way through my lifeless body. I couldn't even trust women, something I realized when one forced herself onto me while she was heavily intoxicated. Over and over again, I was taken from.

I was angry with these people, all of whom I had trusted, many I had loved, and one I had shared my life with. They all took a part of me away and I could not get it back. They all stole my *time*. I wanted that returned to me but instead of my open wound getting healed, it got infected. I punished and used men in a sadistic way to make up for my suffering. I wanted to inflict the same pain that each and every one of them had caused me. In fact, I took pleasure in it. Seeing men suffer at my hands as I used sex as a weapon helped me cope with the pain. I sought revenge but, in the end, here I was: broken and lost, cycling through pain. I became addicted to suffering, lingered in pain, and grew bitter. I was unlovable. I created a monster, one that was sick with an illness that only I could find a cure to.

We are told to love our enemies, but that can be hard to do when they've caused this kind of trauma. No one seems to understand or want to know what it feels like to be me. Once I tried telling the truth, and I was shamed for it. "It was your fault; you allowed it to happen," they told me.

I made a choice to not close myself off anymore; I didn't want to become bitter. I realized that these people who hurt me will never come back into my life and say, "I hurt you, and I am sorry." In a perfect world, it might have happened. The truth is I don't fucking *need* any of these people to tell me how painful my experience with them was. They tortured me and left me traumatized by flashbacks and nightmares. I have PTSD.

I finally acknowledged that these people who broke me into tiny little pieces cannot put me back together. And honestly, why would I want them to? When I chose to channel my efforts into vengeance against men, I became their protégé. I realized that I was doing exactly what they did to me. I had become the predator. They fucking Miyagi'd me! I can't expect anyone else to rebuild me. That is my job, and I must do it alone.

After another failed relationship in 2023, I felt ashamed. This man was perfect, until he was not. The odds were against me: he was younger and broken by abuse himself, another alcoholic. I attracted yet another man who needed to be fixed. It dawned on me then that my addiction was clouding my judgement. I was an addict myself, addicted to toxic men. This time, I reached out for help, a skill that took me years to learn. Feeling ashamed, I went looking for my sister's compassion.

"Ashamed? Ashamed of what? Wearing your heart on your sleeve? Having the ability to recognize a toxic situation and walk?! You should be proud of yourself," she told me.

I suggested it wasn't his fault entirely, admitting that I bore some responsibility for seeking out another "fixer upper." My sister wouldn't have it though. She would not put up with my lack of self worth.

"*You* know your worth! You wrote a book about it, remember? Never dull yourself; be true to yourself. Then the right person will see you," she told me.

I felt transformed by my sister's words. She always sees the best in me; she sees beyond my past mistakes. In fact, she always makes it clear that without those missteps, I would not be who I am today, and that I should be grateful for them. "Noticing that your 'peace' is not peaceful and having the courage to change it? That is special," she said. My sister's strong yet gentle persuasion began to lift my spirits. My heart was already feeling lighter when she finished her pep talk. "So! To be clear, are we feeling ashamed? No! We are feeling empowered, bold, and courageous! Are we full of light? Yes! Now *that* is contagious!" she exclaimed.

My sister is the true wordsmith, and her wisdom always shines bright. I try to follow her lead, but healing is bittersweet! Now that I've done the work to heal myself in the wake of the abuse I suffered, and I have forgiven the people who caused it, I find it nearly impossible to date. I see so many red flags, so many things I am not willing to compromise on, because I have such trust in my own worth. I know early on in a relationship when things will be an issue. Logic takes precedence now over my feelings and my desire to be liked. I cut off the union before it gets to that point. I immediately recognize the shallow connections and the people who are unwilling to grow.

I trust my intuition and my healed heart. I respect myself too much to beg or to ask twice. I will not value any love that is not offered freely! Not many people will work on themselves; few are looking to improve as a partner. The worst situation is a relationship where the other person expects you to lower your sense of self worth to validate their shitty fucking treatment of you because they are too set in their ways to change. I have reached a point in my life where I will not settle or waste my time and energy.

Every relationship is a two-way street. When the time you put in isn't matched, it's time to walk. If a person wants a relationship with me, they must put some effort into it. Otherwise, I'd rather be alone. Do you know who I am most connected to? Me. I am in love with who I am. I fall in love with her more every day. I connect with and work for *her*. I am dedicated to understanding and supporting her. She healed my soul and rebirthed a woman who is no longer a victim of feeling forever less.

The smell of sweat and beer is so strong, I almost choke. I back away, looking up into his eyes. He looks right through me, as if nothing is there. I am being led into another room. I look behind me to make sure my brother will be ok.

This man smells nothing like my father. Throughout the ordeal, I keep thinking of my mother and her voice. I hum her favourite song to drown out the sounds he's making and count the flowers on the shower curtain to ease my discomfort.

After he is done with me, I go into my brother's room, scoop him up into my arms, and tuck him into my sister's bed. I grab all the sheets off my bed, throw my mattress onto the floor, and push the bed against the door. I go over to my dresser and do the same thing. Anything I can get my hands on goes in front of that door behind which my sister and brother are sleeping. No matter what happens to me, I will protect them. I fall asleep on the floor in front of the door.

"Elisha!? What is going on in there?" my mother shouts. It is the next day, and it's light outside now. She is trying to push open the door and in frustration she is calling for me. I come over and start taking down my fort of stuff. She finally pushes her way through and takes in the mess. "What is all this? *Look* at your room!"

I glare at my mother with hatred. She is getting mad at me for protecting my sister and brother? Doesn't she understand what just happened?

"I don't ever want to see this again. Do you hear me?" she demands. I storm out of the room without saying a word. "And what is your brother doing in your sister's bed?" she asks.

After that, any time I heard my mother's parties in the middle of the night, I would collect my brother, place him in bed with my sister, and make a barricade in front of the door. I'd usually stay up most of the night, afraid to go to sleep. I needed to guard my siblings. Dad was not there to help, and Mom was busy entertaining, so I knew it was up to me. At times, I would hear the door handle rattling and a deep voice saying words I couldn't understand. But that smelly man never got in. I kept him out.

I was in control.

God is simple.
People are not

The Building with a 't'
6. *Pentecostal Church, 1996*

"Very bold move of her, that dress."

"I agree. Flamboyant!"

I am going pee in the lady's washroom at church, trying to make out that word, *flam-boy-ant*. I wonder what it means, but I mind my own business while the two ladies wash their hands and continue their dissection of yet another victim—someone at church they disapprove of. Whenever I would go to the bathroom, I'd often find the same two ladies gossiping.

"Joey, on the other hand, is a darling, and a true man of God!"

I pause at hearing my father's name and peek through the crack in the bathroom stall. I start to listen more intently.

"How God saw fit to pair those two together is beyond me," one lady comments.

I watch through the tiny slit as the other lady agrees, nodding her head, and replies, "Did you notice the dresses are homemade? Even the dresses she puts on her daughters!"

A *tsk* sound comes from both women simultaneously.

I look down at my dark blue cotton dress. It has a blue bow at the back where it zips up, and in the front, there is a white and pink ribbon that I am twirling around in my fingers. I pull up my white stockings and flush the toilet.

"Shoot! Someone is in here?" one lady gasps.

I exit the stall, pulling up the ruffled sleeves of my dress and brushing the front down to smooth it. I look up at the two women who are both staring at me. Soft, fake smiles form on their faces.

"Elisha?! You surprised us," the shy one says.

I push by them and start washing my hands.

"What a beautiful day God has blessed us with," the snobby lady remarks.

I move past them both without replying and grab some paper towel to dry my hands. When I finish drying, I walk straight to the door to exit the bathroom.

"Elisha! You are being disrespectful by ignoring your elders. What would your Father in heaven say to that?"

I open the door, but hold it open with my back, turning very slowly to face the women. With a vindictive smile now on my face, I reply, "My Father in heaven would tell me to say..." I pause, taking a breath and narrowing my eyes, "...he hears everything! And he is disgusted with you."

I leave them standing there in shock. We were never supposed to speak out. The church ladies expected a head bow with a curtsy and for us to always agree with them as they were wiser. At ten years old, I have decided to challenge that nonsense. Skipping my way up the stairs, I see my beautiful mother in her homemade, bright green dress. It was tailored to her curves and the collar was trimmed with lace. She is holding my sister's hand as they wait for me. I walk up and grab my sister's other hand.

"Are you ready?" my mother asks.

With the brightest smile I can give her and looking into her blue eyes and seeing her soft, pink smile and long, curly, blonde hair, I reply, "Yes, Mom!"

My mother, guitar in hand, leads my sister and me down the church aisle, walking past my brother and father. My sister and I are to join my mother in singing a song she wrote called "How Far is Heaven?" We take our place in front of the church where at least a hundred pairs of eyes are upon us. With one hand holding my sister's hand and the other resting on my mother's shoulder, I search out the gossipy women and sing as loud as I can, never taking my eyes off them.

I have gone to church since I was a baby, and not just on Sundays. I attended youth groups, prayer groups, and community gatherings on weekdays too. I was told it was our family. My father insisted we all went; however, shortly after our performance that day, my mother stopped attending church altogether. She mentioned it was nice for her to be home alone and have time to herself. But deep down, I knew the truth: after a long battle, my mother decided to walk away from the toxic women who were so cruel to her.

They would scold her then ignore her and silently punish her. They knew of her past failures in her marriage to my father and condemned her. She wasn't worthy of entering the house of the Lord. The worst woman of them all was one of the fellowship leaders of the church.

My father sought counsel from the pastor. Many times, we would sit and wait for hours while my father had his sessions with him. After my parents' second separation, we stayed with my father. When my parents reconciled, my mother was constantly subjected to ridicule about her past from the "godly" women of the church.

For her health and their marriage, my mother stayed far away from the church. As a little girl, I witnessed the false representation of love from the other women at the church.

"Where is your wife? We sure do miss her?" This from the same catty women I caught gossiping about her. I rolled my eyes every time I heard those lines, making sure they saw it. The best was watching them pour themselves onto my father in their pathetic attempts at flirting.

"Joey! It is so good to see you!" they would purr, making eye contact and rubbing his hand tenderly. These self-righteous cunts knew nothing about this man, my father. His handsome face and money-filled pockets blinded them all. My father always tried to donate to the church anonymously, but everyone knew the chicken scratch handwriting on the envelope was his. My mother may have made some mistakes in her pain and grief, but it was in part due to my father's hands. He played a major contributing factor in my mother's downfall from being a strong woman and honourable wife.

"This darling man, a true man of God." I would hear these words about my father all the time. The truth, however, was that he was also a violent man who used his hands to beat my mother. And he couldn't even blame alcohol like my grandfather. My father experimented with drugs and booze as a teen, but he never followed through with the lifestyle. He was completely sober when he abused my mother, using his words to control her and his anger to terrify her. My mother had moments of bravery; she would speak out and defend herself, but then his hand came next. He was a crazy, raging, lunatic when he got angry. She wasn't any saint, not by a mile, but at least my mother was honest about the things she had done. My father knew hitting was wrong but would often say that my mother had provoked him; it was his way of justifying what he did. My father simply didn't know how to control his anger. Years later, when I was in my twenties, a judge finally sentenced him to anger management classes. That was when he finally realized the truth and his part in it all.

When I was twelve, my father withdrew from the church. Years later, I asked my father why he left church, explaining to him how hard it had been for me to be taken away from the only community and lifestyle I knew. He told me he became disillusioned with the church because it no longer seemed to be about becoming "Christ-like," the literal meaning of Christianity. He said he didn't like the teachings being practiced as the church spoke against doctrine and decided to let his family make their own choice as to whether they wanted a relationship with God.

I thought for the longest time that my mother was a coward for letting those women get to her, until that day in the bathroom when I heard what they were saying about her. My mother is a God-fearing woman who knows God's love, but most of all, she knows her worth. The church isn't for women like her and me.

I am a sinner, an adulteress, a vain woman, a liar, and I deserve to burn in hell for all the pain I have caused others. But I have learned to devote my life to God, Jesus, and the Holy Spirit. This helps me understand the truth about life and provides me with a love that is powerful beyond measure. It helps me to understand how full I am and forgive myself. It gives me peace—a peace I believe is not founded on earth but in God.

Religion is very simple; it's the people who are complicated. I am anything but simple, trust me. Not a day goes by when I don't swear at God. My prayers aren't what you see in the movies. It's often more like, "Ok, God. What the fuck?" I have argued with

God more times than I can remember, and I challenge his ways often. For example, "Fuck off, Lord. I am not writing a book!" I often beg God to let me die in my pain. "Pity me and just let me die in my agony." When I worry about a hard choice or committing a sin, I make sure to check in. "Smite me, Father!" I absolutely fear God. I don't fuck around. He scares the living shit out of me. I have read the stories in the Bible. I would hate to be turned into a pillar of salt because I chose to look backward and not forward. Or have my beautiful long, purple, mermaid hair ruined from living in a whale's belly for months due to my stubbornness and defiance of his will. I hate feeling alone and know in my heart something would be missing. To me that is the worst pain imaginable: not living a full life or believing in something greater than yourself. People are often surprised when they hear about my faith and beliefs.

"But you are nothing like those religious fanatics!" they say. I get blamed at times for my God and what he has done.

"I hate your God and your people," they say.

Some people pester me with questions about scientific theories or other religions. I use the word "pester" because many struggle with the idea of God's existence. "Seeing is believing," they tell me, forcing their indifference onto me in a manipulative tone, daring me to validate what they say. I love to hear other people's opinions and share mine, but I won't forsake my values and morals. Now people see me coming and run the other way. I don't take it personally. I choose to live this way. My favourite question of all is "How do you know God is real? Let me guess: your faith!" This is always followed by a sneer and cruel laughter.

I had a girlfriend who was celebrating her university graduation at a local pub with all her fancy, preppy, highly educated university friends. I respect, admire, and frankly envy people who pursue higher education, but I despise those who arrogantly prey on those who didn't have access to the same level of education. This was that sort of crowd. One young man stood out as a complete douchebag know-it-all. After gawking at my collar bone tattoos, which say "Hope" and "Faith," he decided to start a debate about faith with the group. I smiled in silence as this person prattled on. He wasn't trying to engage with me; he wasn't talking *with* me but *at* me in front of his pals. I had to gently tap my girlfriend's leg to calm her down as she tried to defend me. She knew what was happening. We endured a long twenty minutes of this guy convincing himself of his own argument. It was getting uncomfortable; many in the group were looking at me with pity, while others seemed to agree with his argument. I decided it was safe to share my own insights.

"True or false?" I asked the group. "If you can see it, then you believe it?" I slapped my girlfriend on the arm as she started to giggle. All of them replied, "True!" except for my friend. She covered her mouth with her hand to hold in her laughter.

"How many of you have seen a million dollars?" I asked. Nobody in the group admitted to having seen a million dollars.

"And yet, you believe it's real!" I exclaimed. Silence followed, but after a minute, the wise guy piped up.

"Have you seen a million dollars? Because if you haven't, that isn't a fact you can use," he posited. As badly as I wanted to throw a punch at this guy or hurl an insult, I knew I had to keep my composure and lead by example.

"Fair enough!" I replied. I took a seat right next to him so people would have to lean in close to hear the rest of our conversation. I could tell this made him *very* uncomfortable as he stiffened his shoulders and inched away from me. He would not look me in the eye. *What a coward*, I thought.

"Do you drink coffee?" I asked. He nodded. "Does your coffee maker have one of those fancy timers you can set up at night, so it makes coffee automatically for you in the morning while you're still in bed?"

"Uh, well yeah!" he replied arrogantly.

"So, you wake up every morning knowing there will be freshly brewed coffee waiting for you? The smell wakes you, the lingering aroma a pleasant tease of what is to come?"

He looked exasperated and gave me a "get to the point already" face. Meanwhile everyone else was puzzled by my detailed description of the coffee. I turned my attention to my girlfriend, and keeping my eyes on her, I said, "*That* is faith! Believing that the coffee is made and waiting for you. You can't see it or touch it or even smell it necessarily, but you know it's there."

He wasn't going down easy and as the rest of the group took all that I said into consideration, he wanted to respond. I politely cut him off.

"Do you want to know what the difference is between you and me? I stood up, reaching out my hand to my girlfriend who was passing me my coat. "Wisdom. Wisdom is the perfect balance of intelligence and love. Your arrogance blinds you to the point where faith cannot exist. Without love, there is no truth behind your false intelligence."

I pulled on my jacket, making sure to expose my "Faith" and "Hope" tattoos. My girlfriend and I exchanged looks as we walked towards the door.

"Did you just call that guy an idiot?" she asked.

I looked back at the dude and said out loud with a smile, "If the shoe fits." Making eye contact with the bartender as we were departing, I shouted, "Our drinks are on him!" I knew he'd be too intoxicated to notice.

Like I said, people are the problem, not God!

Pentecostal Church, 2014

    I am standing before the same building, the one with a pretty "t" on top of its roof, the highest point in the sky, so people can see it from the highway. As a child, I would see the letter "t" in all sorts of shapes and sizes. I used to wonder what was so special about a "t." Was it God's favourite letter? Why did every church have that "t"? Before my father took us away from the church, I found out the letter "t" was a symbol meant to represent a cross that some man died on, a very important man to God and everyone.

    Now I'm a grown woman and I have my son in one hand and my daughter in the other, and we're walking beside my father, approaching the same ugly, heavy, brown doors to the building. I take a breath and smile at my father who still changes when he enters the house of the Lord. *Why does he do that?* I wonder. I guess it's a matter of decorum: his voice deepens, his goofiness disappears, and his hair is combed back with gel. It's almost like he feels like he has to change in God's house. I find it fucking weird and worse, fake. Here I am, divorced, a single mother of two, with my purple hair and my crazy makeup. I am covered in tattoos and I'm wearing all black. It feels like I am going to a funeral.

    I notice the church looks exactly the same, and I am immediately disappointed. What happened to all the fucking money my dad has poured into this holy dump! It has the same shitty green and brown Berber carpets, the hard, brown pews, and the big "t" in the middle of the wall in front of the church. I watch my dad make conversation with someone and overhear him mentioning,

"This is my eldest daughter, Elisha!" I giggle as I look past their faces, paying no attention to their obvious shock when they take in the sight of me.

We take our seats in the pews on the right side of the aisle as the service starts. This church was once the centre of a community of hundreds of people. Now, less than thirty are present for the service, all of them gawking at the sight of Joey's daughter! The children are called to Sunday School, and I listen for another ten minutes before making my way downstairs to the kitchen where I help myself to a cookie and some tea. I have just finished pouring milk in my tea when I hear footsteps enter the kitchen.

"So, you're Joey's eldest daughter?"

I close the fridge and turn, not surprised at all to see that familiar snot of a woman standing before me. She's older now, and more obtuse.

"I am," I reply, not looking away from her.

"Oh my! You have changed a lot!" she exclaims, her eyes looking me up and down.

"Funny. You haven't changed a bit!" I giggle, but my tone is direct and sharp. She twitches and shifts her weight to her other foot.

After a short pause, she says, "I see you have two children. And where is your husband?" I take a sip of my tea and decide to ignore her question. "Well, it is nice to see the children in church. We most definitely need more Christian children!" she continues.

"My children are not Christian!" I snap.

"I beg your pardon?" The shock in her voice is clear. I swear she has shit herself. I put down my tea and face her.

"Cut the shit!" I bark. She squeaks at my profanity. "Religion is not the problem. *You* are! I am divorced, but you already knew that. I don't raise my children to be like you so-called Christians. I teach my children to have a relationship with God, Jesus, and the Holy Spirit."

She stands there, frozen in place, her eyes bulging.

"I know what went on in this building. I witnessed the corruption and heard the lies spread about my mother by you so-called Christians. There was nothing 'Christ-like' about it! Now you come before me with that 't' around your neck when you haven't the faintest idea what it truly stands for."

Her hand reaches for her necklace. Out of all the deceitful people there, she most needed to be put in her place.

I continue, "I don't hang a cross around my neck. I wear one on my heart. 'Love one another.' Wasn't that Jesus's final commandment? And yet here you are, still passing judgement, except this time we're standing in the kitchen instead of the bathroom."

She just stands there while I slowly turn to pick up my tea.

"Aren't you tired?" I ask quietly.

She leaves the kitchen without a single word. Complete silence follows. I collect my children and father from the service. As we walk to the vehicle, my father and I notice this same woman crying in her car, alone. Concerned, my father wants to go to her.

"Father! Leave her be. This is between her and God!" I demand.

Healing doesn't mean the pain never happened

Daughter of a King
7. *Sisto Road, 1998*

My cousins and I are horsing around in the bedroom my sister and I share, making too much noise for my father's liking. My uncle is visiting and talking with my dad in the living room, which is down a short hallway from my bedroom. My father opens the door and tells us to keep it down or he will spank us. I am older now and haven't been spanked in years. I give him a questioning look.

"You will spank us?" I inquire.

"Not just you, but your cousins too!" he replies.

I immediately call his bluff, knowing full well he can't touch someone else's kids—whether he is family or not. We continue to play, and the door opens minutes later. Dad comes in and charges at my younger cousin; she is tiny compared to my sister and me. Shockingly, he grabs her legs and lifts her off the bed and starts striking her. *What the fuck?!* I say to myself. I can't believe what I am seeing. Pushing my younger sister out of the way, I race to her aid and grab my father's arm. Then he turns on *me!* Suddenly, he is hitting me, missing my ass completely and hitting my lower back. This makes me angry. He finally stops and leaves me facing the wall as he leaves the room. I turn around and see my cousin in the fetal position on the bed. I look to the side to see my sister, her bright green eyes red from crying and her hands clamped firmly over her ears.

That's when I lose it. I turn around and start sprinting full speed for my father. I catch him in the hallway and push that mother fucker as hard as I can. He stumbles over his feet, barely catching his balance. Next thing I know, he grabs me by my neck, lifts me up, and throws me against the wall. He punches the wall inches from my head, leaving a hole in the drywall. He is squeezing my neck so hard, I start to breathe deeply through my nose, trying to conserve oxygen.

"I could snap you like a twig," he growls, staring at me with his green eyes.

"Joe?!" my uncle gasps.

My father ignores him entirely, keeping his eyes on mine. Angry tears start to slide down my face, but I maintain eye contact even as he squeezes tighter. My feet are dangling inches off the floor. With all the strength and will power I have, I muster three words:

"GO FUCK YOURSELF!"

He instantly lets go.

Later that late evening, when I know both of my parents, my sister, and my brother are asleep, I go over to the hallway closet. I pause, making sure the house is still, before slowly opening it. To the left of the closet is the hole his fist left before he let me drop and walked away like a coward. I reach deep inside the closet, pushing aside the jackets. *Where is it?* I wonder. Then I feel the cold steel between my fingers. I pull out the rifle, holding it in my hands, feeling its power. I hear my father's words again: *snap you like a twig.* I load the gun and start walking to my parents' room. Quietly, I open their door and go to the right side of the bed where my dad is sleeping. I have no tears now. I look down at this man, lift the gun into position, and point it at his head. I place my finger on the trigger.

BANG!

It took me twelve years to stand up to my father. Nothing was the same after that. I knew who was in control. He was just a bully, picking on someone half his strength and size. Such a tough guy. I was able to distinguish my father from the tough guy act from that moment onward. In his anger, he became a monster to me, something unlovable. I wasn't afraid anymore. However, my mother was.

When I was a teenager, I had little respect for my mother. She seemed lazy and weak to me. She was not my role model, and I almost disliked her. I thought she was weird with her homemade, embroidered denim skirts. She always smelled of weed and seemed to spend most of the day laying down on the couch eating chips or the kernels out of the popcorn, then discarding the puffy part into a separate bowl. I treated her something awful whenever I could. I blamed her for the things that happened to me in apartment 18. Because of my parents' separation, I ended up having to act like a mother to my siblings, and I resented her for taking my childhood away.

It wasn't always like this, though. I inherited my voice from my mother, and she taught me how to sing. At five years old, I sang along with her as she played the guitar. She is still the most talented woman I have ever known. She draws, she sews, she can read and write music. She will never admit it, but she is like Marilyn Monroe. She can act, sing, and model. She is also a talented writer. The short stories she has written are the most beautiful pieces I have ever read. She wrote one about my father and titled it "Gentle Rock."

Time allowed me to understand her as the woman she was before she became my mother. I was finally able to see *her*—her long, curly, strawberry blonde hair, her bright blue eyes that sparkle when she smiles, her vintage cowboy style. She is the very essence of originality. There was a time when I didn't understand her, and for years, I made the most of every chance to take from her. I broke her heart. She wasn't ever a weak woman, but a woman who would constantly make sacrifices for others. She always placed her happiness second to everyone else's. She judged her value as a woman based on how she benefited someone else. She didn't ask for perfection. She did ask for unconditional love. Unfortunately, most of the time, she was given condition-based love, and many over time broke her trust.

One particular family member took advantage of my mother's mistakes and tried to turn me against her. The second time my parents separated, we lived with my father, but he was working out of town for two weeks at a time. So, he asked this person to stay in our home and look after me and my siblings. This individual was so cruel and very mentally unwell. She called my mother a whore and tried to convince me she wasn't my real mother. She carried out horrific verbal and physical abuse on my siblings, once even kicking my sister down the stairs while she was attempting to put her winter coat on. She stole my sister's birthday money, but when my sister confronted her, she called her a filthy liar and an evil, little witch and told her she was possessed by the devil. She was always slapping my sister in the head, pinching her, or dragging her by the arm. She would lock my little brother in the closet for hours at a time.

She starved both my siblings as punishment, but I was served lavish dinners and invited to late night tea dates. She never laid a hand on me, not once. Instead, she tried to twist the truth and turn me against my mother. My sister begged for my help. When I refused, she told my father what was happening. But, when my father asked me about it, I lied to him about everything. I realize now that not only was this woman trying to destroy my relationship with my mother, she was also turning my siblings against me.

Luckily, my mother learned the truth of what was going on with her children, and she fought for our lives. She restored the peace. My mother rehabilitated her home and children with her powerful love and a lot of forgiveness. Once again, she placed her health to the side for all our sakes.

My father has since changed, but for many years he was not safe to be around. It took three separations and a lot of forgiveness from both of my parents for things to change. "Forgiveness does not change the person who hurt you or mean that you forget. Forgiveness changes *you*, and it's there to cradle you when you remember," my mother once told me. I've never forgotten her words.

Now I see her as a woman battling, fighting for equality. And I realize I want to be just like her. Within ourselves, we find our purpose as *women* before anything else; however, men have made us a commodity for their entertainment. I think a woman's strength lies in her wisdom and gentle spirit. I believe a woman's calm presence and serene mindset can overpower any man. Following my mother's example, I have learned to simply be still, to be silent, and that less is more. I try to inspire without force and guide without control. I create my existence without the hustle. What is that saying? "Behind every great man, is a greater woman." I believe it! Because it's the woman who is stronger, not the man. A woman can soften a man's heart. A woman will allow a man to win his own argument to conserve her strength. I understand the word "surrender," and I'm not triggered by it, because I believe acceptance is the real superpower.

Before I was a woman, or a mother, I was first a daughter of a king. This is what I believe: I am of royalty, and I claim my crown and power to walk purposely through life as an independent woman. No prince necessary! Do you know who else is a daughter of a king? My mother. My father was a bitter tyrant, but she never gave up on him. She continued to love him. This came at a price, and at times she had to leave due to the violence. For a while, she lost herself, engaging in drinking and substance abuse due to the pain. She had every opportunity to divorce him and start again, but she never took it.

For the longest time, I blamed her for the molestation I suffered that night, and the many nights after, in apartment 18. In my early thirties, after some intense counselling, I finally told my parents about that abuse. As I recounted my trauma to them, I let them know that I blamed them both.

"I hold you equally accountable, Dad, because Mom was unwell as a result of your abuse. She couldn't take care of me. She was being held captive in her ongoing nightmare of the suffering you caused her," I told my father.

Reconciliation comes through honesty and integrity. My mother's acceptance of my father and all his pain meant that she bore the responsibility for his welfare. She took on all of his pain as well as her own. He was her "gentle rock," but she helped him find that gentle side of himself.

My mother once shared a story with me from when she was a little girl. She was in her room feeling afraid and decided to pray. She could hear her father strike and her mother wail in pain.

Looking out the window, she prayed to God, asking him to protect her mother. She also asked God to send her a man when she was older who loved him because she knew if that man loved God, he wouldn't bring harm to her. My mother teared up as she recounted this episode to me. She explained to me that my grandmother loved a broken man who took his anger out on a helpless, yet fearless, woman. My mother said my grandmother was fearless because she fought from her heart and loved unconditionally, despite the agony. I questioned my mother's faith, pointing out that her prayers weren't answered. My father was an abusive man.

"Yes, but show me a man who isn't?" she answered with conviction. "Your father loves God; therefore, what harm can he do to me?" she asked.

Her ability to forgive, her endless love, and her obedience to a higher power is something far *greater*. Is she the reason I learned to love the unlovable? Was it her meekness, gentleness, and righteousness to see the truth behind God's plan? She sought a relationship with a man as his daughter before she became any man's wife. She was the daughter of a king.

Today, I grin from ear to ear with twinkles in my eyes. I have the most loving parents anyone could ask for. They truly love each other—and me. That love, together with the truth, has reunited our bond. They have dried my tears and helped heal my wounds. I no longer carry any blame in my heart. We decided to change together. My father is no longer an angry man, but a humble and soft man. He is no longer violent, and it's been over twenty years since he struck my mother. Now he takes his anger out on anything mechanical he's trying to fix, still beating himself up even though he is a retired mechanic. After all these years, his hands are still bloody and scarred. His voice is still deep, and his words are thick when he needs them to be. But now my mother can call him out on his shit, saying, without fear, "You're a fucking asshole, Joey!"

I giggle. He needs to be told that. It's hard to believe that this once menacing, angry, violent man could now be so docile. She's helped him get in touch with his softer side, and now he cries the most in the family. My mother teases him often about it, calling him a "fucking little cry baby." It's hilarious. My mother has adopted some small dogs, in part to fulfill his need for physical touch. That's his love language. Otherwise, he won't leave her alone and gets too clingy. She encourages him to dance and sing along to the music. She is so smart. After all these years with him, she understands him in every way. She has become the leader in his world.

He built her the dream home she always wanted and calls her "Munchkin." He completely and utterly adores her and everything she does. He bows his head in silence and thanks God every single day for her. Their marriage hasn't been easy, and at times it seemed downright impossible. It was painful for me to witness the anger and violence that occurred between them. I can't unsee that, and it remains with me to this day. But I don't linger there. In the end, they endured a total of three separations, but their commitment to one another survived. After a lot of work, growth, forgiveness, and love on both sides, they are now looking forward to their fortieth wedding anniversary.

"Bang!" I try to say it, but no words come out.

I slowly lower the gun, take my finger off the trigger, and quietly walk out of the room, shutting the door behind me. I start to shake uncontrollably. I have to pause and take a knee before unloading the gun. My heart is racing, beating against my chest so hard it starts to hurt. I place my hand over my heart to slow down my breathing. *In through the nose and out through the mouth.* I repeat this in my head until the shakes stop and my breathing returns to normal. I unload the gun, place it carefully back inside the closet, and close the door. I stare at the ground where I was helpless hours ago.

"Who's the mother fucking twig now, bitch!?" I start to giggle.

Suddenly I remember something from a moment before. I was there again, holding the rifle in place, aimed and ready, but then I saw her, my mother. Her white skin was glowing in the moonlight so vividly. I watched her breathe and noticed her hand draped around my father's shoulder. I had the power to end the abuse, the pain, and the monster, but I would have destroyed her. I would have lost her.

PART II

Wake

I will arrive in clarity—not confusion

A best friend and forgiveness

Green Eyes
8. *Chief Lake Road, 2004*

"Shut the fuck up, you fat, stupid bitch!" I scream.

My brother is in the back seat, eagerly waiting to be dropped off at school and praying my anger settles. I had offered to take both my sister and brother to school on my way to work. She and I are arguing about something, but it's different this time. She rarely raises her voice or has anything to say back. I am speeding down the highway in my parents' new, dark blue van, cursing as my anger pulses through my hands and into the grip I have on the steering wheel.

"Slow down, Elisha!" my sister yells back. I ignore her completely. I begin to accelerate, feeling the gas give more juice to the engine. The slight grin on my face is quickly taken away when my sister punches me in the face. The sudden, sharp, stabbing pain spreads from my ear onto my cheekbone. Before I can fully comprehend what's happened, I slam down on the brakes. My brother's backpack flies forward from the backseat onto the front dash of the van. Both of my siblings' bodies look like rag dolls, lunging in a quick jerk movement due to the rapid stop. I slam the van into park and throw myself into a full-on rage fit as I exit the vehicle, flinging the door open, flying out of my seat, and slamming the door shut.

I am parked on the highway close to the right-side ditch where morning traffic merges onto the highway to beat the rush of the day. Not a good place to pull over, but I don't care. I rush to my sister's door, screaming like a frantic lunatic. I grab her door handle only to find it is locked. I pull harder and harder, hoping somehow it will magically unlock. I see my brother in the backseat, his face ablaze with panic and confusion. I go to his window.

"Let me in!" I scream at him. He stares at me, not moving.

"Open the fucking door," I scream louder. With fear in his eyes, he rushes to press the button and unlock the door. I am so quick that I manage to pull the handle to my sister's door the very second he presses the button. I grab the biggest fistful of my sister's hair and try to pull her from her seat, but her seatbelt is still buckled. Undaunted, I shove her head down into her legs, reach over her back, and unlock her seatbelt. Using the same hand, I grab her mid section and throw her out of the van. Her body tumbles through the thick grass, the tall bushes, and finally into a muddy puddle. I charge after her like a wild animal and find her lying facedown in the mud. I grab her shoulder and flip her over. I pin one of her hands with my right knee and jam my left knee into her chest. I hear a gasp of air escape from her mouth followed by a cry of pain. Her free hand tries to lift the weight of my knee off her chest. I raise my fist, priming it with all my strength, ready to strike her so hard that she never forgets who is more powerful.

All I see is green.

She was born with the darkest hair and the most beautiful olive skin tone. From what I was told by my mother, my sister was adored by everyone the very minute she was born. The nursing staff at the hospital would dote on her, playing with her hair. When my father first saw my sister's features, he gave my mother a questioning look (I was born white as fuck, blonde, and always mistaken for a boy.) All my mother did was return my father's look—that was all the reassurance he needed that this was his daughter. When I strolled into the waiting room to see my mother and my new baby sister, I was a toddler who had just turned one and was now a big sister. Apparently, my mother cried her eyes out at the sight of me. I was no longer the baby.

My sister and I are sixteen months apart. For a while, I was a good sister to her, but that all started to change once I grew older. My father's abuse of my mother left me angry, and I released it onto her. She became my punching bag, a place to unleash all my rage. I learned my lesson the hard way though when I let my anger loose outside of my home.

I was in grade nine and had already endured several months of torture from a particular group of girls. I had tried everything: I had attempted to avoid them, sought out counselling, and spoken with the principal about the bullying and how it affected me. I even broke down and cried in my father's arms. Nothing worked. One day, we were warming up to play volleyball in gym class. I hated volleyball—all the girls from this group that was torturing me looked the same with their short shorts, tight, see-through, white shirts, and bleached hair. We were sharing the gym space with the grade nine boys, and I was getting into ready position for a serve when the "Queen Bee" of this group of twats pulled my shorts down. My shorts weren't the only thing that came down either. I was fully exposed, the beef taco with extra sauce was on display for all to see. I happened to be on my period at the time.

I have never screamed so loud and so hard in my life. It startled the whole gym, even the boys in the weight room came over to see what had happened. I collapsed right there on the gym floor and didn't move for the longest time, using my baggy t-shirt to cover myself. I was in shock, and it wasn't until a gym teacher came over to escort me that I could finally retreat to the girls' changing room.

I disappeared from school for two days, the whole time lying to my parents that I was sick and begging them to homeschool me. The experience was so traumatizing. That is when I started cutting. The self-inflicted harm distracted me from pain inflicted on me by others. I found pleasure in it and experienced a kind of ecstasy. I wanted to be nothing but high in that moment. I didn't cut myself on the wrist where my parents would see; I cut the skin on my inner thighs. I accidently cut too deep one time and couldn't get the bleeding to stop. There was so much blood. Holding my leg, I rushed outside and threw dirt into the wound and climbed on my bike, allowing the blood to pour over the seat and metal. Then I raced around to the back of the house to find my father chopping wood and convinced him I had fallen off my bike onto a sharp stick.

"Here comes the bloody virgin Mary!" This is the nickname I endured when I returned to school after the incident. The name was actually quite clever as most of the students had known about my faith in God since elementary school. Now, over half the school knew everything: not only that I was a virgin and that I grew up believing in God, but also how bloody I got every month. After enduring this torture for a while and nursing my wounds, both physical and mental, I felt ready to heal them. I wasn't afraid anymore. I was just numb at that point. I walked by the common room to my locker, head held high and feeling powerful for the first time.

"Bloody virgin Mary!" the "Queen" shouted from the common room. Between the common room and the hallway, there were over fifty students around. Most of them laughed, some stared, and others who understood my pain looked away or rushed past. I refused to be intimidated. I pretended to ignore the Queen as I usually did, placing my books carefully inside my locker. I closed the door shut and locked it. Instead of walking around the long way to avoid her, I proceeded directly towards her, but looked past her as if I couldn't hear her. She was still mocking me and yammering away as I approached her table where she sat with all her fake-ass friends. My heartbeat was so strong I thought it would pop out of my chest and give me away.

It happened so fast no one knew what was going on until it was too late. I grabbed a handful of her blonde hair and with all my strength I slammed her face as hard as I could into the table. Her nose broke immediately. I heard a loud *crack* as blood exploded onto the table. I continued and the more force I used to crush her face into table, the more the blood sprayed everywhere. It covered her friends who had stopped laughing and started screaming in terror. I felt nothing, I heard nothing, but for the first time ever in my life, I felt that I was more than nothing. Later, I was told by a friend that it took three guys to pull me off her. I don't remember that.

I was terrified of my parents finding out, so I made a deal with a friend's mother. She did not hesitate to help me. She agreed to pose as my mother when the school eventually called about the incident, and I pledged to do outside farm work for her for free all summer. She knew about the bullying that I had suffered and felt I had been justified in my reaction. I was suspended from school for a week. The parents of the Queen wanted to press charges, but I was a minor. In the end, my friend's mother defended my actions to the authorities, and I got my wrist slapped by the RCMP for the assault. There was evidence that I had asked for help from everyone including the school counsellor and the principal. The school had a record of my counselling sessions. No one cared, so I took matters into my own hands and defended myself.

"Elisha is a quiet girl who has no record of violence in her past. She did everything that she was told to do and asked for support. Now we are going to punish her for defending herself when ultimately the school and faculty failed her?" my friend's mother argued.

Breaking my parents trust was usually a line I never crossed. Thankfully, they never found out about this. During my week-long suspension, I woke up, packed my lunch, and left for the school bus with my siblings every morning. When I got to school, I walked to the McDonalds and did the schoolwork I was missing. I didn't fall behind, I didn't mind missing class, and I felt free. The first day back after my suspension, everyone moved out of my way when I walked the halls. There were no more whispers, no more nicknames, and the group of squawking Sallys never bothered me again. They couldn't even look in my direction. Perhaps it was because of this episode that I never really had girlfriends in high school. Instead, I gravitated towards the boys. They were my best buddies, and I found they were funnier and more fun to be around, despite the fact that they often teased me. It was always lighthearted teasing though, and I didn't mind it.

The girl I assaulted came back to school a month after the incident. I didn't see her much though as now she was avoiding *me*. I would enter a room, and she would run out of it. I hated that feeling. One afternoon, I was doing some research in the library for a school paper. I pulled the book I was looking for from the shelf and all I saw was black staring back at me from the other side of the bookcase. Her eyes were so swollen and bruised and there were dark purple patches on her nose. Her usually pale skin tone was now so dark. I felt a knot tighten in my stomach as I took in the sight of her. She didn't see me as I rushed out of the library to the nearest bathroom. I locked myself in the stall and started to cry. I cried so hard. I didn't want to believe that I was the one who had disfigured her nose and caused the bruises on her face.

Rumours spread through the school about "the fight." *How in any way was this a fight?* I wondered. The poor girl had her face beaten in. I heard the reason she was gone so long was because her jaw was dislocated. She had to eat through a straw for weeks on end. I threw up when I heard this. I wanted to apologize to her so many times, but how could I? I was so ashamed for what I did to her and the trauma I caused her. Knowing she would never be the same after that, I swore to myself I would never hit another person in anger again. I didn't want to be like my father. Her eyes, the terrible sounds, the blood, and the terrifying silence that followed that day haunt me still.

My sister's green eyes are full of desperation as I, the monster, tower over her. She is frozen in terror, neither blinking nor moving, preparing for what will come next, as tears start to form. The pain marks a spot in her eyes. She watches helplessly as my fist comes down toward her oval face. My fist is already in motion when I hear a sharp, deep sound.

"Elisha, stop!" The voice halts my movement, and I throw my fist down into the water just missing her face. Suddenly, I'm back in the high school library and I see that bruised face and swollen eyes again. After years of torment and unresolved guilt, I realize I am about to do it all over again. I scream as loud as I can, throwing all my hate and anger into the puddle, grass, and bugs. I start to weep and realize I am still on my sister who can't move. Immediately I lift my knee off her and her breath starts grabbing at the air. As she feels my weight lift, she pushes the rest of me off her and makes a dash for the van door. I stay in the grass and release my pain in tears.

"I wasn't taking any chances with your psycho ass!" my sister giggled. A few months later, we were walking on the road in the sunlight, our arms linked together. I was laughing so hard my stomach started to hurt. She was explaining that this was her reason for leaving me behind in the wet grass that day. She continued to tease me.

"How did it feel? Being all wet with mucky water. Try having your head submerged in it. I swear I swallowed a bug too!" she exclaimed. Even after such a terrible experience, she kept her sense of humour.

We were laughing and joking, but I turned away from her gaze and teared up. The pain I caused her and the high school girl due to my acts of rage still haunted me. She caught me pulling away. "Elisha, don't do that!" she said, checking me before I had a chance to apologize again. Then she said something I will never forget, something that put me on the track to healing. "When you start drifting into the past, you lose your purpose in the present. I understand where the anger comes from. You're in pain, and I think it took you hurting me for you to realize it." After hearing this, I expressed my love for her and made her a promise to never hurt her again or allow anything or anyone to hurt her.

"I freaking hope so. You kinda owe me," she replied in her goofy voice. I started laughing and turned to face her to hug her but then suddenly I saw something black running towards us. Alarm bells sounded in my head. *It's a fucking bear!* In a moment of panic, I pushed my sister very hard towards the bear and made a run for it. I have never run so fast in my life.

"What the hell?" my sister yelled. This "bear" was now beside her and she was petting it. I started walking back towards her trying to catch my breath. When I reached her, I saw the bear was actually a three-legged black labrador.

"Holy hell. I am so sorry. I thought it was a bear!" I gasped.

"Are you fucking kidding me? You thought it was a bear and pushed me towards it!?" she asked angrily. I couldn't help but laugh at my pathetic self. This right after I promised to protect her from harm. I totally botched it.

"You are the worst sister ever," she snapped.

My sister shared this story at my wedding to my first husband. She had the crowd laughing so hard. She's funny without even trying. I love that about her. She is way funnier than me. In my eyes, she is also the better mother. She commands obedience without yelling. Her patience, compassion, and capacity for acceptance make her the best mother. I think she gets this from always feeling trapped in my shadow when she was growing up. She wanted to play piano and go to art classes. I wanted to play ball and get dirty. I was always very competitive, but she just didn't have that in her. If a ball came flying her way, she would close her eyes, duck her head into her chest, and randomly throw her glove up anywhere in the air. Or she would scream "Nope!" and run out of the way. It was fucking hilarious.

I was horrible to her when we were kids. When my father built our shared bedroom, I insisted he add a barrier wall between us for privacy. I could not handle clutter in my room or closet, but my sister didn't mind it. I hated our room. We used to share a light, airy room upstairs, but then we moved to this new room in the basement that had no window. It was so dark, it felt like we were living in a cave. The only thing I was excited about was choosing the wall colour. I wanted blue. Then one day, I came home and saw my mother had painted it fucking baby *pink* with green and light blue froufrou sponge accents. The last straw was the tacky, flowery wallpaper border. I had spent my whole life trying to escape that damn colour *pink*. I spent as little time as possible in my room, whereas my sister spent most of her time there.

She would often beg to borrow my clothes, but I always turned her down. I was convinced she would ruin my clothes because she was bigger than me. She had inherited my mother's genes and had her round hips and booty. Her thighs were as thick as my torso and her waist size was three times bigger than mine. She never asked to borrow pants, only shirts and sweaters because deep down she knew pants were out of the question. And yet, I was still the cunt who said no.

She never held it against me, and she never pushed me away.

Her compassion knows no bounds and defies my understanding. She just bided her time and patiently waited for me to come to her. Finally, in my early thirties, I did.

"I want to go to Las Vegas for your fortieth birthday!" she said recently while exiting my closet seemingly wearing every piece of clothing I own, including a pair of pants. We are very similar in size now.

"Whatever you want, darling," was my immediate response. A smile crossed her face as she twirled in front of the bathroom mirror. She caressed the fabric with her hands as if it were Chanel. She was in my black trouser pants that feel like you're wearing a pair of pjs, a white shirt with a floral pattern, and a mid-length, green, open cardigan.

"How often do you wear this?" she asked politely, indicating that she wanted it. I smiled. She knows that smile means she can have whatever she wants. She went back to the closet to grab more, creating a pile of clothes on my bed. I watched and listened as she began acting like she'd won the lottery.

I spoil my sister. She doesn't ask for a thing from anyone, so I fill her cup as often as I can. She always places herself last, taking care of everyone else's needs before her own. I will buy an item of clothing even if I know I won't wear it much, but my sister will love it. If she mentions a lipstick, hair product, or any kind of beauty product, I buy it for her because she never buys things for herself. I spend so much money on myself, it feels good to spend on her sometimes. She shows so much love to her children, cutting up their food into all different shapes for their school lunches: little pineapple stars and perfect circles of melon. I love the way she talks to her children and her animals, changing her tone in mock formality: "Oh, thank you, good sir!" My all-time favourite though is when she speaks for her pets who have a voice through her. "Pup, pup," she says delicately, pretending to be her black and white collie. "Meow, meow," she purrs for her black and white cat.

Her voice is the only one I seek for compassion when I have a broken heart. She's the one person I can go to for support for family struggles. She was there for me when I initially doubted my ability as a writer. "I can't do this. I am not smart enough. I cannot put a sentence together to save my life," I told her. She laughed and admitted this is true but told me that God commanded me to do this. "What is scarier? Obeying him or disappointing him?" she asked me.

She knew the right question to ask me. When I faced my fears and published my first book, going so far as to plaster my face on the cover, she called me and confessed, "Ok, so just know I always believed in you. Like for real, Elisha. But I have to say when I first heard about you writing a book, I honestly thought that you were just going through a mid-life crisis." I burst out laughing, knowing she will always support me, but also be honest and real with me.

She continued, "I encouraged you initially because God was involved, and you don't mess around with the big guy upstairs. But it's actually really good! The book is so well-written, I am in shock." When I heard those words, I could tell she was relieved, and a weight had lifted off her shoulders. But that wasn't what made me hold my stomach in pain with laughter.

"Did you know I am in the book? *Me!* Your sister!"

She is still in shock about it all but what I don't think she knows is that later that night I broke down and cried when I realized it was her voice that had carried me through it all. Her voice helped me to find mine. Her gentle wisdom and support breathed life into me. Her love and intelligence kept me grounded and in balance. I could never have gotten over the enduring pain of my past without her. She was the girlfriend I never realized I had in high school. I always thought I was the strong one because I was tough and hard, but now I realize that just made me brittle and easily broken. She is the truly powerful one because her softness means she can bend without breaking. Her resilience has taught me the true meaning of strength. It's why after all I put her through, the way I treated her when we were younger, she is still able to be my sister, the greatest gift God ever gave me.

Liquid courage, two old souls, and a promise

The Truth According to...
9. *Beauty Salon, 2016*

"You are such a selfish *bitch!*"

This is the second time I have been called this name by my employer. I have been working for this woman for almost three years and knew shortly after my grandma passed in the spring, I would soon gather up the courage to leave. It was only a matter of time.

She is towering over me as I sit on the salon bathroom toilet, staring at the floor in disbelief that she is yelling at me, and I feel my body slowly melt into a puddle. I feel helpless and defeated. My heart is pounding so hard in my chest as I take yet another round of verbal abuse from this woman. I think of all the sweat, blood, and tears I have shed for her. I think of the *time* I have given her, precious time I should have been spending with my kids. I think of all the nights I returned to them, exhausted after another brutal day of work, with little to give them. I think of the toll it's all taken on my state of mind: the stress, the anxiety, the depression, the overall deterioration of my mental health. My body aches all over from the weight gain and the excessively long hours without breaks.

Yet here I sit again. She can't even leave me alone in the bathroom! As I wait for her to finish her tirade, memories of verbal abuse from my past flood my mind.

"Pass the goddamn ball!"

"What the fuck are you doing?"

"Are you stupid?"

I remember all the other people I have worked hard for but for whom my best never seemed like enough.

"Clean yourself up. You have a client in forty-five minutes!" she tells me.

Thank fuck! I think to myself. I let out a gasp of air as she closes the bathroom door behind her. I hadn't realized I was holding my breath. I sit there on the toilet for a long time without moving, running my hands through my hair and going over every detail in my mind. *What did I do wrong? The client asked for me. I did what I was told to help the new stylist.* I feel wetness tickle down my cheeks as the tears spill onto the cold bathroom tile. I take a deep breath and slowly stand up, telling myself, *I can do this! Just a little longer.* I walk towards the door and place my clammy hand on the doorknob. I cautiously turn it clockwise.

Prince Rupert, 2012

I walked through the doors of the local pub to yet another split shift. As a single mother of two children under the age of five, I was exhausted and feeling defeated. I was not a fan of the community in Prince Rupert; everybody knew your business. You couldn't fart in the wrong direction in this small town. I have to say though that the scenery is mesmerizing. I loved walking along the Cow Bay boardwalk, watching the sun set as it slowly descended behind the boundless ocean, the water acting like a gigantic mirror floor, creating an identical second sunset. White shapes move up and down, side to side, gliding above the water. Some purr, some grunt, but most seagulls laugh. They laugh at the people who foolishly bring food to the boardwalk. "Idiots," I mumbled to myself as I watched the tourists coming off the cruise ship.

Because Prince Rupert is made up of hills, you can see the cruise ships miles from shore. Houses of all shapes and sizes dot the hills—small and tall, fat and wide, long and steep. They're all character homes, all very old but usually slightly updated to modernize them yet still keep their authenticity. Bright green moss grows everywhere: on roofs, pathways, trees, and even light posts. It rains nine months out of the year, which was my second most-hated feature of this town. You don't get sunlight. The book *Twilight* is set in the fictional town of Forks, Washington, which is described as the wettest and cloudiest place on earth. I'm convinced the author was inspired by Prince Rupert. "The City of Rainbows," the locals call it. Typical! Let's call the rainiest, most depressing place in Canada something romantic.

I will say, however, that the most beautiful drive I have ever taken is the one from Terrace to Prince Rupert. You're in the middle with mountains on the right and the Skeena River on the left. The rich green of the dense, life-giving forest is shot through with endless white veins—waterfalls that pour forth from the mountain and feed all below. The beige sand of river shoreline in September, when the river runs low, seems never-ending. Driftwood piles up for miles, with surfaces carved into various shapes and designs by nature. Little creatures venture out onto the dunes, smelling new land, as the eagles soar above, ready to hunt their prey. When I make this drive, I like to pretend I'm a Viking warrior who has lost her love in battle and is making the long trip home. I'll admit my imagination gets a bit overactive on long drives through romantic scenery.

I had moved to Prince Rupert with my first husband for his career. By 2012, we were separated, and I was working hard to make ends meet. I chose to walk away from my marriage; it wasn't for me. I really made an effort to be his wife and a mother to his children, but honestly, I was just left so empty. I was so alone all the time. I didn't recognize the overweight person with the blonde hair and pale skin I had become. I really worked at being a good mother, but I was a terrible wife and not a great friend. I was so fucking lost, I didn't know who I was anymore. I had recently left a job working for the government that paid triple what I made as a server. However, I knew by leaving that cubicle I could feel a little bit of my soul spark again. I was around people again in a fast-paced environment, not isolated in a little box.

I was judged harshly for leaving my desk-bound, office career for a minimum-wage server job, but I was beginning to find myself again, and that was important. Little by little, I started to recognize the person in the mirror. It wasn't easy at all though. I worked longer hours, barely saw my children, and most nights I was plagued with doubts about my decision. I cried myself to sleep a lot.

This particular evening, I looked over my section and saw the two ladies who come every Thursday for their draft beer hang out. They were the sweetest, kindest locals, the lifeblood for a small-town pub. Mary loved extra foam but Cindy wanted very little. Sometimes they would come with their husbands, but mostly it was just the two of them. Cindy spotted me first.

"Well, hey there, my darling!" she called as she leaned into me for a hug and a kiss on the cheek. Mary came right next to her and gave me a tighter squeeze, pushing Cindy out of the way.

"Goddamn, you're a pushy bitch!" Cindy snapped. Mary just started to laugh.

"She doesn't want your lame-ass hugs," Mary replied. I left them to their corner seats overlooking the harbour and poured their draft beers. Making my way slowly to the table, I placed their drinks down on coasters. "What is wrong, dear?" Mary asked.

"You look like someone pissed in your cornflakes!" Cindy barked.

I smiled but teared up at the same time. Cindy's face softened as she got up from her seat. Mary stayed silent. I turned away. Later, as I was walking towards the kitchen to pick up an order, I saw Cindy exit the manager's office. I gave her a shy smile, embarrassed that I had let her see me cry. She came over and grabbed the food out of my hands and placed it back under the heat lamps.

"Your shift is over!" she exclaimed. Panicked, my eyes darted towards my manager who had just come out of her office.

"Elisha, it will be slow tonight. Take the rest of the night off," she told me. I wanted to protest, but Cindy's glare stopped me in my tracks. I cashed out, nervous about what had just taken place. I was about to leave, coat in hand, when Mary asked me, "Where do you think you're going?" Taking me by the arm, she walked me to their table where I noticed a third drink had appeared—my favourite, a Paralyzer. Cola, coffee liqueur, vodka, and milk served over ice: the ultimate. Now I was bawling. Mary put her hand on mine while I completely broke down, crying out all my sorrows. Cindy remained still, silently sipping her beer, and occasionally indicating to the bartender to keep the Paralyzers coming. I vented about my shitty life in that small town, how I'd left my husband and two kids, how I was broke and feeling like an absolute failure as a mother, wife, but mostly as a woman.

"I never saw myself here. I feel so alone," I sobbed.

"I understand, sweetheart," Mary replied. Mary always knew what to say. Cindy was the opposite. She was more about action.

"Are you done coddling her?" Cindy snapped, looking at Mary.

"Oh, shut up!" Mary shot back.

Now on my third drink on an empty stomach, I was feeling pretty good, and I giggled at these remarks. Usually, I would have been fearful of Cindy's tone. She reminded me of my father in the direct and blunt way she spoke.

"Elisha, you lack purpose. So, quit whining and go find it," Cindy told me as she looked me in the eye. I returned her look without moving. I had too much respect for her to try to argue, using any of my million excuses. *How do I find my purpose?* I thought to myself. Finally, I felt free to really say what was in my heart.

"I am done feeling guilty for wanting to lead a purposeful life. All I have ever done is what everybody else wanted me to do. I love being a mother, but I need to be more than that. I need to find something that drives me. I don't know what talents I have, but I recognize that I can either decide to start to explore this or remain sitting still," I said. There were no more tears. My voice was not shaky or weak, but strong and powerful. I watched as the biggest smile spread across Cindy's face. She held up her glass and tipped it towards me.

"Cheers!" she said, before she took a drink. "Now *that* is the Elisha I know."

"You're still a cunt!" Mary chirped. Mary always had the last word. I sat with these two souls all night, laughing and drinking.

The next morning, I woke up with the worst hangover. I don't even remember how I got home. I was still wearing my clothes from the previous night, and I felt something in my pocket. I reached down inside and pulled out a piece of paper. The writing was terrible. It was chicken scratch and all smudged, but I could just make out what it said: *Don't forget your promise.*

What the fuck? I wondered. I didn't remember making any promise. *Oh my God, did I promise a guy something? What the hell have I gotten myself into?*

I headed to McDonalds for my hangover cure: six hashbrowns and an orange juice. Back at home, I sat on my couch and stirred some electrolyte powder into my juice, my solution for dehydration. My phone started to ring. I saw it was my best friend, but I didn't pick up. I knew that if she found out I was hungover, she'd give me so much shit. She called again and still, I didn't answer. *Wait*, I thought. *She knows!! How the biscuits did she find out I was drinking?* Before I could answer, there was a knock at the door. *Holy hell, it's her! Fuck!* As I walked to the door, I secretly prayed to God that it was my neighbour coming to complain about the deer eating his flowers. I would actually have given anything for it to be him at the door. Then I could have finally confessed that it has been me pulling the fucking heads off his precious damn plants the whole time, ever since I saw him shoot a baby deer in the butt with a pellet gun. I delighted in taking revenge for that poor baby.

The banging was getting louder and harder. I unlocked the door, but before I could open it, it swung open pushing me back. Jenny stood before me, laughing.

"How are you feeling this morning, cupcake?" she giggled. "I noticed you didn't answer your phone, so I thought I'd come over."

Goddammit! I thought to myself. *I know better than to not answer my phone when she calls.* She pushed her way through me and kicked off her shoes. I closed the door behind her as I slowly rolled my eyes. *This is going to be a long day*, I sighed to myself. I turned to see her sitting in my spot on the couch, eating my hashbrowns. I just smiled.

"Great fucking breakfast. Did you get ketchup?" she asked, enjoying herself. I finally laughed out loud. Her eyes were wide in excitement, and I could see the ginger freckles on her white skin. Her light, coppery brown hair was cut in a short, graduated bob, the ends dangling at her chin line. I sat down beside her. "So, where is your laptop?" she inquired.

"Why?" I asked.

"You don't remember do you?" Her grin was as big as Jack Nicholson's Joker's in *Batman*. I became anxious and unwillingly went to go grab my computer. I handed it to her, and she did her thing while I nervously stuffed hashbrowns in my mouth. Finally, she placed the computer in front of me, and I started to read: *Your application has been received* was written there on the screen in bright green, bold letters. I started to choke on my hashbrowns. She handed me my "baby juice," as she liked to call it.

"What the fuck is this, Jenny?!" I coughed through my words.

She began to tell me about the previous night. I had made a promise to find my purpose and apparently that was applying to cosmetology school while intoxicated.

"The note!" I exclaimed. "I can't do this, Jenny. I have kids! I have no money, nothing!" I was shouting at this point, and the panic was setting in. Jenny just smiled. I started to pace back and forth, trying to figure out how to undo the mess I had made.

"Elisha, your promise wasn't *applying* to cosmetology school. Your promise to Cindy and Mary was that if you got accepted, in three months you *must* go—no questions asked!" Her eyes held mine. She knew to hold me there. By now, my mouth had gone dry.

"Jenny I can't go to hair school. I don't know a fucking thing about hair!" I was desperate for her to see reason and help me terminate the application.

"That is why you go to hair school, dumbass! To learn," she replied. She wasn't there to help me undo anything I did while intoxicated the night before. She was there to make sure I went through with it! She was the one who had driven me home and made sure I would find the piece of paper in my pocket.

"You left me the note about my promise, didn't you?" I asked.

"Nope. *You* did!" she laughed.

Within two weeks, I learned my application was successful. I would be starting hair school in the fall. In less than four months, I packed as much of my life as I could into my Jeep Patriot and took off to spend a year in Kamloops. I left that small, rainy town, my best friend, my house, and my children with less than one thousand dollars in my bank account. I cried the whole way there. It may have started with a bit of liquid courage, but I kept my promise to Cindy and Mary.

Cosmetology school was a fucking joke. I hated every minute of it. It was nothing but long days, boring, mindless studies, and the worst: perm roller sets. I did not sign up for this: to set, roll, and hope the curl sets in with this god-awful, stinky perm solution? Ugh. It was terrible. I knew it was not a service I would ever want to offer to my clients. Nevertheless, we had lists of tasks that had to be completed by graduation—foils, haircuts, and you guessed it, perms. Your mark got reduced if all the little squares beside these tasks weren't checked off by graduation day. They expected something stupid like a hundred rolled perm sets.

Yeah! Sure! I cheated and most definitely checked off more than I did. As part of the program, you even had to do a perm set on a customer who would come to the school. When I found out I was scheduled for a perm set with an actual person, I skipped school that day. I *never* touched a perm set again after I finished cosmetology school.

The director at the school I attended in Kamloops was the funniest looking man I have ever seen. He had white hair cut in a mohawk with the sides shaved. He was shorter than me, and I am five foot four. He had absolutely no clue how to run a school let alone work with hair. He owned a white poodle that would shit in the classroom and the work areas, but he'd still walk the halls with that dog in his arms. The man was ridiculous; there is no better word to sum him up.

Only two things made my time in Kamloops enjoyable. One was an instructor named Dawn. She was heaven and so beautiful from the inside out. She saw my drive and my talent, and with her soft voice, she pushed me to do my best. There were days though when she was so tired she would ask me to help teach the newcomers. She would sit behind her desk and guide me as I tried to demonstrate whatever techniques were to be learned. I wasn't the best student to choose for this task, but I think she chose me repeatedly because I made her laugh so much. I didn't do it on purpose. I was just a bit of a goofball. "Oh, Elisha!" she would giggle.

The classroom would roar with laugher over my theatrical sense of humour. I fucking hated working on a mannequin, especially this particular one I had nicknamed "Suzy Cream Cheese." Dawn loved that name and always asked me to demonstrate using Suzy. I had wanted to name her "My Bitch," but Dawn pointed out that Suzy Cream Cheese was more elegant. I would sulk as I went to get her off the shelf, grabbing her by the hair and drop kicking the mannequin head across the classroom. Dawn would smile while calmly telling the other students not to follow my example when moving their mannequins. Finally, I would slam the head into the holder and start my demonstration.

One day, after one of my performances, I noticed Dawn wasn't her usual self. She appeared even more tired, and she didn't seem to have her trademark patience. Gone were her warm smile and lovely laugh. When the class ended, I went to her and saw her hands were shaking and sweat was forming on her forehead.

"Dawn, is there anything I can do for you?" I asked. I reached for her hand, which I noticed was cold and clammy. I bent down to meet her eyes and was struck by a detail I had never noticed before. Her chin length bob, accented with soft, delicate beige-gold streaks that blended into her light blonde hair, was netted around her head. I realized it was a wig.

I felt so guilty for not having noticed it before. I left her for a moment and came back with some water. I watched her drink slowly and listened to her tell me to get to my next class. I didn't see her for the next two weeks. No one knew anything, only that she took some time off. Then she was back, smiling, laughing, and allowing me to drive her crazy. Dawn was at the heart of my time in cosmetology school. Years later, a colleague informed me that she had passed. Dawn left this world after battling cancer for years. She became an angel, creating another heaven as she did for me during my time with her. I will never forget her or the love she gave me, and I will always be grateful for her belief in the stylist and artist I would become. I know I make her proud.

The second greatest part of my time in school was finding a kindred soul named Katie. On the first day of class, she showed up in a mini skirt and bright pink stilettos. I laughed out loud at the sight of this broad. I stared at her as I started to dissect her look: her mid-length brown hair coloured with tacky, blonde, zebra streaks, her hands edged with pink stiletto daggers. I had never seen such long nails. *How the fuck was this chick going to do hair with those monsters?* I wondered. I judged her very harshly based on her appearance and decided we would have nothing in common. We would just be acquaintances, nothing more. At that time, I hated the colour pink, and she was covered in it. At five foot eight, she was always blocking my view during instruction. Her booty was the size of my torso, her tits the size of my head, and her skin made me look white as a bed sheet. I decided I hated her.

But she always took my side in debates and told me I was the best student, the one who was actually going to leave school and make something of myself. She pumped up my tires pretty well. She laughed the hardest when I was clowning around, cheering me on, encouraging me to provide more entertainment to make the day go by faster. To my surprise, she was my biggest fan. She used to call me her "purple freak."

I didn't do a single thing to deserve her, but she got me through hair school. I really struggled leaving my children behind and no one knew I was a mother of two until she saw me crying one day at school. I was in the lunchroom feeling upset, tired from work, lonely, and homesick. A teacher called my name for class and Katie popped her head around the corner to see me sitting down on the floor, knees to my face, bawling my eyes out. She made eye contact with me for a second before turning around and heading back out the way she came.

"She isn't in here. I think she may have gone home for the day. She mentioned she wasn't feeling well." Katie's reply stunned me.

Another ten minutes went by, and then I heard her footsteps

thumping down the hall. She burst through the door out of breath.

"Come on, lets get the fuck outta here!" she panted. She helped me up, grabbed my shit out of my locker, and told me to follow her. She handed me a tissue she had fished out of her cleavage and led me down the hallway. A big exit sign glowed above my head. Below it, there was another sign saying *DO NOT OPEN*.

"Ready?" she asked.

"Ready? Ready for what?" I asked.

She pushed open the door, setting off the alarm, and started to run. I scampered after her, and the two of us rushed up a hill to get around the corner before we were seen. I had gotten ahead of her when suddenly I saw a pink shoe in my path. I looked back just in time to duck her other shoe.

"Grab my fucking shoes, you fast bitch. I can't run in them," she gasped, her face red and sweaty. I started to laugh so hard at the sight of her I couldn't move. I was holding my belly as she grabbed my arm and hauled me to the top of the hill. I had one of her shoes in my hand and the other tucked under my armpit. There we were, both out of breath, both sweaty, and both realizing we now had a free day together.

I ended up telling Katie everything about my life and what I had left behind. "You have fucking kids?" she squeaked in shock. "You're sexy as fuck *and* a MILF?!" It was her turn to make me laugh. She took care of my tears, fed me pachos (lattice fries with cheese and green onions) and got me a Paralyzer—my favourite snack and my favourite drink. As I stuffed my face, it struck me that she knew everything about me, but I didn't know a thing about her. I felt ashamed that I had judged her so harshly based on her appearance alone. The saying "never judge a book by its cover" hit me hard in that moment.

"Katie, I owe you an apology. I have been so mean and judgmental towards you," I said, staring down at my hands as tears started forming. Looking up at her, I continued, "I'm sorry for being a bitch!"

She took her glasses off and, at that moment, I noticed how much she reminded me of my sister. Just like my sister, her eyes were all out of focus and one was kinda crooked. I started to giggle.

"Girl! You be trippin'. You don't owe me a thing," she laughed. "Sounds like this is more of an iss-*you* than an iss-me. But you know who is an issue? That ho in school, Daniella." She went off about this chick for the next forty-five minutes. We laughed and laughed. I teased her about the fact that she speaks like a washed-up cowgirl who is pretending she is Black but also loves singing to country. Katie and I were best friends from that day on. Her energy continues to match mine in every way.

The next day the director of the school was giving a speech to the students about the alarm going off and disrupting classes. He gave a warning that if caught, the perpetrators would be dismissed from school. As Katie tried to hide her smile, I stood up and interrupted him.

"Come on, you guys! I take my education very seriously. Whoever did this should think twice about doing it again," I said.

The director was not impressed. Katie almost fell out of her chair crying with laughter. He knew that we knew that he knew, but he had no evidence. We continued to pull off this prank every month. He eventually got pissed off enough that he installed cameras both inside and outside. At that point, Katie decided to really have some fun and bought bright pink and purple glitter masks and a pink wig to cover my purple hair (she knew I *hated* pink). We would put our hair in pig tails and race out the door, setting off the alarm every time. Despite our disguises, it was pretty clear that it was us. But it was enough to prevent the director from being able to positively identify us. So, he would make the same speech the next day with Katie laughing in the background and me being a smart ass with my words. These episodes were the highlight of my time in hair school with my girl Katie.

Straight out of cosmetology school, I landed an interview at what was rumoured to be the best salon in Prince George. I was over the moon and, after graduating as the top student in my school, I was eager to continue to develop my talent. I wore all black to my interview and way too much makeup. My purple hair was down, and I was rocking a double side shave. I walked into the salon and immediately felt intimidated. All the women in the salon were glowing. The hair, clothing, and colours were all incredible. The staff stood out the most, each woman had her own vibe and groove. I watched as a taller lady softly tossed her client's hair, turning her chair slowly so she could admire the unique and exquisite cut and colour in the mirror. Each element in the stylist's design brought out a feature in the client's face, and the smile on her face showed how much she loved it. Walking in the doors of that salon, I realized that this is not just "hair dressing." This is a professional career.

My train of thought was interrupted when my eyes fell on the hair products for sale. I had never seen such a palette of colours on bottles of shampoo and conditioner, all with the big letter K, which as I moved closer, I realized stood for "Kevin Murphy." The packaging was gorgeous, but everything was tiny compared to other salon products I had worked with like Goldwell, Redken, and Joico. I figured Kevin Murphy must be pretty fancy stuff.

"Excuse me? Can I help you find something?" asked the lady at the front desk. I suddenly remembered I was there for my interview.

"Yes. I am actually here for my interview," I answered. This lady's face turned sour, as if she just drank spoiled milk. She caught herself just in time to cover over it with a fake smile.

"Have a seat. Can I get you anything while you wait?" she inquired.

"No, thank you," I replied, my eyes meeting hers and a big fat smile on my face. While I waited, I decided to familiarize myself with this Kevin Murphy. I noticed he doesn't used the word "shampoo" for his line. He uses "wash." I went to turn over the square bottle and saw the tiny thing before tax was thirty dollars.

"Fuck! What a rip off! Who in the world would buy this shit?" I muttered under my breath. I was startled by a voice behind me.

"Did you know that the square packaging holds more product by volume?" The taller lady who I had seen earlier standing behind the chair styling was now reaching for the bottle in my hands.

I gave her my smile and hand to shake.

"You must be Paulina?" I asked.

"Yes. I am the owner of the salon," she responded as she reached for my hand.

I was hired and found out grumpy snot pants who greeted me when I entered was my manager. Anytime I was put on phone duty, she would glare at me, watching as I fucked up the names I couldn't pronounce properly as I left messages for clients on their voicemail. Everyone else got a kick out of it, but her? She was not amused. She didn't care to take the time to get to know me. She had already stamped "I don't like you" over my picture in her books. As for me, I knew I had to treat her with respect to her face, but sometimes I couldn't help but stick my tongue out at her behind her back. She was, however, magnificent in customer care, a specialist in my eyes. I would watch carefully how she interacted with clients. People honestly fell in love with her. Her words and beauty could lift you up in this special way.

The owner, boss, and master stylist, Paulina was mesmerizing. She was an artist and had it all going for her: a successful business, a strong team of stylists, and people who loved her. She was at the forefront of the hair industry and always on top of what was current and fashionable. She taught me the trends of the season, the importance of clean, high-quality products, and the value of winning the client's trust. I was most impressed with her business mindset. In my eyes, that was her greatest asset and strength. Her marketing and advertisements brought in the exact clients she was after. If you worked for her, she would talk you up, as if she were your own personal agent. She knew about money and how to invest it wisely when it came to running a salon. I watched her every move and absorbed every piece of information like a sponge. Her success at running a successful and profitable business was something I admired. I looked up to her, as a woman, a mother, and a friend. This was Paulina.

At the same time, there was a dark evil that came from within her at times, an ego that wouldn't accept responsibility for any of the pain it caused. I called her Mrs. Hyde. I have never been written up at any past job ever in my life, but working for this woman, I was written up twice. The first complaint was over me leaving earlier than normal on a Monday, a day the salon closed. Every eight weeks, we had to come into the salon for a fucking "hair day" when we would all do each other's hair. We did not get compensated for this, and I had to put my kids in daycare for it.

That particular day, I had been explicit about my need to leave by 2:00 pm. In fact, I mentioned it three times to be exact! And yet, I still got yelled at.

"You are such a selfish bitch! Get the fuck out of my salon!" Paulina bellowed at me. I showed up the next day to find an intense, two-page write-up. I didn't agree to everything that was written, but at the time I wasn't ready to leave. So, I signed the fucking thing. She made matters worse for me after that, hovering over me all the time. She was a bully.

The second write-up was due to a conversation I had with a client who inquired about two staff members who no longer were employed at the salon. I mentioned very casually one had moved away and the other started her own business. I was honest and told the client where she could find this individual. She was inquiring after all.

Well, fuck me in the ass. Here I was again being written up for what? Being honest with a client? I was told I was unprofessional and a gossip.

The truth was it was about her ego, her pride, and the vanity of the idea of "owning" a client. How dare I send clients where they truly want to go?! In my training, I was taught to sell—yourself and the products, but I longed for more in my career. I wanted to be an artist and fall in love with the person in the chair first and then with their hair. I wanted there to be a foundation of trust. I wanted it to be intimate. I was promised that if I worked hard and built up a clientele, I could have what I wanted most: a flexible schedule that would allow me more time with my children. I clung to this ideal.

As my talent and career grew, so did my clientele, but Mrs. Hyde would seek to destroy it. Instead of being inspired by me and learning my gifts as a successful colourist, she would tear me down continually, always underestimating my knowledge and questioning my decisions because I was "just a junior stylist." Mrs. Hyde acted as if she owned me, and she would try to control me. I did things differently. I took my time with the person in the chair and treated them like a human being, not a way to make money. I wouldn't talk to them through the mirror. Instead, I would sit in front of them, face to face, to build their trust by asking about their life. I wanted to understand their personality before I asked about their hair: a woman's beauty security blanket, one of her most valuable assets. I gave my clients my time; I wanted to gain their trust and make them feel cared for.

Unfortunately, the more time I devoted to these free consultations, the less time I was devoting to making Mrs. Hyde money. I saw less and less of the sweet, kind, and compassionate Paulina and more of the "time is money!" Mrs. Hyde. She wasn't happy about my approach, or the success I was having. I was outgrowing her. She countered by sowing seeds of doubt in me, based on lies. She told me I could never have a salon of my own until I became a master stylist. I'd have to go to business school if I hoped to run a successful salon. Finally, the ultimate cutdown: we were all being dropped off after a coworker's bachelorette party and when we arrived at the new house I had just purchased, she opened the door and got out so I could exit the limo. With a sarcastic smile, she said, "Nice house. It's too bad, you won't ever be able to have a salon in this terrible neighbourhood."

Still, I stuck it out at the salon. After two years there, I had grown a wonderful client base and developed a reputation as a talented colourist. I had also made Paulina a shit ton of money. Sitting down at my year-end evaluation meeting with my boss and manager, I finally felt justified in asking for more flexible hours so I could cope better as a single mother. To my disbelief,

I was denied this request and told it was "not good for business." I argued that I had been working hard, had been successful, and that another stylist who was also a mother had been hired after me but was allowed to keep a flexible schedule. Paulina told me, "She is a senior stylist with ten years of experience."

I tried to argue that my knowledge of colour more than made up for my lack of years behind the chair. Plus, my education was more recent and an asset for clients looking for the latest trends and styles. No one else in the salon understood the colour techniques I had mastered. "Wouldn't that make me a so-called 'master stylist,' at least in colour?" I countered.

"You are nowhere near a master stylist," they told me.

I was denied, and before I knew it, the meeting was over, and I was leaving the room disappointed and exhausted. All my hard work and preparation had gone down the fucking drain. I started to cry. I couldn't believe after all my effort and all that time that it still wasn't enough. My poor little babies; the mom guilt I felt for never being around when they needed me was overwhelming.

The harder I cried though, the clearer the truth became. I realized Paulina, a woman I had grown to love despite her tough character, would never be happy with my work. She had hired me knowing that I was a mother and how important that was to me. This was the final blow. Or so, I thought…

I exit the bathroom and head to my cubby by the colour bar to take a long drink of my smoothie. *I can't get another write-up and endure months of torture again*, I say to myself. I had already made plans to leave this woman, but I just needed a little more time. Paulina whips around the corner and I shoot my eyes down. My heart is racing. She ignores me for a split second while she starts mixing her colour formula. Suddenly, she turns around and as she does, I look up into her green eyes. "You and I will be talking again after work. You will need to stay late," she tells me curtly.

I feel my face burn up and my sweat tickle down my back. With my eyes never leaving hers, I finally stand up to this woman. "No. We will not!" I say firmly. I quickly and quietly collect my most expensive items: my shears and clippers. Then I grab my purse and the smoothie. Just before I leave, I lock eyes with a coworker who had always helped me so much during my years there. My eyes say it all, and with a soft smile and a head tilt, I vanish through the door.

Elisha Rose Beauty & Style, 2017
Location? In my fucking *home!*

I walked free after three years working under that woman. I left with no references, no clientele, and no job. It was my first stylist position, and the last time I had a boss. In the fall of 2016, with help from my family, I built a 400-square-foot salon in my home, that very same home in the supposedly bad neighbourhood. I didn't need a business degree or a master stylist title. I just didn't need to be around people telling me I couldn't do it.

Now I am in charge, and I threw out the rulebook. Titles no longer matter. I value my time and those who give me theirs by sitting in my chair. I take as many breaks as I need to eat, rest, and be with my children. I never double book myself: one client, one conversation, and one-on-one quality time. I offer a safe space and an exclusive experience for all of us, myself and my customers. I provide complimentary consultations, something that is unheard of in the industry. I created the Rose Café, a coffee and tea bar at the salon where I can pamper my guests with homemade drinks and treats. I care about every single detail and express this, not only in the way I do my job, but also in the space I built. Lavendar-grey painted walls, antique mirrors I salvaged, and my greatest accomplishment: my grandma's dresser. She passed shortly after I started building the space and left me some of her things. I took her dresser and painted it white, and the drawers three shades of purple faded from dark to light. On one set, I installed white rose handles.

"You know what happened today, Mom? I accidentally kicked the soccer ball right into his face and broke his glasses." My daughter, who is eight years old, is telling me about her day while I'm blow drying and styling a client's hair in the salon. The salon has been in operation for three years and is now thriving with a full roster of clientele. All my clients know I am a mother first and understand that my children are my priority. I built my business through hard work, study, and experience, and my recipe for success is simple: give my best without compromising on what is important to me. I broke the rules that had constrained me when I first became a stylist and implemented new ones that I can live with.

My time is precious, and I've built a schedule that puts my needs first: especially my need to look after myself and my children. No longer do I miss hockey, judo, or any other event. I make time in the mornings for meditation, reading, and taking my fur baby for walks. At the same time, I do not allow myself to be rushed through conversations with clients. I am always fully present with them, and many of them feel safe enough to cry and express their problems and heartbreaks. I am not just a stylist; I am a therapist. I want to care for my clients in every way: hot towel massages, deep scalp therapy, and sharing what I love most in the world: my beautiful children.

"I missed you today, Mom!" my son said one day, planting a kiss on my cheek as he walked into the salon. I paused and pulled the shears away from my client as I looked into his eyes. I'm on the verge of telling him how much I love him when he cuts me off. "I know, Mother. I am your whole world." I smiled as he left the salon and turned back to my work and the client.

"Thank you for your patience and understanding," I said politely to the client. I never apologize for my children's presence in the salon or the occasional time they pull my attention away.

"You don't need to thank me, Elisha. Children come first, and I am truly honoured to be a part of your experience!" she told me.

Shortly after I left Pauline and her salon, I heard rumours that she lost most of her staff within that same year. She ended up selling her business to a new hire and constructed another salon within her home. It broke my heart to hear how much she lost. She once owned the top salon in all of Prince George but lost it all. When I heard, I sent her a text to let her know how sorry I was, although I didn't apologize for walking out on her. There was no response until she heard that my partner had passed away.

"Elisha, I'm so sorry you lost Brad. My thoughts are with you and your kiddos. You're a fighter. You'll get through this. I believe in you," she wrote.

I now realize that no matter your first impression, people are never all good or all bad. We're all somewhere in between. Paulina was a monster to me at times, but I was also immature and needed guidance. She took a chance on me and gave me my first job. She was tough on me, and at the time, it was hard. But I learned a lot from her and in the end, it helped shape me into the stylist I've become. After working for her, I not only had the skills I needed. I had the gumption. I wouldn't have the career I have today had I not worked for her. We had our differences, but that doesn't mean she was a bad person. We just thought differently about things. And now I realize that encountering an alternative point of view can be a great opportunity. It might mean you try something new. Or it might make you even more convinced of your original mindset and give you the strength to pursue your dreams.

Small price to pay for some pussy

Wanna See a Big Dick?!
10. *Prince George, 2021*

I can barely get the key in the door lock. I have weight up against me from behind. I feel a pinch in my crotch and drop the keys. I bend down to grab the keys, the weight increases. I feel something hard push up against my butt. I lift up slowly, pushing back firmly. I am grabbed by the elbow and spun around to face this boy candy I picked up from the local pub. I pause for a brief moment as I flashback to the first time I met him, before I let him stick his dick near my ass.

"Elisha, this is my daughter, Paige and my son, James." This woman has come to me for years to get her hair done. She's decided it's time for her teenagers to get their hair cut by me as well. James was so shy and cute; he spoke very little that day. But now, years later, his innocent tongue is down my throat. I stroke his cock, which is so hard I can trace its imprint on the outside of his jeans. He pulls away from my lips, his hand grabs my neck, and I feel his teeth on my throat. He is kissing, nibbling, and sucking down towards my tits. I feel every fucking emotion of pleasure. *Goddamn, this feels so fucking good*, I say to myself. I try to turn away to get the key in the lock, but he pushes hard against me, ripping open my cheap, see-through, black blouse exposing my black tube top. He grabs the centre, between my boobs, and pulls it down. His mouth feels so good on my nipples. I feel myself getting wetter and wetter. I could get off with just boob foreplay, and this kid had it down. I push him away and off me and quickly turn to open the door. The same door he has walked through many times for a haircut now bursts open and is hastily slammed shut and locked behind us.

We kiss as we peel off our shoes. His hands go to my ass, and he grasps me firmly just under the cheeks. He lifts me up as if I weigh nothing and carries me into the house, placing me down on the stove while he continues kissing me everywhere. He is so young and healthy. Alive and spicy. I undo his belt, unzip his jeans, and reach deep down inside his boxers pulling out his cock. I stroke it gently and realize it needs some juice. I withdraw my hand pulling back my head from his, detaching my lips and bringing my hand to my mouth. I spit loud enough for him to hear and seize a hold of his erection. A groaning sound releases from somewhere deep within and I see his head move like a bobblehead you place on the front dash of a car. I listen intently, making sure not to give too much. I don't want to spoil my dinner with dessert. I grab his neck and pull him towards me. As I loosen my grip, still stroking but more slowly and softly, my lips reach his ear.

"What do you want, James?" I ask in a seductive whisper. I rub my lips along his ear and lick the side of his ear lobe. He doesn't answer. He grabs my hand off his penis and picks me up again. He makes his way to the couch and places me down very gently, sliding his hands up my sides before pulling down to remove my pants. My underwear is still on as he spreads my legs and moves his head into the kill zone. I feel his warm breath on my silk panties. I gasp at the tingles I feel as his mouth touches my inner thighs, and he takes big bites into my flesh. Holy fuck he is eager to please me.

"I understand what you are going through," James is saying. We were dancing hand in hand to some music at the pub. He had been buying me drinks all night after finding out that my partner had passed away. He said this kind of loss was familiar to him. He knew the pain of losing a loved one.

How in the hell can such a young guy know all of this? I wonder, blinking rapidly trying to understand what is happening to me. Meanwhile, James's tongue twists and turns like a tornado inside of me. He retracts his tongue and licks the sides of my meat curtains, up and down, then slides down the steep slopes of a very slippery mountain and into my taint. I start to shake uncontrollably and clasp my legs around his head suffocating him in my pussy.

He knows I am close and pushes my legs apart. He stands up, takes off his shirt, unhooks his pants and pulls them and his boxers down. His hand reaches for me, and I grab a hold of it. He lifts me effortlessly into him as he turns himself around to sit down on the couch. I am about to mount him. *Dear God, I hope I remember how to do this.* I take a deep breath and exhale.

The Rum Jungle, October 2006

The hotspot in Prince George was a nightclub called The Rum Jungle. I had decided since I didn't party or drink, why not make money off the people who do? I was nineteen and had no plans for the future, aside from saving money. So, I started working in the newest and most popular club. I wasn't popular in high school but here everyone knew me and adored me. Some even fell madly in love with me. I had my hair cut to my shoulders, dark underneath with blonde and dark streaks throughout the top.

"Can I get two vodka cokes, two holy waters, and four gladiator shots?" I was filling the order for a regular of mine who comes every Saturday night. He tipped me well and kept me busy. My boss insisted that I make him a priority. She knew the money he brought into the club. He was a drug dealer, and his clientele kept us steady.

The club was hopping that night, and I was rocking a glittery, sparkling bikini top. It was tight and revealed my football shoulders and muscular arms. I was medium in the chest, a 32B. Nothing crazy. My toned ass was my greatest asset, and it looked great in the mini booty shorts that came with the bikini top. I made my way to the bar, collecting empties along the way. I spotted my favourite bartender and ran up to her. She and I were in sync, same mindset, rhythm, and best of all, there was no bullshit between us. She appreciated that I came to work and not to flirt. Well, at least not in front of her bar, wasting her mother fucking time.

"Hey girl!" she yelled to me as I approached her. The other servers were standing there, waiting for their orders. I grabbed the empty glasses around me and cleaned, moving the beer boxes and shuffling some bottles around. I punched in my order but said it out loud to her at the same time. She was already pouring and mixing. She knew by the order who it was for, and we knew never make him wait. I treated her fairly and split my tips 50:50 with her every time. She handed me my drinks before the other servers.

"What the fuck, Jasmine? I have two fucking drinks and was here first!" one of the servers barked and then glared at me. Jasmine didn't take shit from anyone. She would chew you up, spit you out and then pick you up, chew more, and then spit you out again.

"Maybe if you would stop picking at your nails and bring me some glasses to clean, I would make your fucking drinks!" she spat back. The other servers got the hint and while waiting for their drinks, took some initiative. She smiled at me, and we exchanged looks.

"Danny is in tonight, busy as usual for orders. Denny's breakfast on me?" I suggested.

"You got it babe! I made you your special," she replied, handing me my drink: a vodka Red Bull sour—without the vodka, of course. The energy drink always brought life back into my very sore feet. She knew I worked three jobs and that I'd already worked all day before coming to the club. She was a lifesaver. She took my tray as she said, "I got this, go take ten!" She tilted her head in the direction of the cooler. God, I loved her. I took my drink, opened the back storage room door, and slipped inside. I searched in my purse for the snack I had stashed away for emergencies: a mini jar of peanut butter and Oreo cookies. I opened the beer cooler door and felt the cold entice me in. Sitting on a stack of Coors Light, I laid out my spread of cookies and began dipping them in peanut butter, one cookie at a time. I was in heaven as I sipped my Red Bull sour, covered in peanut buttery cookies. Suddenly, Kyle, a bouncer, barged into the cooler.

"Well, what the fuck do we have here?" he asked. This guy, a super fit health nut was always making fun of my eating habits. He stood before me all judgmental and grabbed my cookies. At that moment, JJ walked into the cooler and snapped the cookies out of his hands and placed them gently back down in front of me. Without looking at me, a soft smile spread across his face as he said, "Leave her alone!"

"Oh, settle down there, JJ! I wasn't going to eat her fucking cookies. I ain't the fucking cookie monster," Kyle said with a laugh as he grabbed a stack of five cases of beer and lifted them like they were nothing. JJ followed behind him empty handed, knowing Kyle liked to show off whenever he could. He paused at the door, still looking forward. "Peanut butter and Oreo cookies?" he asked, with a quizzical look on his face. I handed him one and he took it. He took a bite and the look on his face said it all. It was like I had discovered the moon or something. I handed him another with extra peanut butter. He looked at me with genuine gratitude as he said, "Thank you!"

"You are most welcome! And thank you," I answered. He always guarded my space. He knew I was different and quiet. I could tell his mouth was dry with all the peanut butter and handed him my drink.

"Holy hell! This is a deadly combination. What is it?" he asked.

"Vodka Red Bull sour," I answered. He gave me a suspicious look because we weren't allowed to drink on the job even though he knew most servers did. "Virgin style: no vodka!" I replied. I gathered my things and told him to finish it. He declined and opened the door back to the blasting music. The number of patrons had doubled, and we were in for a long night. We gave each other a look and went our separate ways.

Some sort of UFC-style fight was in town. Jasmine was making good money from a guy who was ordering ten rye and cokes every thirty minutes and tipping her a twenty every time. We had a system for that. She would hand the money to me instead of putting it in the jar to split with the other bartenders. I would keep track on a piece of paper in a tally style making sure I gave her the correct amount at the end of the night. I made another line on the sheet, number seven.

The boys were busy, bouncing out the drunken messes and the flighty, punchy bitches. One girl was throwing her shoes and hair extensions at another girl who had decided to go commando. Her mini skirt was over her ass cheeks and her "hairy berry" was exposed, flashing the whole bar. This was another reason I liked to work there: not only was it damn good money; it was free entertainment! I was ringing in another order when Jasmine slipped me another forty.

"I have to make a drop!" I told her. She handed me my zipper bag, and I took my cash caddy off the tray and headed into the storage room and then the cooler. I knew I was getting full and started counting out the cash: fifteen hundred, the most I have ever taken out. I zipped the bag back up and headed out of the cooler and the storage room, closing the door behind me. I quickly handed the cash bag back to Jasmine who grabbed it and shoved it deep down into the beer storage mini cooler behind the bar. I never took chances. A server got jumped outside the club once after closing and all her cash was taken. That was the good news. The bad news was what they did to her face. She was left with a nasty scar along her jawline. The poor chick never recovered mentally. The other servers seemed so careless to me, putting their cash caddies on the far side of their trays. Stupid if you ask me. Not worth the risk at all. All it takes is a fight breaking out, you get pushed or caught in the middle and there goes your cash.

I placed my drinks on my tray and was about to head to the floor when I felt a hand around my waist. I turned to see it was Ricky, another popular drug dealer in town. Danny dealt the hard stuff: cocaine, crack, and meth. Ricky played it light with Molly and was always surrounded by women who slung themselves all over him begging for water.

Two waters, darling!" he begged as he leaned in to kiss my cheek. I felt sticky, hot, and gross sweat touch my cheek. *Fucking ewww!* I said to myself. Jasmine saw him coming from a mile away and handed me the waters. We both rolled our eyes. These guys never bought drinks, just tons of water. As a result, none of the servers liked to wait on them and ignored them outright, but I managed my own system. It took some time, but I got good at making money off those druggies. My trick was to bring an extra twenty dollars and buy a whole case of water at the beginning of my shift that Jasmine would store for me. She would enter it into the system showing that many waters sold so my employers were paid. I would then give them out for free. How did I make money? By taking a gamble at first and winning them over with my charm. I always had bottles of water on my tray. *Always.* I would watch for the telltale signs: sweat, spun-out eyes, non-stop chatter. The biggest give away? They would never be drinking. There would never be a single drink in their hands or on the table. And they would be dying of thirst! So, I knew. Sometimes I would buy two cases of water. My employer always made fun of me for wasting my money on water, but what she didn't know is that I actually tripled my profit. Between my good looks, steady pace, and never letting them thirst, it all paid off. One individual high on Molly can sometimes drink five to seven bottles of water in an hour.

"Here you go, sweetheart!" Ricky yelled as he tried to shove a twenty in my hand. Another trick? I always turned down their money the first and second time because by the third they would always be offering *more.*

"Ricky! I told you this many times before. Your money isn't good here," I said as I gave him back his twenty. He smiled, placing the money back in his pocket. He took the water, offering one to the cream puff beside him who looked dryer than a fish on land. I continued to make my rounds, carrying my extra four bottles of water and dropping off other orders along the way. When I came around the corner, I found Ricky waving me down again.

"Hey darling! Can I get some more…"

Before he finished his sentence, I handed him all the waters I had on me. With a smile, I once again pushed his money away, turning his tip down again. I turned on my heel and left. Like clockwork, he chased me down, grabbed my hand and shoved a fifty-dollar bill into it. I pretended to say something, but I didn't let words come out. I just moved my lips. It was enough.

"I don't want to hear it! You're the best server here," he said as he shoved more money into my cash caddy. At last, music to my ears. It worked like a charm every time. I looked at him with thankful puppy dog eyes and walked away slowly. Once around the corner, I skipped my way through the crowd. Boom, shakalaka boom! I was almost at the bar when I suddenly fell forward onto my knees and felt a heavy weight on me. The floor was wet and smelled of beer. My head started pounding as I stood up and searched for my cash caddy. I saw it getting kicked around on the floor by frantic feet. I heard screams and glass breaking.

I knew the drill: cover your head, duck down, don't panic but get the fuck out of there. I had just reached the caddy when something grabbed me from behind, locking me in place. I couldn't move and I started to panic. I screamed and kicked ferociously, thinking, *this mother fucker isn't going to take me or my money without a fight! There won't be any scars on this face!* Suddenly, I got pushed into the wall. I managed to reach my knee up high enough to push off the wall as hard as I could, hoping to escape by throwing this person off balance. I tried to push off but slipped, smashing my knee into the wall.

"Fuck!" I screamed.

"Elisha! Stop it!" a deep voice commanded. *Wait a second, I know that voice.*

"JJ?!" I asked.

"Yes! Stay the fuck still. I am trying to protect you," he said breathlessly as he was buffeted around by the crowd. He pushed me harder against the wall, his hands now encircled me, his shoulders protecting my body and the wall my face. I saw a small opening to the bar and the storage room.

"JJ!! Over there!" I screamed. I stuffed the cash caddy into my tits, turned around to face him, and jumped as high as I could, spider monkeying my legs around his waist. He made a run for it. My head was tucked into his neck. I felt his heart racing and heard sounds that made me curious. I peeked over his shoulders. It was a massacre. Blood everywhere. Faces getting smashed in, bottles to the heads, and clothes flying off from every direction. I must have made a sound.

"Get your fucking head down!" JJ barked at me.

We got to the storage room, and he threw open the door, shoving me in there. Before he left me, I saw him smiling. *What the fuck could he possibly be smiling about?*

Eventually the cops broke up the fight. At the end of the night, I was closing out my sales. It was a big mess all around. The servers were complaining about everything. The fight, the lack of good tips, the lost money, and the fact that they had to tip out the bouncers who were only doing their jobs. I sat there quietly in my soft cotton jumpsuit and sandals. The best feeling in the world was getting into my cozies after a long shift. My manager was making a statement to a soft-spoken police officer who I noticed was very young looking with dark hair. He was handsome. I found myself mesmerized, trapped in a trance. I loved the idea of becoming a police officer—it was part of my life plan: to work hard, save money, and apply as soon as possible. I had never considered dating an officer, until then. He looked my way and smiled. I blushed immediately, looked away, and continued counting my cash. I had to recount my cash three times; it didn't seem right with how much I had in leftover tips. Kyle and the other bouncers were so distracting it made counting hard. Aside from JJ, they all teased and poke fun at the servers, always flirting and play fighting. They picked on me the most.

"Elisha blushes when a guy smiles at her; she won't know how to suck a good dick!" Curtis laughed. I hated fucking Curtis. He was always so mean to me and treated his lady like shit. Well, they both treated one another like shit. "Elisha, do you even know what a blowjob is?" he asked. I tried to ignore him, but felt my skin tingle and go red. Everyone was laughing: the other servers, the DJ, the bartenders, and the bouncers.

"I bet you she is still a fucking virgin!" Kyle chimed in. I started to tear up.

"That is enough!" JJ yelled.

I looked behind me and his face was red and his fists were bunched together. He didn't look at me.

"Oh, now, now. Calm down there, JJ. We are only teasing," Curtis laughed.

JJ always protected my space. He knew I was not a flirt or interested in being a form of entertainment for men. I also knew that he really liked me but had never made a move. Now all the attention was on him. His buddies Kyle and Curtis started to tease him. Everyone at our work knew he liked me. *Holy fuck. Twelve hundred dollars*, I said to myself. That meant my girl Jasmine made two hundred. I still had to tip out the bouncers. I always rounded up with money. All the other servers gave the bouncers change, all twoonies and loonies. I gave bills: all fives. I gave Kyle and Curtis fifteen dollars, but JJ got a fifty. He looked at his friends with a smile. Both Kyle and Curtis were shocked.

"Maybe if you guys weren't such assholes...," JJ said unapologetically.

Jasmine came up next to me. "You ready for some breakfast?" she asked.

The following Saturday I had promised my girlfriend Cara that I wouldn't work on her birthday. She wanted to go to the club as a special treat. It was weird being served by my coworkers, but Cara ate it up. I was watching her on the dance floor when I noticed some familiar dark hair dancing on the floor as well. Well, not really dancing, more shuffling from side to side, awkwardly. *Holy chicken guts!* I said to myself. *It's the police officer from last Saturday night.* He wasn't in uniform and was with what I presumed were a bunch of his cop buddies, all off duty. He recognized me and made his way through the crowd. *Shit! Holy fucking shit! This cop is coming to talk to me!*

"You want to dance?" he asked. I giggled at him. He was clearly asking with liquid courage in his veins. All his cop buddies were laughing and teasing him. "Shut the fuck up!" he yelled at them, turning away from me and giving them all the finger. I decided to put an end to their teasing and agreed to dance with him. He might have been shy when he was sober, but he was lippy and funny as hell when drinking. He made me laugh all night. We exchanged numbers and in a short while started seeing each other. Robert proved to be a wonderful man: direct, kind, and always injecting humour into situations when it was needed. He was also a great police officer. Many officers highly respected him. I respected him highly. He actually convinced me to eventually quit the bar scene. He wasn't comfortable with it. I think as a police officer he had seen too much shit in bars.

I gave my notice but still worked at the bar for a few more months after meeting Robert. One night, I came on shift, and I noticed JJ sitting by the bar. He looked so upset, so I sat next to him.

"Hey JJ! How are you?" I asked.

He didn't answer, but asked, "I heard you are quitting." I was stunned. I didn't think he would take it so hard.

"JJ, it's time for new chapters…," I started to say before he cut me off.

"I am going to miss you," he said.

I realized he was heartbroken by it all. I never gave him a chance to date me, he had to see me with another guy, and now I was leaving.

"JJ, I am so sorry. You are a great guy…," I started to say.

"Just not good enough," he said, finishing my sentence for me. He left as fast as he said those words. I never forgot that smile he gave me after he placed me in storage that night.

In the end, I married Robert, and we had two children together. Unfortunately, it ended in divorce after ten years of being together. Living the life of a police officer's wife was very hard. I felt caged up, and I decided I would rather be alone and single and live a life where no one knew me, where no one knew I was a mother, where no one knew I was someone's wife once upon a time. I moved to Kamloops for cosmetology school and to begin a new life. As they say, be careful what you wish for.

At first, I felt like a queen in Kamloops. At twenty-six, I was fresh off my divorce and queen of all the dick I could eat, queen of the sorrow suckers. When I arrived, I landed a serving job at a strip joint. It was the only serving job available. There, I hid behind pounds of makeup, black clothing, and my vagina. My pussy was on a platter, and I was handing out free samples all week long, with extra on the weekends. My long purple hair made me exotic; I rocked a side shave and had a body that could bend like a pretzel. My skin was covered in tattoos. I wasn't this virgin Mary server from Prince George anymore. I worked my way into a bartender position at a strip club. A smorgasbord of men from an all-you-can-eat buffet was presented to me as I mixed drinks and poured shots. When my shift came to an end, I would always have some young, rare meat waiting by my car for some afternoon delight.

I liked them young. They were new and fresh and let you be in control because they lacked the confidence. The best part was they never called to bug you afterwards. It was always one night only. Tickets for sale: One Night Stand! Get them soon for a limited time only. I would play the part, telling them, "You were amazing!" I'd say anything to get them out of my way so I could devour my next victim. I could never be myself with any of these men; something deep inside was always missing. I've seen every size and shape a dick comes in; I even had mantras for them all. Small and skinny? "You're cute." Long and skinny? "Let's pick my teeth." Fat and nubby? "Your dad hates you." Fat and long? "Your momma hates your dad." Turtleneck? "Fuck off!" No neck? "I will fuck and suck you dry." The perfect combination? Fat, long, no neck, and 6.5–7 inches hard. Translation: "I will let you fuck all three of my holes, put a baby in me, and cum all over my face while screaming your momma's name."

If I didn't acquire a one-night stand over the course of my shift, I'd swing by A&W to grab a couple of burgers before driving back to my basement suite. I'd have to shower twice to remove all the booze, the sweat, and the disguise. When I looked in the mirror, I didn't recognize the woman I saw. All I saw was emptiness and loneliness. I would cry every time I looked into that mirror, missing the spark I used to have. I compensated with food, stuffing my face with mini burgers before fading away into the abyss. I was secretly ashamed of what I had become. I took from everyone and had no respect or dignity for myself.

I fucked a lot of boys in that time but never dated any men. They were always the "half n' half guys," just like the cream we use for coffee. They were boys disguised as men in grown-up clothes who pretended to want the responsibility of a relationship, and used all the right, seductive words, but never followed through with any action. They were like toys that come with all the bells and whistles but not the crucial AA batteries. I knew these half n' half guys, or "midways" were good for short-term use but not long-term commitments. I actively sought them out as they offered entertainment that I could turn on and shut off like a remote control for a television program. The purpose was to amuse myself whenever I pleased. I took from them what I needed and wanted.

I lowered myself to this game for many years, this roller coaster of men and their emotions. It was satisfying to call the monster out to come and play—to twist, poke, and pivot in any direction I wanted to for that false sense of accomplishment. This monster inside of me was powerful and beyond my control for a long time, and I knew one day I would meet my match. Karma *will* come to bite you in the ass. And I did meet some equally bad people over the years, but nothing too damaging. It was like a taste of bittersweet chocolate, until I realized I had started becoming the bitterness.

I refused to heal from the trauma of my divorce. The result? I fucked, screwed, and manipulated anyone I could. I think most times it was to feel something. I used sex as a coping mechanism and avoided the pain. For the men I fucked, it was a small price to pay for some pussy, a short-term loan with a high interest rate. The interest part was my cooter. I felt unloved so I did anything I could to give myself a false representation of love. The high-rate part was giving away a piece of my soul and spirit every time I spread my legs.

I drifted further away from the life of intimacy I longed for. I became an addict.

James and I fucked all night. I didn't have a single orgasm, but I was relieved I still knew what I was doing. He ended up passed out on the couch, buck naked, exposing himself with no shame or covers. I laughed. He was just a boy, and I was a woman. I thought to myself, *this was fun, but it ends here*. I didn't like the idea of sleeping with intoxicated men. It reminded me too much of my last relationship before my partner died. We used each other to shut each other up. The abuse played back and forth, like a ping pong match. A small part of me wished I had not listened when a friend told me, "You need this. Go get some dick!"

Now I am stuck trying to wake James up before my daughter comes home. Do I kick the mother fucker? I bend down and rub my hands through his hair like I do with my own teenage son. *This is fucking gross*, I think. I pull away immediately. I place my foot on the couch near his head, pushing up and down.

"James, get *up!*" I say loudly.

The noise I hear next sounds like a dead donkey, and the smell is like a dead fish dipped in whiskey. The fucking guy farts and turns over still passed out.

"You have got to be kidding me?" I say. I feel like I just fucked my fourteen-year-old son. "Ewwww!" I scream. I need this twenty-three-year-old kid out of my house before I lose my mother fucking mind. I bend down, hovering above his ear and yell, "Fire!"

He shoots up so fast his little pecker stands at attention. Meanwhile, I am laughing my ass off. He just stands there, looking all confused. With a soft smile, I politely say, "Time for you to go."

He picks up his pants, boxers, and shirt. I feel better he is on his way out the door. Then suddenly, when he reaches the door frame he turns around.

"Can you give me a ride home?

The dead don't give a fuck

Grief Is for the Living
11. *Mexico, 2018*

I am in the bathroom at yet another strip club. I don't really have to go, but I am feeling very overwhelmed and self-conscious. A stripper had just coaxed me onto the stage, and Bradley had pushed me so forcefully, it was clear: I was to entertain him. The stripper had encouraged me dance in front of Bradley while she kept trying to lift my shirt. Any time she would expose my skin, I would pull away to cover myself. I didn't feel right; something felt very wrong, and I raced off the stage.

Now, I am sitting on the toilet feeling so broken. It's our last night in Mexico, and Bradley chooses this? The whole trip was meant to mend us, but instead, I have spent most of the time alone: walking the beach alone, sightseeing alone, meeting new people alone, and waking up alone. Bradley has spent every night at the local pub, drinking. While there, he has been friendly and social but upon returning to our hotel in the late morning, sauntering in as I am eating breakfast, he ignores me completely, and heads to our room where he sleeps all day. Then he wakes up and repeats it all. I purposefully avoided an all-inclusive resort because I didn't trust Bradley to manage well with the unlimited drinks. In the end, it didn't matter. He still found a way to get more alcohol, and it is costing me triple.

I have been starting my day in this beautiful country by walking from the condo we are renting to the waterfront. As I walk, I listen to the palm trees swish in the wind, smell the spice in the air, and look for baby iguanas. If Bradley is awake during the day, he prefers the stuffiness of the casino over sitting at the beach. There was one day he walked the beach with me for five miles, but we didn't say a single word to each other. I watched other couples walking hand in hand, laughing and teasing each other, kissing and embracing. I could not have been more depressed.

I open the bathroom door slightly and see the stripper's tits in Bradley's face; she's straddling him and taking off her clothes. *He bought himself a lap dance?* This shatters me. He hasn't touched me all vacation—not a single hug or kiss. He hasn't even held my hand, not even during what should have been a beautiful, romantic walk on the beach. Now I am looking at a dark haired, beautiful, exotic dancer all over him. I look down at my body and pull at my clothes and skin. I have put on a lot of weight in the last year. My relationship with Bradley did not satisfy me, and so I replaced intimacy with food. I don't understand what I ever did to annoy him to the point where he acts as though I don't exist. I feel he drinks too much, but I don't know anymore. Deep down, I believe it's my fault he always seems upset and has become so distant. Who would love an overweight, uptight, and depressed woman? I am convinced he drinks so much because of me, and my depression has forced him into this state.

I had hoped this trip would fix us. I wipe my tears away and walk to the table. The stripper is sitting beside him now. Bradley is hard as a rock. I don't remember the last time he was erect for me. The only time he manages a semi-hard cock with me lately is when he is completely obliterated. I feel nothing when he is in this state. I am repulsed by his heavy body on me and his breath, a mix of stinky beer and Jägermeister. I hold my breath to stop from throwing up. Meanwhile, he pants over top of me, his sweat falling onto my face. Eventually, he ends up jumping off me in frustration, pushing my legs closed and to the side. "It's your fault my dick won't get hard for you," he always yells, stomping away in anger. Then it's weeks upon weeks of him ignoring me until he needs or wants something.

    He leans over and asks for something. I don't understand what he is asking but the stripper stands up and signals for both of us to come with her into a back room. I try to pull Bradley away, my eyes pleading and my heart racing. He finally reaches for my hand but instead of showing any tenderness, he abruptly jerks it forward, squeezing it tightly. I have no choice but to follow him into the back room. We come to a set of stairs that lead into another room where there is a small bar. The stripper is wedged in the middle of the two bouncers. I start to panic and look around the room for something to defend myself with. *I will fuck up that stripper's face and pop her fake tits if I have to*, I think to myself. One of the bouncers makes eye contact with Bradley and points to four perfect white lines on the bar counter. Now I see what he was asking for. Bradley puts his nose to the counter and in one big breath sucks up a whole line of cocaine.

Traditionally after a loved one passes, you grieve them. I think at least that is what everyone thought I was doing when Bradley passed in April 2021. The truth is, I was beginning to grieve the life I had lived up until that moment. The moment he was taken out of this world, I promised myself I would never be the same, and I started to grieve that. It is interesting to live someone's life, to learn different perspectives and reflect. I no longer go by "what ifs." Instead, I have been forced to live by "this is." This is the uncertainty: what is my life without Bradley?

To answer this question, I need to put into practice the truth. "There is no love without truth" is as accurate as "there is no truth without love." When I was addicted to self-pity, I was content to live a life standing still. I became my grief. I was flooded with the pain of my past, endless stories that I hid from and left unwritten. I couldn't grieve Bradley until I faced the pain I inflicted on him.

I have to go back to when Bradley had an affair and why it hurt so much. When I learned about that affair, it was by far the hardest I've ever cried. I cried harder than when he died. I still cry for him, so I guess his death resulted in the longest cry, but not the hardest. It's not the actual act I cry over or that I struggle to forgive him, because I had forgiven him long before his death.

Why did he run into the arms of another woman? Because I was part of his suffering, and this is what hurt the most. I stripped parts of this man away and created more pain because *I* was in pain—constant pain. I was an insecure mess of a woman, and I recognize now that I could sometimes be cruel towards Bradley. He was my punching bag at times, and I would hit him below the belt with words I knew would break him. What's more, on multiple occasions I actually physically abused Bradley to regain control of him. I was afraid of losing him to drinking, and not understanding the disease he was battling with, I became angry when he lapsed. I didn't realize that he didn't have control over his actions. So, I'd punch him in his chest, or I'd push him so hard he would fall over.

My words were the real lethal weapon. "I hate you!" I'd scream. "No one loves you when you're like this, Bradley!" I'd yell at him. He put on so much weight due to how much he was drinking, and I would not shy away from telling him he was disgusting. Many times, I felt like I was part of his brokenness because I caused some of it. My criticisms and the suggestion that he was unlovable just fed the monster and drove him to drink more. Eventually, he turned to drugs and finally, another woman. He didn't walk into the other woman's arms. He ran.

Honestly, I'm not sure I blame him. I am haunted by the role I played in his destruction. We both were suffering souls, and it was a bad combination. Bradley never recovered from the betrayal; he allowed the affair to define him. He went from one woman to the next, abusing his body more and more with drugs, drinking, and sex. He filled his empty bed with a parade of partners and escorts. Unfortunately, it all weighed on him, and he became sicker and sicker by the day. I watched this unfold from a distance and knew in my heart I was partly accountable for this man's suffering.

At the same time, Bradley was responsible for some seriously shitty behaviour in the relationship as well. I guess in the end the problems in our relationship were not one person's fault. We both played a role. When we separated, I swore that everything would change. I vowed to stop causing him pain. I realized we were both addicts: he was addicted to alcohol, and I was addicted to him. I was addicted to this toxic, harmful, and broken man, and I realize now that it was all I'd ever known. The men in my life had always been abusive, whether it was physical violence, sexual abuse, or sex addiction. When Bradley showed up, I didn't know any different. This was the line up, and I was the first batter up.

It was time to *wake up*. When Bradley called to beg to come back after we had been separated for months, I took him back and gave him all of me because he deserved nothing less. He never looked at me the same though; he wouldn't forgive himself because deep down the truth was, he only created more pain for himself knowing how much he had hurt me. That is how sadistic the disease was for both of us. The love he tried to give me was always second best, but he couldn't understand that. Because I believed I was the problem and fully blamed myself, I even considered a suicide attempt. This episode opened a new reality in me and was the real wake-up call. I finally forgave myself and all that I'd done to Bradley. I had peace. This peace allowed me to treat him right and try to restore him to the man he needed to see again, a man he deep down needed to believe in. It worked for a while, but the disease claimed him in the end.

Then I had to contend with self-pity, that dark entity that creeps up after rejection and the feeling of being completely cut off: *I am unlovable*. But then the truth came knocking even harder. I realized that rejection represents the opposite of reality and results in the ultimate amnesia: we forget who we actually are. Our wounded souls are trapped in a state of suffering. When I transitioned into *self-honesty*, I found my relief and secured my quality of life. It was through self empowerment that I was able to heal. Translation: acceptance.

Within months of Bradley's passing, I was watching a movie called, *The Children Act*, which stars Emma Thompson. Her character, Fiona, is a successful judge and a very hard-working woman. In the first twenty minutes, you learn how dedicated to her career she is. But when she comes home after a day of work to her husband, you can see there is no relationship between them. It's just a façade, a play, an act for other people. One day, the husband greets her when she gets home, and his bags are packed. I was sure he was finally leaving her for good. Nope! Instead, he openly confesses that he is leaving for the weekend with one of his colleagues. "I am going to have this affair!" he states. There are no lies and no deception. The saddest part is when, just before he leaves, he asks her a question, hoping she will fight for him. "Do you remember how we were?" She doesn't answer him.

I paused the movie. Why did this feel familiar? I saw a parallel. Fiona threw herself into her work for years. Over time, it caused division in her marriage. Her work numbed her pain. It's no surprise when her husband comes home from the weekend, she has the divorce papers ready and his shit packed. But then he confronts her with the *truth*.

"I have been waiting for you to be my wife and partner for fifteen years of this marriage, and you completely walk away over a weekend?" he asks. He tells her *she* is the one who has been having the affair for the last fifteen years, and yet he stood by her the whole time!

Bradley having the affair was the best thing to happen to me. Because I realized that all along, all that time, for so many years, *I* was having an affair too. Just like in the movie, my career as a new stylist took all my time and energy away from being a mother and a partner. My wall of control was so high to keep everyone out including him. The rejection made me indestructible but not in a good way. I wouldn't let him love me. At times I used his drinking against him. I would not admit that I was also having an affair and instead pointed all my fingers at him. I stripped him raw for so many years with my abuse, my wall, and closed myself off from the truth. Am I to curse him until the end of time over some pitiful month-long affair? By the way, he couldn't even do it sober. He had to be intoxicated to even follow through with it and took a shit ton of Viagra. He confessed that to me. I, on the other hand, *was fucking sober!* Who truly is the monster now?

The affair opened my eyes to the truth: what exists in the heart and core of love. I was living a life without truth therefore love could not exist. Living a life without understanding and honesty, a life where partners beg or say "yes, dear" is a punishment. There is no peace in that lie. Rejection no longer controls who I am. I have broken down the wall and all the barriers that surrounded my heart and now love a free man. Bradley's indiscretion forced me to make a choice: control or intimacy. I choose intimacy.

The stripper snorts the other two lines. I am paralyzed and can't move. *Is this really happening?* I wonder. The bouncer catches my eye and points to the coke.

"Would you like some?" he asks.

Bradley quickly answers for me in a deep voice: "No!"

He uses his arm to push me away while he snorts the last white line on the table. I have never seen Bradley do drugs. I have witnessed the high, him telling me stories, or him stealing money, but this is the first time I see the white powder turn him into something unnatural. His eyes change to all black, like you see in horror movies about demons. He appears possessed and looks through anything in front of him. I am right in front of him, and he doesn't see me or hear me talking to him.

"Bradley, I want to go!" I beg. I am afraid. I go to the bathroom and throw up. My nerves have gotten the better of me.

When I return, Bradley is nowhere to be found. I feel my heart sink; I try to get into the back room, but the bouncer won't let me through. I start to tear up. He eventually takes pity on me and allows me to see what's going on in there: Bradley is getting sucked off by the stripper. The bouncer has two hands on my shoulders to protect the woman whom he is paid to protect.

"This is just business for us," he says in a cold and bitter tone.

I understand very well what he means. Bradley has paid for her. I place my hand over top of one of the bouncer's hands and gently pat it—my only way of indicating that I surrender. I grab my bag and walk down the long stairway to the front entrance. No more tears come, just the vision of what I have just seen repeating in my head. I am in a trance, a twilight zone of numbness.

I get outside and reach in my bag for money to get a cab to the hotel. That's when I realize Bradley took the money to pay for the stripper. I stand on the sidewalk, destitute and alone. I walk towards the highway not knowing or caring where I am going. *I would kill to be hit by a bus right now*, I think to myself. I start to fade into the night like the ghost I am. Suddenly, I feel those same hands on my shoulders again; they are leading me back to the club. I try to resist; I don't want to go back there. I am picked up and cradled like a bride would be on her wedding day. I feel the warmth of the sun on his skin, I rest my head on his shoulder, slightly tucking my head into his neck and I start to weep. Soft, slow whimpers come from deep inside me. I smell his copal spice and sandalwood cologne. I feel wetness on my forehead and realize he is kissing me like a father would his daughter, gentle pecks to soothe and bring comfort. I feel his weight shift and realize he is bending down as he carefully puts me in a cab. He says something to the cab driver in Spanish and hands him some money. He buckles my seatbelt but avoids eye contact. Just before he closes the door, I come back to life and reach for his hand.

"Thank you," I say quietly as tears cascade down my cheeks.

He turns to face me, bends down, and cups my face with his hands. Finally, looking in my eyes, he says, "You are a cosmic treasure and deserve to be loved." His sharp accent doesn't get in the way of me making out those words. My tears flow and he catches them and sweeps them away with his thumbs. "I am not a good man. You are a good woman. I have never seen this. Gracias, angel!" He kisses me on the lips and holds himself in place. As he pulls away and turns to leave, I see tears form in his eyes. He closes the door. The cab pulls away and I look back to see if he waves goodbye, the man who called me "angel."

On my last day in Mexico, I give myself something to remind me of my experience here. Sitting on the beach, listening to the waves crash, watching the palm trees sway in the wind, and looking at the sky change into pink and orange tones, I feel a slight tingling on my right cheek as the salty air hits it. I gingerly touch my cheek in the spot where a fresh rose had been imprinted. The word *love*, handwritten, makes up the stem, which traces along my jaw line and ends with a small "t." I got a new rose tattoo in honour of the man who protected me. He gave this angel her wings of worth back through her faith.

How can I heal these painful memories? I carry them still; they are a part of me, but they don't define me. They refine me. The dead don't give a fuck; they are dead, and the pain died with them. It's the living who keep it alive. Why do I keep it alive? Because it's a reminder that there is still good in the world. I could tell you it gets easier, but it doesn't. Bradley's death haunts me, the trauma lingers, and the pain echoes constantly. It doesn't matter how many times I repeat, "I am safe," I still struggle with what happened. The wounds have healed, but the scars still sting. How? He is dead. The truth makes it so hard: you never get over the loss of a loved one. You learn to be with them in spirit, where pain no longer exists. We experienced the pain together and the willingness to grow from it all.

"That is why you were so perfect for each other. You filled in each other's blanks," Jenny once told me. She saw the truth long before I did. I just wish death was celebrated more, and that we could gather the living when there is death. A human wants to be believed in before they pass on. *What* you believe isn't important. What's important is that you believe. Isn't that faith? Author Jamie Anderson wrote, "I have learned that grief is really just love. It is all the love you want to give but you can't. Grief is love that has no place to go." Grief is for the living, and love is a reminder for the dead. I hope all the grief stays with me because it's all unexpressed love.

Sometimes, when the house is quiet and the children are still sleeping in the early morning, I open an old storage box where Bradley kept every single letter I ever wrote him. I hold each one against my heart while my teeth chatter and more tears flow. There are love letters, angry letters, letters of hope, but mostly there are letters of truth in love. Shortly after I published my first book, *I Am Worthy*, I found all these old letters inside this box, even the few letters I wrote him back in high school along with my grade 12 photo stuffed in his old wallet. All this time, he kept me close.

"I digest and reflect on your words and get to know Bradley in a way he would only let you know," a reader of my first book once told me. It made me realize in turn that he only let me see him, the truth of him: the addict and the monster we both became.

Was Bradley my karma? Why couldn't I just let the mother fucker die? Instead, I wrote a book about him to face the pain while I'm living. As I read the reviews of the book after it was published, that fact became apparent. To some who knew us both, I am a villain; to others, I am a hero who inspires them. I wonder who I am to Bradley? Who am I in my own story? A hero or villain?

Bradley kept a journal, and his last entry repeated the phrase "I am worthy" ten times over. It's emblematic of his story. His repetition of this phrase only made it clear that he struggled to believe it. He feared it the most. He lacked the wisdom to trust in it, to find the will to live with it embedded his heart. It was hard to tell our story. He was an ill man who fought a courageous battle, and I loved him through it all.

Once a cheater, always a cheater

A Monster Calls
12. *Prince Rupert, 2012*

Black as the night sky, dark as a raven, a deep, elegant ebony, the endless streams of beauty move between my fingers as I move my hand along her temple. The silky strands of hair fall as I gently push them with the tip of my first finger, which guides my path. My middle finger caresses the round shape of her head as my index finger joins in. She sinks into the movement, and I smell her soft, sweet, candy breath as she drifts off into a heavy, peaceful, and innocent sleep. I call her Abby, short for Abigail. She is not mine by blood, but I feel like she is my daughter. I scoop her up in my arms and carry her to her bed. She wiggles the moment she feels my warmth leave so I sing to soothe her back to sleep.
 "You're fair as the dew on the roses…"
 I quietly fade my voice as if someone is turning the volume knob down and turn to go. With one last look, I check to see that her long, dark lashes remain closed. Her snow-white skin glows in the moonlight. Little brown freckles are the last thing I see as I close the door.
 I gather my things to take my leave. I don't want to deal with her father tonight. I just want my own space, to go home and be alone. I hate leaving her; she is too pure to be trapped in this

lifestyle her parents have given her. It breaks my heart. Chris, her father, comes out of the bathroom glassy eyed and looking through me. I know what comes next.

"Where are you going?" Chris asks.

"Home!" I reply sharply, which jolts him.

"You're leaving me?!" Chris asks, his voice tightening.

"Eventually," I mumble under my breath.

"What!?" Chris asks in a panic.

"Nothing. Go to bed, Chris!"

He is still talking at me as I slip through the back patio door, ignoring anything else he says. I walk the seven blocks home, which is mostly uphill as it is Prince Rupert after all. The whole way I think to myself what a man baby Chris is. He sucks the living life out of you. All addicts do. The best thing Chris and his ex-wife did was create three beautiful daughters: Sam, Claire, and little Abby who is the youngest. I love his girls as if they are my own, but I've made a huge mistake getting involved. Recently separated myself, I couldn't cope with the pain and distracted myself by breaking one of my biggest rules. Dating someone I work with is a big bust and always complicates matters. I wanted a fling. Chris pretended he wanted the same, but it turned into more for both of us.

I walk home in the night feeling the salty, cool air and bearing the guilt. I don't see my life with this man; he has nothing to offer me but empty promises. His cup is never full, and he expects others to fill it constantly. His daughters have been doing this for him for most of their lives, but then I came into the picture and took some of that weight off of them. Why do I stay? For her. Abby. For them, my girls. I want to give as much love where I can before I leave. One day, I will leave this place. I can feel it down in my soul that I am meant for more. The town, the people, all of it is too small and I am growing tired of feeling small because others think small. I start to cry as I open the door to my own house. I hate this house and everything about it, but it is all I have. I wipe my tears as I open my daughter's door and see an empty crib. She and her brother are with their father; it's his week. I find comfort by grabbing some peanut butter and a package of Oreos. I sit outside on my back deck and look at the stars. I wish I could disappear into the abyss, live among the stars, galaxies, and little green men if there are any. "Take me away!" I whisper into the night, shoving down my last cookie covered in peanut butter before I end the night with a glass of milk.

I go inside and see my phone glowing. I pick it up to find ten missed calls and a shit ton of text messages. I roll my eyes and head for a hot shower and my bed. I will not engage in Chris's tantrums tonight. He's the monster who calls in the night when he has had his favourite flavour of juice—a juice box he cannot give up. I fall asleep dreaming about my little Abby.

Shortly after I left The Rum Jungle, I got a job serving at Boston Pizza. I wanted something that was less stressful and more conservative. I wanted to impress my new boyfriend, the police officer. I wanted to prove I was committed to the relationship and make more time for it. We bought a townhouse together, and I very quickly moved my way up into a manager's position at the restaurant. Everything was going smoothly and according to plan. For years, I had planned my future. I was going to become a police officer, not have kids, save tons of money, and move around Canada, happy in my new career. The bonus was I got to be with my very own officer. I didn't expect that at all.

It was a very slow night at the restaurant, and I let most of my coworkers go for the evening. Instead of disappearing for the evening, most of them stayed and hung out. They were laughing, drinking, and entertaining themselves while I tended to them, making drinks as the night wore on. I watched Ryan, my boss, flirt with the young, new hottie. He always went for the fresh meat, the new hires, before they found out what a dog he was. I used to laugh as I called the play-by-play: He will fuck her, she will get attached, he will not, she will find out he is also fucking three or more other servers, she will cry, and she will quit. As I'm pouring a rainbow slush drink, I look up to see the scene: Beckie, the last woman Ryan screwed, is now staring daggers at his back. I bring the slush drink to the new girl and then proceed to the far end of the table to drop off the fifth shot of vodka to Beckie. Without taking her eyes off of Ryan and the hot totty, she picks up the shot I only just placed down before her and slams it back before slamming the empty glass back on the table. Everyone felt the table shake and looked in her direction—everyone but Ryan. This pissed her off even more.

"Fuck, I am bored!" she slurs.

I had already called her a cab ten minutes ago. This was all too familiar to me. I saw the yellow car come through the parking lot. *Perfect timing*, I thought to myself.

I turned to Beckie and said, "I am really glad you said that! Your cab is here." I then explained to her that she had asked me to call her one, which was a little white lie on my part. I gently told her she must have forgotten. With a soft smile, I gathered her up and took her out the front door. I handed the money to the cab driver and gave him the address. After sending her on her way, I walked back to the bar and went to the computer to find her bill.

"I got it!" Ryan said.

Shaking my head, I printed Beckie's bill and handed it to Ryan. He was wobbling back and forth, unable to hold himself steady. He gave me cash, paying for his bill and Beckie's but not the new conquest who was still flicking her hair and putting on a fresh coat of lip gloss.

"Ryan, for fuck's sake! Can you just keep your dick in your pants at work? I really like this new chick's work ethic," I exclaimed. He laughed in my face. I turned and walked to the back of the kitchen to get more ice for the bar. "Fucking low life sleazeball. One day he will knock up one of these poor girls. Such a loser," I said out loud while I scooped ice into a bucket. I looked up and saw Ryan going out the back door. Curious, I decided to follow him because he never went out that way. That's when I saw Ryan hop into the same yellow cab I placed Beckie in. *You have got to be fucking kidding me!* I said to myself. I crossed my arms at all this horseshit, promising myself never to get involved in drama and any sort of relationship at my workplace.

"Was that Ryan getting into a cab with Beckie?" Keith, another coworker asked. We got along more or less, although he always thought he was right about everything, and I put him back in his place. I didn't care how long he'd been working there, when I was wearing my gold pin that said *MANAGER*, he needed to respect me. I still worked as a server sometimes, so when I switched to the white pin that said *SERVER*, I would ignore Keith and carry on my merry way. When I refused to engage with his immaturity, it pissed him off more. He got a rise out of starting arguments. My trick was never to argue with him. I didn't want to indulge him.

I'd look at him and just walk by without answering his question. I grabbed a handful of ice, poked my head in the kitchen, and gave the cook, Gus, my eyes. He knew my order and with a gap-toothed smile said, "I gotchoo, boss lady." I giggled and walked upstairs to the office.

I grabbed a towel and placed it on the floor in the office. Hanging my head down, I took the ice and pressed it against my neck, massaging my upper and lower neck in a circular motion. That's where all my stress lived. I moaned in pleasure at how good this felt. I didn't hear anyone come up the stairs, so the soft knock at the door startled me.

"Chicken guts!" I screamed at Keith as I dropped the ice, and it exploded all over the office floor.

"Did you just say chicken guts?" Keith asked with a laugh.

"Keith, go away! You are not allowed up here. You are not an employee right now, and you've been drinking," I said, ignoring his laughter.

"I just came up to tell you your food is ready!" Keith replied.

Why? I thought to myself. Gus usually stood at the top of the stairs, holding my food as a server himself and yodeled in song to me. It always made my night. Why did Keith take it upon himself to come and tell me instead?

"Go tell Gus I will have my usual please," I ordered. Keith was confused so I told him to trust me, just do it, and watch. Keith stood back after telling Gus exactly what I had said, and the performance began.

"C-A-E-S-A-R-S-A-L-A-D, E-X-T-R-A-D-R-E-S-S-I-N-G," Gus yodeled in an extra high voice. I ran to my locker and grabbed my twenty-five-foot-long braided Rapunzel wig that I had made myself along with my bright pink and purple cape laced with gold that my mother had helped me sew together. I ran to the top of the stairs and threw Gus my lock of hair but only halfway. Gus needed to impress me. "I-C-E-C-R-E-A-M, V-A-N-I-L-L-A-B-E-A-N."

I laughed as I threw down the rest of my hair. Gus picked up the braided hair in front of Keith who was witnessing this for the first time. He had his hand over his mouth to stop from laughing as he watched Gus pet the hair tenderly and rub the golden locks along his jaw line. This was what I found fun and amusing. Gus and I worked a night shift twice a week when I was manager. Our sense of humour matched perfectly. His overweight, soft, marshmallow-like body was so enticing to hug. I fell in love with his character and attitude. He had a heart of gold. I ran down to Gus to kiss his cheek and give him a big hug.

"T-H-A-N-K-Y-O-U, S-W-E-E-T-G-U-S!" I yodeled in return.

Gus walked back into the kitchen with a big smile but then gave a serious look and head nod to the dish pit guy, indicating it was time to get back to work.

"This is none of your business! Are we clear?" I said to Keith.

"I have no idea what you are taking about," Keith answered, acting like he hadn't seen anything while he grabbed my bucket of ice. He turned to look at me briefly before opening the door to the restaurant. He smiled and waved his arms mimicking my performance. I looked down, blushing and giggling at the same time.

Later, I was sitting at the bar and overheard a group of intoxicated coworkers asking Keith where he had been. He told them he was taking a smoke break with the kitchen staff. I looked over and saw Keith was still smiling at me. I looked down and tucked my hair behind my ear. When I looked up again, I caught the new chick looking at the kitchen doors, obviously hoping Ryan would walk through them. I ate my Cajun chicken Caesar salad with no croutons and vanilla bean ice cream in complete satisfaction, exchanging three bites of salad with one spoonful of ice cream.

The next evening, I walked into a closing shift as a server. I was changing by my locker and saw Keith was doing the same.

"You're not supposed to be working tonight!" I exclaimed.

"And you are not a manager T-O-N-I-G-H-T," Keith yodeled back at me.

With the office door right beside us, I mouthed the words "fuck you" instead of saying them out loud. I pushed the blonde wig and cape in my locker as deep as they would go. Keith told me Beckie called in sick.

"I bet!" I said. I closed my locker and brushed by Keith as I headed into the office. *Oh, wonderful.* Ryan was sitting in the chair. I looked past him towards the cameras and saw Beckie was on the floor working. "What the fuck?" I said. I must have said it a little loudly because Ryan turned to face me with a puzzled look on his face. "Keith told me Beckie called in sick!" I exclaimed. Ryan laughed.

"No. She is hungover but didn't call in sick," Ryan giggled.

What a fucking pig of a man, I thought to myself. I really disliked Ryan and took pleasure picturing myself as a cop, pulling him over, and slapping cuffs on him one day. "Keith asked Beckie to switch shifts with him," Ryan said with a smile. I ignored the smile and walked away.

I was so busy most of the night I could barely keep up with myself. I forgot all about Keith and the shift change. I started folding pizza boxes as the evening slowed down. Beckie went home right after her shift, and another staff table with Ryan and his side chick formed after hours. I heard all of them laughing as

Keith served and entertained them this time around. I needed to cool down, so I went to the ice machine and filled a towel with ice and then went through the back outside. I felt the cold ice on the back of my neck, dripping down onto my undershirt. I took my apron off so I could feel more of the wind blow against my skin. The cool breeze gave me a flashback to that night in the beer cooler at The Rum Jungle. I felt my heart prick remembering JJ and his last words. I tilted my head up and lifted my eyes to the night sky as the tears started to form. I decided I needed more of a cool down and took my hair out. My long, dirty blonde hair fell over my shoulders, reaching the middle of my back. I *loved* my long hair but wore it in a bun to keep it from smelling of food or grease. I allowed myself to daydream about JJ and a life with him for a time. Water trickled down my cheeks as I closed my eyes and asked the air to forgive me, the woman who let him go.

"Elisha, are you ok?" The question startled me. It was Keith. I had no energy left to be disappointed. Only soft words came from me.

"I am fine," I said.

I had no understanding of the outside world around me. I was drifting away into my own space and time. I felt my hair push forward and off to one side. I felt a warmth on the shoulder that was left bare and another soft touch on the back of my neck. My white, see-through beater shirt was blowing against me when I felt wetness on my neck. I laid back against him willingly.

"You are a fucking idiot for switching your shift!" I snapped.

His hand moved to my torso and across my belly. He slid one finger along my pant line.

He lifted his mouth from my neck and whispered in my ear, "Then I guess I am an idiot."

Keith and I began our secret affair shortly after I started working at Boston Pizza. It was instant attraction, and we both couldn't keep our hands off one another. When the manager opportunity landed on my plate, I knew I had to hide the relationship at all costs. I felt like a coward, but I wanted a life Keith couldn't give me. My fiancé gave me protection, physical and financial, but Keith gave me the touch I longed for, the love I needed desperately, and made me feel beautiful every waking second that I was around him.

"I will see you later tonight!" I said, sliding away from his embrace.

I got home around 2:30 am, praying Robert was asleep. I inserted the key into the door lock but didn't turn the key. *You are a monster. Yeah, go home to your future husband after fucking your side guy's brains out in the back of your car.* The monster called and I answered. A deep guilt inside me made me wish I could just disappear.

I took a deep breath, exhaled, and turned the key. Robert was waiting up for me. He came right over and started kissing me, telling me he was happy to see me. He was showing me more physical attention than normal. I was undressing, about to get into the shower, as he shared his day, which had ended with a late-night poker game with his other cop buddies. *Drinking*, I thought to myself. That explained the extra attention. Robert started undressing as well. *Fuck! He wants to shower together!* This always led to sex. Keith had just been inside me an hour ago. I raced into the shower while Robert undressed himself. He was still talking away as I lathered and scrubbed the soap three times over, washing my body, even inside my vagina, to cover the evidence.

Later, as I laid naked beside Robert who had passed out after

I made love to him, I felt sick to my stomach. I mean, I really felt sick. The next thing I knew, I was racing to the bathroom and hurling my guts out. Over the next few weeks, the sickness got worse. The smell of cheese and peppers made me throw up in an instant. I'd hold my breath with Vicks VapoRub under my nose just to get through a shift. I made sure to avoid Keith. I was bloated and felt like I'd been on my period for weeks. He had become very annoying lately too, asking me all sorts of questions that I was too tired to answer. I was always so darn weak and sleepy, and I felt nauseous all the time. My body felt like it weighed a ton as I moved from table to table. Out of nowhere, just as I finished taking payment from one of my tables, I turned and ran right into someone. I stumbled backward and looked up, about to apologize, and I saw it was JJ! I screamed inside my head.

"You don't look very good!" he said with a smile. I was in shock and stood still, like a dead whale floating. I ignored the comment, wanting to know about him.

"JJ, it has been a long time. How are you?" I asked.

"No, seriously! You don't look good. Why are you still working?" he asked, ignoring my question.

Suddenly, I felt faint, and JJ grabbed me softly by the arm and placed me down on a chair next to my customers' tables. I was sweating all over the place in areas one should not sweat.

"I do feel like death. It's been going on for weeks now, but I am too lazy to go see a doctor. And too busy," I replied. JJ didn't say a word but just stared at me. I stared back in silence, but then realized I had better just say what needed to be said because I might not ever get another chance.

"I am sorry, JJ…for everything," I said, my voice cracking as I sobbed through the tears.

"Elisha, I think you might be pregnant!" JJ said out of nowhere.

What the fuck? As if? I said to myself. *JJ doesn't answer my questions, refuses to let me apologize after all this time, and now assumes I am pregnant?* He gave my hand a quick squeeze, got up, and went to leave. But something stopped him. He turned to look at me.

"I only wish it was mine."

My pregnancy was confirmed, and I gave work my two weeks' notice. I left like a dog running away with its tail in between its legs. I also confessed everything about my affair with Keith to Robert, so he had a choice to stay or go. I am a lying, cheating cunt, but the baby, our son, is all Robert's. How do I know this for sure? Because I still had a tiny bit of class left in me, and made sure Keith wrapped his dick any time we had sex. I may be a lot of things, but I ain't dirty! Shortly after Tanner was born, Robert and I did all the necessary testing to make sure he was our son together. And thankfully, he was.

After Tanner was born, Robert suggested we move closer to his hometown of Prince Rupert. I had never heard of it, but it sounded like a great plan to me at the time. Little did I know it would be the beginning of the end for us. Was I looking for an escape? Or did I still feel guilty and want to make amends with Robert by doing something he wanted? Maybe it was a mix of both. Our daughter Hailey was born in Prince Rupert in 2011.

By 2012, Robert and I were separated.

I wake up to Chris pounding on my door. It is 7:00 am, and I know he hasn't slept a wink. I open my window.

"Chris, go home! It is 7:00 am," I yell.

"No! Not until you fucking talk to me," he screams back. *How the fuck did I get in this mess?* I wonder. If it wasn't for his girls, I would have just fucked the dumbass, fuck and chuck style. Chris had the biggest penis I had ever seen. Like damn! It was nice and no turtleneck either. It was like sucking on a lollipop, a big one. Now I am losing my cool with this big dick loser and know exactly what to say to get him off my front lawn.

"I swear to fuck, if you don't leave, I will call Jenny!" I bark at him. Jenny is my go-to problem solver when it comes to him. They have a history from years ago, and she is still lethal at putting him in his place. It makes him uncomfortable to be around her. I love it, especially in moments like this. I hear nothing and peek out the window. Chris has already started walking away back home. "Thank fuck," I mumble. I know I will see him somewhat sober tonight at work.

Walking along the boardwalk to work I take in the ocean scene: coast guard ships, navy vessels, and a cruise ship are all docked. I instantly smile realizing it will be a busy night with lots of money. That isn't why I was smiling, though. I know I will be too busy to talk or deal with Chris. I can't believe I've made another stupid mistake by getting involved with someone at work. *When am I ever going to learn?* I think it's the thrill. I love the ride but hate the aftermath. It's like a roller coaster: the anticipation of the build-up and doing a daredevil move. However, once you get off the ride, the consequences set in, and you are left with a mess. False promises of commitment lead to broken hearts. The truth is I just like the feeling of being free.

Breaker's Pub, nestled along Prince Rupert's shoreline, has my kind of atmosphere. I started working there shortly after I separated from Robert. The owner knows me because she grew up with Robert's family. Barb supports my schedule as a single mother of two. She also loves my work ethic. And tonight, I was going to need it. It was going to be a full house with coast guard staff, air force, navy, customers both local and non-local. The kitchen will be slammed. As I walk into the pub, I think to myself, *I am going to make a lot of money tonight.*

Later, near the end of my shift, the pace starts slowing down as most patrons move to night clubs for the evening. I had laughed a lot during my shift because the navy boys were all fucking crazy and horny like a bunch of dogs, fighting over the girls they wanted to take home. One sailor was talking in Russian to get some pussy. It made my night watching this guy's desperation to get his dick sucked. I picked out the quietest but cutest navy boy. *Come out, come out wherever you are, monster!* I seductively hum to myself, as I drive down a dirt road after work where I let him fuck my brains out. I will never forget my experience with that American navy sailor. The entire time my legs are in the air, my phone is ringing non-stop. I am having a lot of fun, but poor Chris is not.

I cheated on Chris so many times during our union I lost count. I even cheated on him with my ex Robert, and with my future partner, Bradley. It wasn't until years later that I finally felt the guilt and shame of my actions. I reflected on the pain I had caused these men when I had the same pain inflicted on me. The only man I never cheated on was Bradley. It was the hardest, most abusive, and loneliest relationship I have ever been in, but not once did I cheat. Instead, I walked all over the decent, boring, but better men. I was a whore.

I eventually got sick and tired of my own shit and decided to stop abusing myself and others. I made amends to Robert by being a great mother to our children and taking accountability for my actions. I didn't touch one cent of his pension or ask for any alimony. The court made a ruling about the amount of child support I was entitled to, but I refused it. I asked Robert to draft up a proposal that seemed fair between us. I trusted him with regard to the welfare of the family. We split our debt down the middle and shared any extra expenses related to the kids. Our divorce cost four hundred dollars each. Robert has been a wonderful partner to me, a great father, and continues to be a hard-working member of the RCMP. We support one another any way we can. Today, I can actually say he is my friend, and I love him dearly.

I tattooed the word "whore" twice on my lower back. Yes, I branded myself for what I did to Robert and Chris. It's a reminder of who I once was. I apologized to Chris's daughters for all the grief and pain I caused them. I no longer call this monster to come out to play. Sometimes I sense this monster, lingering in its deep, dark cave of selfishness, but that is where it will remain. To this day, Abby calls me "Mother." She has always had my heart and is like another daughter to me. We are inseparable, and I am so proud of her.

They say, "once a cheater, always a cheater," but I am not a cheater—not anymore.

I refuse to be small because you think small

End of the Season
13. *Beer League Softball, 2019*

Are you fucking kidding me? I say silently to myself. "Fuck! That is the second play he fucked up on," I say out loud.

I hate people who play ball and can't catch or make a throw to the bag. Shit! Get off the field and out of A division. Go join another league and a lower division. I want to win no matter the cost. That is the only baseball I am interested in playing. I don't care about the people, the drinking, or the laughs. I just want to play the damn game well, and by "well," I mean perfectly.

With the other team scoring five, we are now automatically up to bat even though there's only one player out. It is the fifth inning, and we are now behind. I jog lightly from the outfield into the infield towards my team. No smile, no words, absolutely nothing. My energy is dark and closed off. Our team is up to bat: one guy fouls out and one girl strikes out: two away. Two of our players manage to get on bag. Now there's a guy on third and another on second. I am up to bat. I step forward into the batter's box. *We need these runs*, I tell myself. I hear my team calling out my name.

"Let's go, 'Lish. Be a leader!" I hear someone shout.

I am a fucking leader. I will show them all how a real ball player plays ball. I remain calm and focused on the outside, but in my head as the ball is being pitched, I am screaming bloody murder.

"Aaaaahhhhhh!" I swing as hard as I possibly can, and I fucking miss. From the crowd, I hear a roar.

"Ooooohhhhhhh!"

Goddaammit, Elisha! How did you miss that? I am angry, very angry. I hate that sound after I swing and miss. I feel my face flush red as I am embarrassed. I take one step back from the box and breathe. Before I step back in, I hear another voice that carries over everyone.

"Kill it, Linda!" Bradley yells. He knows how competitive I get and how embarrassed I am when I swing and miss. I steady myself before I take another swing, remembering what he once told me: "Just because it's a strike, it doesn't mean it is yours."

"Strike!" the umpire yells.

Two strikes. Fuck this pitcher is pitching to me high and deep. I shift back in the batter's box, choke up on my bat an inch, and lift my back elbow higher than I normally do. I shift my weight more to my back leg, lifting my front leg higher as the third pitch is released. The pitch is so high and it's too close to gamble on whether it'll be a strike or not. I have to go for it. I swing.

"Strike three!" the man behind the plate yells.

I start throwing a tantrum as the players left on base walk to the dugout to grab their mitts. I throw my bat, stomp my feet, and kick the dirt all the way to the dugout. "Fucking bullshit!" I scream.

I never, and I mean never, strike out. I did everything right for the pitches coming in. *The fucking pitcher is a chicken shit for not pitching me a decent pitch!* I think to myself. I grab my glove from the dugout and walk slowly to my spot in the outfield. I stand there holding my breath in anger. The batters take advantage of my state of mind by hitting the ball to me or near me. I miss so many plays, so many catches, and watch the ball go right in between my legs. That isn't even the worst part. At one point I look up to see Bradley leaving the game. Tears start streaming down my face. I am disappointed in myself. How did I become this player? I don't even recognize her anymore.

I started playing the game when I was five years old. My father signed me up for hardball, which meant playing with boys. I was a tough kid and loved the idea. I played catcher as a position. Throwing a guy out when they try to steal on a girl is still to this day a great feeling. I stand corrected: not great. Fucking fantastic. Countering their underestimation gave me a thrill, and at a young age I told myself that no man was better at this game.

I grew out of little league ball, and when I turned fifteen my father begged me to play in the Babe Ruth League. I shut the idea down immediately after I saw how the male coaches treated the girls in the league. The girl players always got ignored or benched, and if they played an inning, they got shoved into the outfield. There were seven innings to a game, and a girl was lucky to get one or two innings because "girls can't play baseball." I had never seen a girl last a year in that league. My father was adamant that I should play, so to prove to him I was dead right about my observation, I tried out behind his back. I figured if I was wrong, I would show him the jersey of the team I made. But if I was right, I'd relish telling him to his face, "Told you so, Daddy!"

When I showed up to the tryouts, I was the only girl in sight. Everyone stared: parents, coaches, and all the players. I wore my ball cap way down, over my ears and low enough to cover my eyes and shoved my ponytail through the opening in the back. I was shaking and hated being stared at. Still, I marched by everyone and went straight to the dugout. I took my runners off and started putting on my cleats when the coach called everyone in.

"Let's get everyone started with a run. Then after stretching we will place you into three groups: Pitchers and catchers, infielders, and outfielders." I stood up ready to start running with the group when the coach called me over.

"Hey you! Girly!" he barked.

I looked at him and barked back, "It's Crosby!"

He called all the other players by their last names. Why should I be any different? After I came over to him, he explained to me the exact same thing he had just said, as if I hadn't been listening. I gave him a quizzical look and said, "I heard everything you said. Can I go run and warm up?"

"Oh no! *You* don't have to run," he answered without looking at me.

I rolled my eyes and started to jog away. I did my best not to rush through my run and stretches, but before long the coach was calling everyone back in. *The fucking bastard!* I thought to myself. *He can't even respect me as a player and wait?* I quickly joined the others and got down on one knee and did my best to let go of my anger and listen. He was saying something about what the coaches were going to evaluate us on, but suddenly I was distracted. I felt something, as if someone was staring. I looked over my left shoulder and caught this kid looking right at me. Our eyes met for a second and then I looked away, turning my head to the front. I noticed he wore his hat down covering his eyes, just like me. The coach started putting us in our groups.

"Kempster!" he shouted.

I heard the boy who had been staring at me get up and jog over to where the pitchers and catchers were supposed to form a group.

"Girl!" the coach shouted. I didn't stand up or acknowledge this remark.

"GIRL!" he shouted again, but louder.

I took a deep breath and sat down on my bum. Once again, everyone was staring, and it was so quiet you could hear the cars drive by along the highway. Suddenly, a much higher pitched voice broke the silence.

"Excuse me, young lady! Your disrespect for the coaches and everyone's time is appalling. You are holding us all up," this woman who was standing beside the coaches said. I started to get up.

"Look, sweetheart," I said, pulling my hat off and letting my long hair fall down to the middle of my back. She twitched at the word "sweetheart." "Oh, I beg your pardon. You don't like being called 'sweetheart?'" I asked. "Well, I don't like to be called 'Girl!'" I snapped back. The rest of the players started to giggle at that remark. "I came to play ball and to be treated fairly, *not* to be disrespected. The name is Crosby!" I stated, making my way to the pitchers and catchers group.

"Where are you going?" the coach asked.

"To my group," I answered.

He shook his head and pointed to the outfield group. I could hear snickering from the boys and even some of the parents.

"I am not an outfielder. I am a catcher," I said. The coach looked directly at me, clearing his throat as he pointed again to the outfielders group.

"Not in *this* league!" he laughed.

I took my glove off and tucked it under my armpit. I placed my hat back on my head and up higher so everyone could see my eyes and started making my way to the dugout. There, I sat in the shade, drank some water, and took a long look out onto the grassy field where I longed to be. *What was the point of any of this?* I wondered. I knew I was right about it all. I was being treated so unfairly. As I started taking off my cleats and packing up my gear, the same boy, Kempster, came into the dugout for a drink of water. I could feel his eyes looking at me, but I didn't want to look at him.

"I have seen you play ball. You are a really good catcher, and you hit the ball hard," he said, stumbling a little over his words. I was so shocked I went numb and stared down into my hands. Then he said the one thing I will never forget.

"Maybe you can catch for me sometime?"

By the time I looked up, he was gone. I didn't know anything about that kid, just his last name and that he wore his hat the same way I did. It would be months later, at the end of summer, before I saw him again playing catch with a friend in Jo Martin's Field. On that hot, sunny afternoon, he gave me some important advice. "Don't be small," he said. What he meant was, refuse to be small just because others think small of you. He taught me to believe I was anything but small, that instead I was mighty, strong, and worthy of the best.

I never told my father I tried out. I was afraid I would get in trouble. I ended up calling the coach a chauvinistic prick before I left. The squealing voice of that "sweetheart" woman echoed after me. I thought baseball had ended for me, but I was wrong. I was introduced to fastpitch by a high school friend who was a pitcher and asked me to catch for her. The ball was twice as big and bright yellow. It took me a long time to get used to it. I'd been throwing side arm in hardball, where the ball is firmer and smaller in size. I had to relearn how to throw and completely change my mechanics. Being a visual learner, I watched the other girls throw just to memorize the movement.

Batting was another story. I was used to receiving pitches overhand—not underhand, windmill style. I learned that the ball rises and then goes down in this game. I was used to playing a game where the ball went faster, curved, slid, and spun. All of this fucked with my mindset. Hitting a fastpitch ball was more difficult for me. It might have been a bigger target, but it came in slower, and I lacked the power to drive a good, forceful hit. I was always ahead of the ball, swinging too fast. If I connected, the damn ball never made it outside of the infield. I got very frustrated and saw my name drop lower and lower in the batting line up. I was so competitive that I begged my dad for a heavier bat to slow my swing down. I took a wider stance in the batter's box and tried not lifting my leg so high so I could get more power. That helped me to rotate my hips forward to connect with more precision. Voila! Hitting was no longer an issue. Soon, I was making doubles, sometimes triple hits.

I was in heaven and proud of the player I was becoming, playing the position I loved with a team of great girls. I didn't miss hardball or the speed of that game. I was just happy I was treated fairly. I played house league for two years until I was asked by a coach to try out for a rep league team: the Thunderbirds. This was a step up, and the next season I showed up for indoor training as a new recruit for the Thunderbirds. The female coach was kind, but I was intimidated by all the new faces. I was a girl but never understood other girls. They always seemed so catty and dramatic. Guys seemed simpler.

We all sat huddled together in the middle of the gym as the coach called out our names and asked our positions. When it was my turn, I said my name, and everyone looked my way. Then the coach asked for my position. "Catcher!" I replied. With my answer the girls started to whisper and looked at one another. Another voice broke up the whispers.

"Not today, junior!" this girl barked. Everyone started giggling. This chick was lethal: brown, mid-length hair in a ponytail, brown eyes, tanned skin, the most perfect white teeth I had ever seen. She was glaring at me and smirking with a devilish smile, as if she was lining me up in a western-style shootout. I half expected her to yell, "Draw!"

"We will see about that!" I replied.

She was better than good. She was unstoppable, and for a moment, I stood there in my catcher's gear and hung my head in defeat. *She is better than me*, I thought to myself. It was my turn, and everyone was staring. Before I bent into position, I said out loud, "There is no such thing as better than." We all have a skill to offer, and I knew I was there to offer mine. I may have been brand new to this league and slower to execute, but I did my best. That was all that mattered to me. Unfortunately, I did not get the position and was really bummed out. My best wasn't good enough, or so I thought. What I didn't realize was that a slice of humble pie was being served my way. I had a choice: I could train to be an outfielder in the rep league with the Thunderbirds, or I could go back to the house league and play as a catcher. Outfielders were losers in this game. How could I handle the shame of going from the best in the house league as a batter and a catcher—an all-around MVP—to the very bottom of the rep league?

Standing in the outfield, I think back to my time trying out for the Thunderbirds and wonder what happened. I realize that ego and pride are scary things. They can get in the way of grace and the deeper understanding of humility. I am the best all-round female player in this league. I can play any position, and I can hit. These things are hard to come across in a co-ed beer league. Yet no one ever asks me to play in out-of-town tournaments. Is it because my fielding sucks? Nope! And having a girl player who can play outfield and infield well is a huge asset. Yet not a single person ever asks me to play.

After walking in from the outfield, I throw my glove again. This time, I sit behind the dugout in the shade. Tears stream down my face as I think about my life: Bradley has left me, the team ignores me, and I am alone. *Alone*...I hold my breath for a few seconds and look up. And that's when it hits me: I *chose* this. I am *still* choosing to be alone. No one wants to play with me because of my shitty, fucking attitude. The toxic energy I am releasing affects the whole team. Being a competitive player is a good thing but not when I expect my teammates to play at my level. I have all the talent to offer but not a single smile to give. I have no sense of sportsmanship, let alone compassion, not for my team or for myself.

Sitting there in the grass, dirt covering my greasy and sweaty arms, I start to laugh at my pathetic self. I go back in time again and see myself in my new black and teal uniform, the word "Thunderbird" emblazoned on the front. *Crack!* I hear the bat connect with the ball, and the yellow fireball comes my way towards centre field. I start running back to the fence. I can see the ball is going to be over my head. In a last, desperate attempt, I leap in the air; my timing has to be perfect. *Smack!* I hear the sound of the ball landing in my glove, the most beautiful sound in the world. The crowd cheers for the play as I dive in mid air, catch the ball, and squeeze the living shit out of it so it doesn't pop out when I slide face first into the grass superman style. I do this all game long and in many games to come. In the end, I chose to play as an outfielder with the better team, and to be the best at whatever position was given to me.

I realize that I have forgotten my values. I love this game, but I have been playing for the name on the back of my jersey instead of the name on the front. No one asks me to play because of my toxic energy and shitty attitude. Who the fuck has a tantrum in *softball?* I think with a laugh. "This is fucking *beer league* ball!" I say out loud, laughing more than ever at my pathetic self. I sit there while the team carries on without me and I allow the tears to outline pathways along my sunscreen-covered face. Tears. Why are they so powerful?

I am still playing the game to this day and am more in love with it than ever. I found myself again and recognize every single bit of her. I don't care about winning or false titles. I care about the people and their time. I am the best because of my heart, not because of my glove or bat. It is nice when people compliment your skill as a ball player; however, when people fall in love with your genuine heart, praise your personality, seek you out to listen to your words of comfort, or express they need your time and advice? That hits differently. That's what I realized as I shed those tears in the dirt behind the dugout, when compliments were scarce.

Today, the ball field is my sanctuary. I play for the sun as it shines on the tops of the dandelion puffs—bright little gold bulbs glowing on the grassy surface. As the sun descends behind the mountains in the distance, slowly fading into the clouds, beams of bright white pierce open a sharp spotlight onto the landscape below—a memory before it sets into the night. *Is this heaven?* I often wonder. Shadows of shark teeth are silhouetted in the far distance along the treeline as dusk moves in. Everything shimmers as a cool breeze begins to replace the sun's warmth. Thousands of flies dance in the last moments of daylight, tiny wings flying around, leaving a trail of light behind them. The grass comes together in green patches—some dark, some light—forming a kind of quilt, like something a grandmother makes for her granddaughter.

You have to get comfortable with being uncomfortable.

Is it easier to stay in a life of comfort, standing on the sidelines spectating? To give in to the fear of failure and settle, stay caged, and never grow? Maybe, but it won't make you happy. I promise you, if you participate in this life, you will experience discomfort many times over, but if you can keep your eye on the possibilities that lie on the other side of discomfort, you *will* find happiness!

I am

I Am Worthy 101
14. *Elisha Rose Beauty & Style, 2021*

After I lost Bradley, I took a leave of absence from work for six months. I walked away from everything. In the fall, I opened my doors again, slow and steady, nothing too big or complicated. I just booked simple cutting appointments and no-brainer colour jobs like root touch ups. Taking that leave of absence cost me thirty percent of my business. Bradley passed away when I was enjoying the most success as a stylist. My books were full for months, and I had finally reached a state of comfort in my income that had taken years to attain. I was so angry at the setback; it was yet another thing I felt Bradley had taken from me.

In the late fall, I was booked for a consultation with a new client. A sweet, kind woman came through the door like a gust of wind. She was very short and had long, dark, curly hair. She seemed sharp, but also soft spoken. Her smile stayed with you for days. You couldn't help but smile back even if you didn't want to. It was intoxicating and instantly made a huge impression on me. She also had a contagious energy; I felt every bit of her. She and I filled the space we were in by being present with each other. I spent half an hour asking about her life, and she openly shared her life with me. She had recently moved to Prince George and felt a need to connect with others. The conversation flowed, and our personalities and perspectives matched beautifully.

"I am so happy you are here, but I guess I should do my part and ask about your hair now!" I finally giggled. She offered a hesitant smile and nodded; it was almost as though I had offended her. However, time is money, and I felt we needed to get moving. I began to ask her when the last time was that she had gotten her hair done when she cut me off.

"Elisha, I have something to tell you," she said softly, looking me in the eye.

"Ok?" I responded, slightly confused.

"Do you know what a medium is?" she asked.

I took a deep breath. My eyes narrowed, and my voice tightened. "Yes. I do, but I must warn you that I am a very spiritual person and I…," I started to say before she cut me off again. She had sensed my discomfort at the mention of the word "medium." I was going to warn her not to fuck around with this shit or with people's hearts. I was about to take a stand with my faith and tell her to be careful about what she said next. But then she spoke these words:

"Bradley has something he wants to tell you."

I Am Worthy made its debut in June 2023. I had planned every single detail of its launch and hosted a private, intimate event. I was terrified. I honestly thought I was losing my mind. Putting my name and "author" in the same sentence seemed impossible. Yet, here I was, holding my book in my hands, feeling the edges of the soft, matte cover, the spine, and staring at the bright blue eyes of a woman I was only beginning to know. This book, these words, my voice…did I really do this?

I pictured a garden party. I wanted to be outside in the sun, somewhere with a view. I had written the book for Bradley and to celebrate him. I made a promise that I would bring joy to his name, that whoever read this book would be a part of us, our truth, and our love. The venue had to be the right setting to capture all of him. I wanted something along the Nechako River. I had walked many miles along its banks in my time of mourning. I shed countless tears there. Hearing the river and watching it continue to flow helped heal me. I spent hours watching the sun gleaming on the surface of the rapid-flowing water, highlighting its power and energy. It was like a magnet, bringing everything closer to it.

I put a lot of thought into what a reader might need to get through my story. I had rose gold gift bags made for each guest. In each bag, I placed travel-size packs of tissues, lavender tea, a bag of candy, book tags, a pen, a bath bomb, and a thank you card. I also hired a local bakery to make cupcakes for the event. All of them had a rose top and were placed in a cute little white box with a see-through heart window.

We held the launch at Northern Lights Winery where my sixty guests could enjoy the view. I felt weightless and at times numb as I sat there signing my name on copies of my book, trying to keep my hand steady, overwhelmed by the sheer ecstasy of the task. I was overwhelmed with gratitude as I saw everyone line up to get their book signed. Requests for photos startled me. *You want a photo with me?* I thought awkwardly to myself. I could hear my girlfriends, who helped plan the event, in the background talking about me to the guests. Their expressions of pride filled me with a sense of self-worth and made me feel like I was a woman they looked up to. The joy was overwhelming, and I had to take a deep breath as I sat back down to sign another copy of *my* book.

"Hey there, hunny bunny. I brought you a drink," Rea said.

Thank fuck Rea always knows what I need, I thought to myself. She was my guest speaker and was there to represent my name and brand. She is kind, a social bird, but also is a master at problem-solving without conflict. She is always direct and follows through with action. She was there to look after my needs and balance the rest. Rea is a rockstar.

"Are you ready for your speech?" she asked.

I nodded in reply. She was saying something to the crowd, but I couldn't hear her. All I heard was my heartbeat and the voice in my head. *I have prepared for this moment for what feels like a lifetime. I want to represent not just me, but all of him, Bradley. I want to make him proud.*

The sound of clapping brought me back to the present moment. Everyone's eyes were now on me, most importantly, my two children; more than anyone, I wanted to impress them.

"Before I say anything, I need everyone to know that without my two beautiful children, I wouldn't be standing before you today holding this book. They hold me so high in worth and that is what made *I Am Worthy* a possibility," I said, finding my son's eyes in the crowd. He is taller than Bradley now and his blond hair is cut just like Justin Bieber. He has the most intoxicating smile; anyone who meets him notes how breathtaking he is in both charm and character. He loves to make people laugh. He is the man in my life who fills my heart.

Next, I searched for her, my eyes darting back and forth around the crowd. My daughter seems shy at first, but once she trusts you, she'll show you her goofy side. She is clever, witty, and loud. I fall in love with all she is every single day. I saw her shyly emerge into an opening in the crowd; she was flushing red with the attention now focused on her. I mouthed the words, "I love you," and she instantly calmed down and a more normal colour returned to her face. I continued with my speech, speaking directly to them, directing my focus and all my efforts so they could hear the power behind our story—the three of us and Bradley.

"I found it difficult to be around people who wanted me to get better. I didn't have a recipe for better. I didn't just lose someone. I lost my everything, my whole world, and a part of my soul. Tanner and Hailey lost a father and I, a soulmate," I said as tears streamed from my eyes and fell onto my cheeks. My son was holding his smile, but his eyes were glazing over with pools of water. My daughter, no longer feeling shy, mouthed to me, "You can do this, Linda." I giggled. "I thought that turning my words into a story was going to be my better. It turns out that better was just the beginning of something extraordinary."

Within two months, I sold two hundred copies. I even had another local bookstore call to request more copies as they kept selling out. I honestly thought my story would only be read by my family and close friends. I never thought in a million years this book would make an impression, and not just an impression but a tidal wave in my community and the province. Before I could comprehend the success I was having, more things started to happen. Many took an interest in my story, and I was offered a book tour. In another six months, in the late fall of 2023, I would take on a new career as a public speaker, promoting the thesis of my book: addiction is a medical condition and not a choice.

I was so new at being a writer and becoming an author and now another opportunity had arrived. It felt like I had taken an overnight train and woken up in a completely new era. The idea of speaking to an audience was daunting, but I never back down from a challenge and it was with this thinking that I embarked on another journey: to find my voice.

I held my breath and held the medium's gaze.

"Elisha, I am only here to offer you a gift, but I need your openness and permission," she said.

I slowly nodded yes but within me I was praying, screaming for God to intervene. I begged God, *if this lady is fucking around, allow me to see the truth. If not, and it is your will, God, if it's really Bradley through her, please, I beg you to give me a sign.* The medium, who had been sitting in my salon chair for the hair consult instantly transformed into something or someone else.

"Elisha, I am a jackass!" she said forcefully. I did not expect this at all, and I was startled by these words. I still doubted, but I gracefully gave the woman my undivided attention. "You deserved to be loved," she said.

Now something deep within me woke up and I gravitated closer to the words coming from this woman. My book would not be published for another two years. No one really knew our story yet, about the lack of love, or the disease. I hadn't spoken a word about it to anyone.

"These tears I shed are not mine but his," the medium said. The thing was, Bradley never cried, ever. I started to get suspicious and began pulling away, afraid that this woman, this so-called medium, was a liar, an impostor who preyed on the weak.

"Bradley wants you to know he is holding you right now," she said, as tears streamed from her eyes. I started to cry, so hurt by what was happening because I didn't believe in any of it. Only God had this power. I felt my shoulders drop, my breath release, and my guard drop. I had no fight for this. I was still very fragile. So, I surrendered. Then I heard him, Bradley, in a soft, faint whisper. "I am here, my love."

My body got warm and light. A beam of sunlight peeked through the small window to my salon and shone down on me. I tried gathering my thoughts together to try to understand.

"I am a coward for the way you found me," the woman said.

Now I knew with all my heart that it was Bradley. I had told no one about how he died or where. It even sounded like him. It was just like something he would have said. Sitting there, I decided I needed to take stock of the facts. You meet a stylist who you have never met before now for an appointment and then call her dead husband a coward? She wouldn't dare. Without realizing it, I was biting my tongue; something was keeping me from speaking.

"I am so proud of you, Elisha, and I know you are going to help so many people."

Bradley knew of my plans. He knew about the book even though at that point it was unwritten. I felt he was giving me his blessing, but he also knew I was battling with a greater darkness: fear.

"Do not be afraid of my family; they are responsible for their own destruction."

I have never dreamed of Bradley since his death. Perhaps that is the way God intends it to be. And after this episode, I never fixated on this woman, the medium. I took what she said as a gift from God. Yes, I do believe it was Bradley's spirit, but

I try now to focus on what was said, not who said it. When I thought about the word "coward," I remembered that the night before Bradley died, he left me a note attached to a marriage licence. It read "How committed I am." I was very angry at this; I felt it was another false attempt to fix the situation he had placed himself in, and it only hurt my heart more. For the longest time I struggled to understand why the word "coward" was what linked this past incident between us. I looked up the definition of "coward": a person who lacks courage. Then it clicked for me. Bradley wanted me to know he lacked the courage to do what was right. He wanted to be honest about who he was, an addict. He saw the truth but allowed the disease to hold him captive. The hardest part about my time with Bradley was believing with all my heart that he was a good man who loved me. He broke me in ways that continue to cause nightmares regularly. At times, when all the bullshit surfaces, I struggle to love him. Most times, I whisper under my breath, "I hate you!" Other times, I scream it. I wallow in self-pity, and picture myself running from the pain of my past and straight into a doctor's chair to demand, "Drug me up!" I don't want to feel anything anymore.

Why come to me through a medium and tell me now? I know Bradley wasn't afraid of dying, he was more afraid of living. When he was high, nothing bothered him; he felt he had a stress-free life, and all his problems disappeared. I watched for years how deranged he was when he woke up hungover. Witnessing the withdrawal from the drugs, which turned all his invisible scars into open wounds for the world to see, was unbearable. Bradley never wanted to leave the feeling of orgasmic release he felt while on drugs, but pain is patient. He couldn't face the pain he caused others and instead chose to escape into the abyss of the emotion anaesthetic. He drank to feel nothing, to become nothingness, as the wounds grew deeper and his soul experienced worthlessness. I vowed not to lack the courage to love others, but most importantly, to love myself. Love is a miracle.

Albert Einstein has been quoted as saying, "There are only two ways to live your life. One is as though nothing is a miracle. The other is as though everything is." I choose everything in my life to be a miracle. I found freedom in my voice. People really wanted to hear what I had to say. One of my biggest concerns was that I wanted to sound like myself, the same me that comes through in the book. So, I articulated my strong points with swear words. I feel swearing gives off a powerful impression, and I leaned into the persona of a philosopher with the mouth of a trucker. My mother strongly disapproves, but what mother wouldn't?

I assumed people who came to my speaking events wanted to hear from me and about my book. But I was wrong. While my story was heard, I realized that many individuals that attended needed to be heard as well. I visited six communities and in every single one there was a story of loss. I listened to all the heartache from those who had lost loved ones and shared many tears alongside those who were broken. I counselled them with encouragement to transform their pain into love and use that power to fight the war against addiction. My story was only one of thousands, and my journey was only the beginning for many more to rise up; however, it wasn't all sunshine and rainbows.

While I was on tour, rumours were spreading back home. Members of my family began to question what kind of mother I was. How could I be a good one if I am away travelling all the time? Many who called themselves friends saw my success as a threat. Some took me for granted and others resorted to gossip. My celebrity caused many to consider me a stuck-up snob.

Jealous much? Then there were the people who wanted to tear me down. I had a man rudely interrupt one of my talks during my tour to state his opinion. "I didn't realize you were a self-published author. Indie authors are not real authors," he said.

With a very polite smile, I looked him in the eye and replied, "Oh, my good sir! And how many books have you written?"

He was entitled to his opinion but so was I. He stormed out of the room and left such an awkward situation. I had to bring the energy back up. Pretending to chase after him with one of my books in hand, I yelled, "Good sir? You forgot your copy of my book!"

Immediately, a roar of laugher came from the crowd. The healthy energy revived, and my presentation continued. I also sold the most books that evening. People saw a taste of my sense of humour, fire, and truth. They all wanted more.

Still, I was the target of spiteful remarks from all over the country through social media. My detractors argued that I was the problem because I said addiction is a disease and that I was enabling the addicts. But I wasn't the first to say this. The American Medical Association identified addiction as a disease in 1987.

Out of all the backlash I suffered, I have a favourite. I was asked to be on a local podcast by an individual who is well known in the community. I wasn't their biggest fan; I thought they were arrogant, but I was tempted to go. I sought some advice from someone I trusted. I needed an unbiased opinion before making my decision. I knew what was at stake. This person's opinion was not glowing. They said the podcast is shit, no one listens to it, the person hosting is a terrible interviewer and always makes everything about themselves. It was enough to concern me, and I wondered why they even wanted to interview me.

"With all due respect, I am confused as to why this person is interested in meeting me? Have they read my book?" I asked the podcast assistant. The only response I received was the sound of crickets as her wide eyes stared back at me. That was the end of the conversation. I had made my point: I didn't care about who this podcaster was or how famous he was or how wealthy. None of that mattered to me. I would give a homeless man my time if he asked for it honestly. Isn't that what we call integrity? What mattered to me was that my book was taken seriously.

Two days before my tour began, I lost my dog, Ayms. Bradley and I had owned three dogs together, but after he passed, I put two of them up for adoption. I couldn't let Ayms go though. He was the last of Bradley's legacy, and he was my baby. I numbed myself to cope and push through the tour. People were counting on me, but the regurgitation of my past life with Bradley, all the pain, all the trauma and abuse left me so vulnerable. I entered into a state of depression that I was only pulled out of briefly by short-term distractions. I had to control my state of mind to accept the new experiences and suppress the old ways of thinking.

While on tour, I always asked the crowd a question: did they think I lost or gained people by publishing my story? Many thought I had gained people, but one woman in the crowd spoke up.

"You lost more people but gained more of everything else."

Bingo! I have gained more of the *right* people in my life. It's all about quality, not quantity now in my relationships. The people I lost are detached from pursuing their purpose. I have learned after much self reflection and healing not to take it personally. Now that I am in this state of growth and awaking, I place many boundaries to conserve my time and energy.

I never understood gossip. It just seems like useless talk and wasted air. What positive can come from tearing another person down? It just puts negativity out in the world and takes power away. The irony is that the negativity has actually empowered me. I realized that people who get together to talk shit about my life gain nothing; they just look like fools. Plus, talking about me only proves that I'm important. That is how powerful I am. Who gives a fuck if you talk about me? Go ahead! Your words will be the kindling to my fire, and eventually you will stop talking and start taking fucking notes.

If it's not making me happy, making me money, or making me better, then I am busy. That is how I do remarkable things. I believe in the possibility of who I want to be. I believe in my worth. That is how I beat the odds and did something worthwhile. I know who I am. Who I am is non-negotiable. Do not pass go. Do not collect two hundred dollars. When it comes to the concept of worth, you have to detach yourself from all the external things. Your worth is not defined by what you obtain or what your neighbour says about you. Your worth lies in what makes you, you—in what you were created to be.

I have asked many people, "Do you know your worth?" Many people respond by blaming others for their lack of worth. Some people don't answer at all. If you don't know what makes you worthy, how can you ask for what you want in life? I work for what I want, and I get what I want no matter how long it takes. I choose the pain of discipline over the pain of regret. I have set my standards and made my boundaries, and people have asked, "You think you're all that?"

And I can honestly respond, "*I am!*"

PART III

Love
A smile is contagious and confusing

Shame holds us hostage
—not fear

A Barbie Girl
15. *House Party, 2006*

Everything is spinning way too fast. I'm not much of a drinker, but I want to show my ex-boyfriend I can handle my liquor in front of all his friends. What a bust! I wobble my way to the bathroom and close the door behind me. At this point I know I need to throw up; I know it will make me feel a lot better. I feel like death as I hurl my guts out. I don't care who hears me at this point. My head is in the bowl of the toilet, which echoes my every upchuck. My stomach hurts so bad. How in the hell did three Caesars do *this?* I lie down on the cold bathroom tile and curl up around the toilet. I keep trying to sit up, but I am so dizzy I just can't do it. I need water badly. I hear the handle of the door jiggle and then I hear a creak, like the sound you hear in a scary movie. I realize I forgot to lock the door. Then I hear a click. *Now* it is locked. Suddenly, I feel wetness along my neck and ear. Then something big and powerful is pulling at me. I keep my hands on my belly; it hurts too much to move.

"I need water," I moan. Why am I moving up and down? Where is my water?

In April 2022, I woke up in a hospital bed. The pain shooting from my stomach was interrupting my relaxed state. It was so excruciating that I started to call out in pain. A nurse came to my aid immediately.

"Hello, Elisha. You've just woken up from surgery. How are you feeling, dear?" she asked sweetly with a soft touch on my arm.

"It hurts," was all I could muster.

The nurse didn't hesitate and shot me up with morphine. I then tried waiting for ten minutes, as they tell you to do, but the pain felt worse at that point. I pushed the button. The nurse approached me again as I wailed out, "It hurts so much."

What the fuck did I get myself into? I wondered as the nurse shot me up again with more morphine. I felt my body relax instantly as the warm liquid travelled through my veins, melting my insides. I drifted off slowly until I was a little girl sitting on a window ledge looking up and out to the stars, the bright twinkles of tiny diamonds that sparkled. In my backyard, I saw the snow glittering under the moon's luminous light. Shadows emanated from all the naked trees. The branches were covered in small spikes of crystalline shapes in various sizes as the freezing snow formed icicles. My window was open, and I breathed in the air, enjoying the cold's touch. I began to sing a song from happier times.

"Tell me of the plans you have for me, Oh Lord, as I lift my hands and pray to be only yours…." Then I closed my eyes, folded my hands together, and prayed. "Please God, make me beautiful when I grow up."

"Elisha? Dear?!" Suddenly, I was pulled back into the present. I opened my eyes and saw a face I didn't quite remember. She seemed concerned.

"How are you feeling for pain now?" the nurse inquired. I felt my lips part and form the biggest grin.

"I feel fucking fantastic!" I exclaimed. She started to giggle. I thanked her profusely for saving me, and then, feeling more and more excited and alive, I decided to have some fun. I thought it would be a great idea to push a whole bunch of buttons like a little kid would. Then I saw these two huge watermelons on my chest, and I remembered what the surgery was for.

"Holy Fuck! Look at these new canons!" I shouted out. At that point, I had everyone's attention, from the nurse's station to the other patients recovering in their beds. "Hot diggity damn! Guess who's the sugar mama now? *I* am, bitches!" I screamed. All I heard was laughter. "Wooohooo! I bet I could snap up a doctor with these babies." I was so distracted by my new fake tits, I didn't hear the doctor walk in. But suddenly I noticed him at the foot of my bed. He grinned silently and looked over my chart and was about to head to the next patient. "Wait! Doctor! Would you titty fuck me with these babies?" I asked, pointing at my new tits he just signed off on. Yes, I asked my poor doctor if he would titty fuck me. That poor man. I made everyone laugh though. Even the doctor broke into a kind of shocked giggling.

The whole point of this operation was to develop more respect for my body, and I had humiliated myself within minutes of my surgery. I had sworn there would be no more whoring around and acting cheap, carelessly throwing away this precious gift I had been given. And then I did just that within minutes, which made everything that much funnier. But then I started to cry. I thought about all the time that had passed, all the time I had spent patiently waiting and asking for the courage to follow through. I felt that as a woman, I deserved to have everything because I had lost and grieved so much. After the birth of my children, I mourned the havoc that process had wreaked on the body God gave me. Now I had healed the scars that marked their place on my skin, mind, and heart. I was reborn.

New scar tissue was developing and hardening over my caesarean section. An addition floated along my stomach, a belly button recreated after all the stretching and pulling. Under the skin, reconstructed abdominal muscles were pulled together like bootlaces, weaving in and out and tied on the end in a nice, little bow. Now, round, silicone gel implants filled the gap where two flat, flapjack pancakes used to be. My formerly sad nipples that used to stare at the floor were now perfectly centred and faced front, smiling back at the mirror.

I spent six weeks in recovery, not lifting more than ten pounds. I had to wear a band just above my new boobs and another pulled tightly around my stomach, like a girdle. I was bent over for months like a hunchback, unable to stand upright. Everything was so tight and inflexible. That wasn't even the hardest part of the recovery. The withdrawal I suffered from the narcotics I was given was something else. I have never been on opioids for a long period of time, and I am allergic to codeine and oxycodone. (I found this out when I got my wisdom teeth pulled and developed a serious gum infection). I was prescribed hydromorphone, i.e., medical heroin. This drug was paired with Toradol, a strong anti-inflammatory. A friend and client had undergone the same surgery a year previously, and she advised me to take the drugs and not to underestimate the pain or the risks. I'm glad I listened. I had my sister-in-law look after me and we created a chart with the dosages and the timing for when I should take these narcotics. I wanted everything a half an hour early to avoid putting my body in pain. When the body is in pain, it is stressed and therefore no healing or cell recovery can happen.

The side effects were scary. I didn't want to eat, and I was always weak and tired. I slept for days and days; I just couldn't do anything else. I just wanted fluids. Eventually, those fluids turned into smoothies, but there were times I had to be force fed. When it came time to shitting, well, it felt like death itself. Nothing is better after weeks of not being able to pass a bowel movement than getting your girlfriend to shove a depository up your asshole. The feeling of crawling into a hot bath on a cold winter day? Feeling a fresh breeze on a hot summer day while you're standing in the outfield playing baseball? Nothing compared to the feeling of finally relieving myself after not being able to poop for weeks.

"Hallelujah!" I screamed. "Liberate the brown trout!" I shouted in excitement.

My girlfriend had never seen anyone so excited to shit. It was like everything had descended from inside me. The relief I got gave me so much joy that I started to cry tears of happiness. The best part for me was when my girlfriend placed me doggy style in the bathtub to sponge bathe me, shooting soapy water up my ass, making fun of me the whole time. It was by far one of the best times of my life.

I tried to cut back my dosage of the opioids after three weeks, but the pain was too excruciating and unbearable. For a month, I had to stay consistent on the medications. Even so, I started to slowly move around, eat light foods, and drink lots of water so I wouldn't get constipated. By the time six weeks came around, I was trying to wean myself off the medications again. I went through severe withdrawal symptoms: night sweats, hot and cold flashes, diarrhea, nausea, insomnia, and tons of anxiety. It was the most horrible experience I have ever dealt with.

I stank all the time. No matter how many showers I took, the drugs were coming out of my pores and seeping into my clothes. Laundry was constantly being done as I was always running out of clean clothes. At one point, I broke down and doubted the choice I had made. I questioned my own integrity. *You are a vain woman, and this is karma for changing your body in an unnatural way. Shame on you for not being happy with what you had naturally*, I told myself. I sat in the corner of the couch in my living room in silence for a long time, listening to my own voice attack me. Migraines would form and it was like someone was taking a bat to my skull. That's when the idea came to me: *Why not stay on the drugs? Then you'll never have to go through this state of doubt and emptiness again.* I liked the feeling the drugs gave me. I felt limitless and unstoppable. These drugs gave me a free way of thinking with no worries attached or responsibilities. The drugs gave me the relief I was seeking for as long as I needed it. *This could be my answer.*

Sometimes you have to reach deep down inside of yourself and grab a hold of what seems impossible. I realized I could never have a healthy and full life with a drug addiction. I had to look inside and picture what that healthy and full life might look like. I realized it meant that I could stay in alignment with my higher self, the true essence of my high vibe vision of what I desire. I desire what is the subject of my heart's deepest longing. I have to remind myself, if I cannot put my heart into it, then I must take myself out of it.

I didn't get this surgery to become a drug addict. My heart isn't into that. I got this surgery to heal a part of my body, to heal a part of me that had been taken from for years.

There were complications beyond the opioid withdrawal. In the months that followed my surgery, I developed a tunnel under my new belly button. Yellow fluid leaked from the sutures used to tie up my abdominal wall; there was an infection. The tummy tuck scar tissue split open exposing what looked like melted skin. A two-inch superficial hole formed, getting wider every day and leaking more and more. I was losing my mind as the fluid soaked through endless medical pads. The pain was gone, and the drugs were out of my system, but now I faced this shit show of a mess. *Will I ever get a break?* I wondered. I was finally referred to the burn and wound clinic. I didn't know it existed but the medical attention I received there put me on the path to healing. Silver nitrate pads absorbed the infection and essentially cauterized the wound. It was the coolest thing I'd ever seen. Within weeks I had a home care set up of saline, soft beige bandages that didn't rip my skin off when I had to change them, and the silver. It was a medical miracle!

Once I had fully healed, I could see abs again: side abs and a lower pelvic line. I hadn't seen these things since before I was pregnant. I also finally could fill out the chest area of a bathing suit properly—pretty sexy, if I do say so myself! The new watermelons brought along some interesting challenges though. I had never had to bat in baseball with boobs before. I found these knockers changed my swing, making it impossible to hit the ball hard, or sometimes at all. I had to adjust. I started wearing two sports bras, and altered my swing, which I now call "wide load." Before the surgery, I would dive for a ball and just land and stay on the ground after I made the catch. Now if I dive, my boobs pop me right back up. No joke! They give me just enough bounce, so I don't slam my face in the grass and give me enough room to make the throw. It was all fucking amazing, the best investment ever.

Like any investment though, it all needs continual maintenance. I decided to build a team for my health. I hired a personal trainer, a registered massage therapist, and someone who specializes in blood analysis; these people gave me the blueprint to my body. When I look back on the money and the time I wasted on fitness trends, I want to shoot myself. I said to each member of my team, "It shouldn't be so hard," and each and every one of them agreed. How did I select this crack team of professionals? I hired them based on their energies. Did they align with me? Were we on the same page? Because I knew if I searched for that, I would have a safe community to confide in. I wanted to be in a room with individuals who inspired me, loved me, and helped me find my balance.

That's the key ingredient: balance. What is balance with regard to lifestyle? For me, it's a connection between the body, mind, and spirit. I do a lot of work with my mind and call on my spirit daily to set aside my ego's fears. Only with all this work can I be present in my body. Movement is for the mind: I walk every day. It has always resonated with me, and I always took long walks through the hayfields when I was a young girl. The best part is that your body partakes naturally. There is no stress, no toxic energy, no music, nothing that would take away from the peace you are cultivating. I firmly believe this is where all the magic lives: being able to listen to your body as it is in movement. When you have a less stressful life, you have less weight gain. And *psst!* Walking is fucking *free*. Exercise is another thing I find many people are unrealistic about because they lack the knowledge about *their* unique bodies. I don't think anyone can understand a woman's body, with its constantly changing, raging hormones, better than another female. No offense, male trainers, but I am in *love* with my girl, Kat. She won me over the minute she told me she did not intend to build me a plan that included a workout every day.

"Three days a week!" she said.

She does not leave my side until she is confident in my ability to execute the exercise correctly. She fell head over heals with *me* when I stated my goals for my body type.

"I want a big apple booty butt and a tight stomach with defined abs to complement my new bongos. I ain't no skinny bitch. I got curves, and I wiggle." I told her. She laughed at my candor and was all for it.

Kat digs my sense of humour and my no-bullshit approach and accepts me as I am. I am confident in her expertise, but more importantly, I feel well cared for. I hadn't stepped foot in a gym in ten years, but she made it happen. It felt possible with her.

I had prayed for the right people to enter my life, to find a community of women who truly support and love me. Besides Kat, May and Tara have been essential. They were right there beside me in those early days at the gym. I remember I was laying down doing shoulder presses with dumbbells, and Kat was guiding me when out of the corner of my eye I saw May who then hopped on top of me.

"Push it! Come on! Five, six…," she yelled, making me lose my focus. I struggled to hold the weights as the laughter poured out of me. On the other side of me, Tara approached, crawling like a gremlin with her hands reaching for me. All of us were laughing by then except Kat who reminded us, "She still has three more to go!"

Tara, May, and I go way back. Before I had kids, I used to secretly think of May as a kindred spirit. She was so strong, she seemed invincible. She was a weightlifter who competed in bikini style competitions and worked on her body with so much discipline, it was like an art form. She never backs down, and her energy continues to inspire my own dedication. She doesn't realize it, but I gravitate to her and want to be around her as often as I can. As for Tara, I coached her in high school basketball and have subsequently played baseball with and against her for years. After she read my first book, she reconnected with me by booking an appointment at the salon. I also see myself in her, but in a different way. She is someone who understands loss, pain, and resilience. She actually led me to Kat. After I told her my fitness goals, she knew just the woman I was looking for. I used to be against hugs, but anytime I see Tara, I reach for her. It is my way of saying thank you for seeing me. Deep down, she understands my soul. A woman who used to look up to me as a coach is now an inspiration to me. My favourite thing about Tara is that she is still a kid. She loves to prank people, including me, and she loves to make me laugh while doing it. We are actually both big kids who love to pull pranks on one another often.

It was Kat who suggested my massage therapist team: a lovely husband and wife duo. They provide the most professional setting and care I have ever encountered. Home-based businesses have always resonated with me since that's what I have myself. The technician I found to analyze my blood was mythical in my eyes. I had never heard of such a thing. Blood analysis as a blueprint to your overall health? It seemed like a crazy, almost surreal concept, but this woman could tell things about my body just by looking at my blood under a microscope. "What did you do to your right thigh?" "You have very low iron." "You are not sleeping well." "Oh girl, you are horny!" I was star stuck. From her, I learned that the reason I am addicted to sugar is because I have an iron deficiency. (It really was an addiction; sugar was like crack to me.) She also warned me that the more sugar I consumed, the more damage I was doing: weight gain, fatigue, thirst, acne, migraines, mood swings…the list goes on. I had to quit, but withdrawal from sugar increases the intensity of the cravings initially; I felt sick. I was always tired. That was only the beginning of my problems.

My body wasn't holding water. I was constantly dehydrated due to a lack of sodium, which actually helps your body maintain its fluid balance and stay hydrated. Who knew? I did not. The blood technician produced a plan for me with strict guidelines regarding what to eat and what not to eat. She suggested I take certain iron tablets along with other carefully selected vitamins. She promised me in three months I would have more energy, fewer sugar cravings, and that I would lose weight. Most importantly, she told me I would glow. She was right and it all just blew my mind wide open.

I found a team of people dedicated to serving my needs with the utmost care, compassion, and expertise. The extra skin I was burdened with has been cut out; however, something remains very powerful to me: this body is new, rebirthed, and its story is now being rewritten.

I feel my body being pulled up and down in a jerk-like movement. My pants are around my knees and hot, sweaty, hard hands are grabbing at my underwear. I am so dizzy that I can't lift my head—it feels like it weighs a thousand pounds. I manage to move my arm from my side to try to hold onto my underwear before I am exposed, but my hand is pushed away and held down.

I hear everything: the voices behind the locked door, the sound of water trickling from the sink, and the weeping coming from inside me as I beg him to stop. I cannot put my body in motion; I am completely helpless.

Open your eyes, Elisha. Let him see your eyes, I tell myself as I feel my panties slowly sliding down my weak limbs. I start seeing dots and everything is spinning so fast. I realize I am going to throw up. I close my eyes, afraid of puking. His sticky, sweaty, stinky body is now on top of me. The drunk idiot has forgotten to spread my legs and is trying to use his knee to do the trick. My pants, however, are around my knees and prevent them from opening, like a thick rubber band with no elasticity. Despite my terror, I can see the humour in this. It is as though I am having an out-of-body experience. My attacker though is frustrated and starts hitting me in the legs and hips. He stops for a brief second and figures out how he can enter my vortex. He begins to turn me over. I am screaming inside, *No! Elisha, do something! Now!* I let go of my stomach and just as my head was turning to the side, I open my eyes as wide as I can so I can be sure to lose control. I barf all over him—in his mouth and on his hair, face, and chest. I don't hear a thing, but I feel a sharp sting on my face and a sudden, overpowering agony. I realize the coward has punched me in the mouth. The bastard then stands up and pukes all over me. Before running out of the bathroom, he gives me a swift kick in the guts. I puke again, and while I feel better, I notice blood mixed in with the vomit.

"Where are you going, cupcake? You sure you don't want any more?!" I yell after him vindictively, after managing to clear my throat. Then comes a scary, cruel laugh as I scream, "Pussy ass mother fucker!"

As I walk home later, I pull chunks of vomit out of my hair

with one hand while I hold onto my pants with the other. I think about the attack and wonder how I managed to escape. How did I know what to do to stop him? I realize that I pulled it off by recognizing that my body was trying to respond to the situation by puking, and I just needed to let it do exactly what it wanted to do. In my darkest moment, it was there for me. It protected me fiercely, violently, and successfully. It was a miracle.

Trauma is a test

Rose-Coloured Glasses
16. *Duplex, 1986*

My father is working as a journeyman mechanic in the mines in Tumbler Ridge, BC. I am three months old and the first born. My mother has just finished filling my tummy with breast milk. I am out like a light. She places me down in the crib for my afternoon nap and leaves the room.

 My mother looks around the duplex with frustration. My father had initially floated the idea of buying this place together with his older brother to her just before they were married, but my mother was against the idea and said no. She had always felt like they, my father and his brother, were too close; it was like they were joined at the hip and at times it seemed like she was dating two men instead of one. It was when they were on their honeymoon that my father finally came clean and told my mother he had gone ahead and bought the duplex with his brother anyway. They had a huge fight, and my mother considered divorcing my father right on the spot. There was something about a betrayal that involved their first home together as a married couple that cut extra deep. She did forgive him eventually though, and now here we all are.

 My aunt and uncle live on the bottom floor and my parents and I live on the top. The co-habitation has been tricky, especially with a newborn now in the house. My aunt has cats, and my mother does not trust them around me. She has warned my aunt multiple times to keep the door that connects to my parents' suite closed. It's another complication to an already strained relationship. My mother and my aunt are complete opposites. They've never really seen eye to eye or been able to relate to one another. Now they are both living under the same roof. My mother sighs, exhausted by the added stress of this situation and her new responsibilities as a wife and now, a mother.

My mother glances at the clock and sees I have overslept, which isn't like me. I am like clockwork: my naps are consistent down to the second. My mother goes to check on me and opens the door slightly to see one of the cats in my crib and on my face.

There have been moments in my life when I was in such great despair I wished for death. Distractions covered up the pain for a short time, but it felt like a roller coaster for my emotions and after a while I couldn't go on the ride anymore. I was so tired, so fucking tired. I was tired of being better. I had pictured myself in front of God, sitting before him, and saying, "Listen, I am done, and I can't do this anymore." I have normalized the chaos and dysfunction. The brain changes after enduring a lifetime of trauma. It becomes less reliable, which to me didn't come across any differently: trauma became my normal. But after dealing with the death of my partner and all the pain associated with it, I was ready to deal with my own demons. Many people have said I've lost my mind. No, I have finally found it. There were more demons hunting me as the pain lingered. I tried to run, but you can only run for so long until you can't catch your breath anymore and you hit that impenetrable wall.

What is trauma? If you look it up in a dictionary, it'll say something like "a deeply distressing or disturbing experience, or physical injury." How do we decipher our trauma? Let's start with the unexplained trauma within our bodies. Our bodies remember everything; it's our brain that hides away the incident until it senses the body is ready to handle the blunt force. I hate cats. I am not a fan and never will be. I can't even get close to one, let alone pet it. My brain has no memory of the time a cat tried to suffocate me when I was a baby. But my body? It says, "We remember you. You cats are all the same, and you want to kill us." The brain tries to rationalize the situation by using logic.

"You were just a baby. You are kinda being a pussy about cats. They are cute, cuddly, and furry."

The body tenses and screams, "Lies! They are evil balls of fur and hide behind the false cuteness."

My brain and body will argue about this until the day I die. I went on a blind date once and found out that the guy loved his cats. Yes, I ended the date because of a pair of cats. I am not afraid of them at all, but I don't trust the critters. Come on. They shit in a box inside your home, for heaven's sake! It's fucking gross to me. No thanks! My apologies to all you cat lovers out there. But did one try and lay its furry body on your face with intent to kill? I think not. Like I said, I am traumatized.

What about the explained trauma? The trauma you recognize causes your brain to react to protect your safety when your body is too busy caught up in distractions or emotions. I remember the first time I gave a boy permission to physically touch me. I wasn't a girl, but I felt so little and young. "Are you safe? Did you give him permission to see you naked and touch you?" my brain inquired. Meanwhile, my body was reeling between butterflies and ecstasy as his hand reached further down my pants. "What is this? I like it a lot!" said my body. But as his finger entered the same tiny hole where babies come from, my brain screamed, "Alert, alert, alert! Pull his hand away! Fart! Fire at will! Do something!"

Suddenly, I thought back to that stinky man in apartment 18, and then the male babysitter who touched me in the same place and in the same way two years later when I was ten. Calmly and assertively my body told my brain, "Be still. It's different this time. We are giving him permission, and most importantly, this is a chance for us to heal." I grabbed his hand, encouraging him to go deeper as I felt my whole being become lighter.

I lost my virginity that night to a boy who had been my boyfriend for two years already. We made love under the stars by a lake to the sound of a crackling fire, the yellow glow of the firelight illuminating my body. I wouldn't have changed a thing. I don't imagine it gets any better than that. Afterward, I took a dip in the lake and as I was floating naked under the stars in that cool pool of water, I smiled. I remembered back to when I was a little girl and would race to the hayfields to find the best view of the dark night sky. I was desperate to escape into its abyss. At that moment, once more naked under the stars, I felt closer to that little girl again.

In the aftermath of all the trauma I have experienced—the abuse, the loss of a partner—many people have said I am doing everything right. "Take it one day at a time," they tell me. Some even say they envy me while others stare with a shocked look on their faces. Most don't know what the hell to think or do with me. In fact, most days I am banging my head against the kitchen table trying to make sense of what is here and now, and *not* there and then. The truth is I didn't become all Zen, start practicing meditation, and build a relationship with God and all that because I did everything right or felt remotely sane. I've had to crack open my history, my trauma story, and travel the journey of it in my present life.

At times, my past traumas wiped the floor with me. I watched myself soak in deep depression for years, all the while missing out on my life. Have you heard about the different responses to trauma? The freeze, fight, and flight responses? Picture yourself standing in the middle of a road, blocking traffic, unable to move despite the horns honking and comments from drivers and other passersby. The paralysis there, despite the anger it causes, is like a freeze response. It causes you to feel stressed, and when you catch sight of a driver giving you the middle finger, you get angry and start swearing; this is the fight response. Finally, you have the sense that you want to run from this danger. This is the flight response. There is another response that isn't as well known. It's called the fawn response. In this coping mechanism, we try to please someone in order to avoid conflict.

Trauma bonding ignites the same parts of our brain that addiction does, and this is why people can't just leave so easily. My mother has told me that to her, it seems the last twenty years of my life have been a sacrifice: an era when I consistently put my needs aside. She saw that I loved deeply and in return all I ever wanted was to be loved back equally. It makes so much sense why I went from relationship to relationship, always needing to be with someone. I didn't know how to be alone. I'll never forget her telling me, in the wake of Bradley's passing, "It's time to find out who you are."

Fear is such a dirty little secret. It can prevent us from pursuing the things we want, which in turn stops us from living life fully. Many people who have lost stay lost. Fear melts us away into a dark, lonely, empty hole. I have been stuck and unable to move forward because I had my eyes trained on the rearview mirror. I kept looking to the past, to all the pain, abuse, and trauma that was inflicted upon me. The death of a spouse had become the death of me, the death of what I was. All that pain is impossible to bear alone, and without even knowing it, I hurt other people. One night I was watching the movie, *I, Tonya*, about Tonya Harding, the first woman figure skater to land a triple axel during competition. When she took her fear out on a rival skater, her skates were taken away. In the film, there's a scene where Tonya, played by Margot Robbie, begs the judge to change his decision, pleading, "Send me to jail but please don't take my skates away!" This scene resonated with me because I could see that for her, and all the trauma she had endured, skating was the only thing she knew.

Generational trauma is the passing down of traumatic experiences or stressors from one generation to another. It transforms us into mimes that mimic the same traits as our parents and the many generations before them. I have this weight on my shoulders that I will never have enough money. I have round-the-clock anxiety and stress that I won't be able to pay my bills or feed my children. I feel I need to find a man to be my cushion and provider to protect the family. The guilt associated with purchasing gifts for myself is real; I feel I am being greedy. Where do these thoughts come from?

Every fucking Christmas, my father gave the same damn speech to us kids. My siblings and I would all be sitting by the tree, excited as always for all the presents, until we had to listen to these words: "There are children suffering in the world without fresh water. The money under the tree could have fed so many helpless children. This disgusts me. I ought to give back these gifts." I know my father meant well, but it was still a major buzz kill. It wasn't until I was in my late teens that I managed to finally speak up.

"With all due respect, Dad, if this bothers you so greatly why get us gifts at all?" I asked. I was sick and tired of feeling guilty. That year I had spoiled my siblings by buying them extra gifts with my own money. I wasn't going to let him tell me what to do with my hard-earned dollars.

"Your mother buys the gifts," he replied in a deep, direct tone. He took a drag on his cigarette and avoided eye contact with me. I stood up to face him. He was such an ignorant bully at Christmas. I had had enough.

"May I offer you some feedback? I asked sharply. He looked at me and I noticed his eyes starting to turn green. He knew what was coming: Elisha's defiance. "If you were really concerned about all those starving children, why did you waste all that money over the years on your addiction to cigarettes?" He did not appreciate my insight.

My mother always went the extra mile at Christmas and birthdays because of her own generational trauma. Alcoholism destroyed many generations in her family. Money was always scarce. Having an alcoholic father made it difficult to acquire food and materials consistently. So, I inherited my mother's anxiety about money and my father's propensity to feel guilty and undeserving.

Fortunately, now I see the distinction and can put an end to this generational trauma. It has to start with me and my identity. What does that look like? I love spending money on myself because it makes me feel like I'm worth every fucking penny spent. I *love* looking good. It makes me feel good, and that isn't about greed or vanity. It's about confidence, baby. I have worked very hard to be a successful entrepreneur and, with courage and discipline, I built a thriving business. I always have enough money for bills and spoiling my kids, and I allow the flow of wealth to enter my mindset.

I have heard before from victims who suffered trauma at the hands of a narcissist that the trauma made them stronger. I do not agree with that. This experience did *not* make you or me stronger. This form of abuse gives a person nothing but suffering—the flashbacks, the nightmares, the triggers, the depression, the PTSD. What makes you stronger? Doing the work. A narcissist traumatizes their victim on a psychological level using forms of gaslighting and manipulation. A narcissist has a very short memory. Using manipulation, they create a false world, a world in which they live. Gaslighting helps maintain the illusion of a narcissist's long-term fable.

We may all be guilty of narcissistic behaviour occasionally. However, when you are facing the abuse, it shouldn't be taken lightly. Giving up a life of control to have a life of intimacy is impossible for someone who's a narcissist. Why? Because they must be in control at all times. Our resistance is what creates more suffering. You cannot fight a narcissist. Trust me. I tried many times. Over the years, I have encountered many narcissists; some were lovers, some were partners, and some were family members. Honestly, sometimes it was me! When I was ashamed of who I was or had become due to the trauma I had suffered, I used narcissistic traits to cover up the pain. The only thing that saved me was my journals. I started writing what I knew in my soul was true. It made me stronger, and now I feel able to disarm any narcissist that comes my way. "I cannot control how you see me. But I know who I am," I tell them.

By establishing healthy boundaries, I can now spot a narcissist a mile away. These boundaries are nonnegotiable to me, but to someone who has to be in control, they see it as a kind of trip wire, and they want to set it off. It is only a matter of time before the bad behaviour starts and I recognize the old patterns. Remember it takes very little energy to converse with a narcissist as they always make it about themselves. I do the "smile and nod" trick because it leaves them confused. A smile deviates from what is the normal response. I don't say a word, not a single one.

But the questions still remain: Can we live a life with trauma? Does happiness exist? How do we find joy and keep it safe despite our scars? Happiness is a state of mind, and being happy all the time is unrealistic if you ask me. We are not meant to be happy all the fucking time; that isn't normal. We can wake up happy, but then something in our day happens and pisses us off making us instantly unhappy.

Joy, however, is sustainable and permanent. I was diagnosed with PTSD after losing someone I love and enduring a life filled with multiple instances of abuse, but I still have joy. I choose to have that. I choose to wake up and smile, not just with my face, but with my heart, my mind, and my eyes. I find joy in a hot bath on a cold winter day. I find it when I wake up to the smell of freshly brewed coffee. If you can find the joy in these little things, these seemingly ordinary things, before you know it, that smile will show up on your face.

Trauma is a test. It asks us if we can sustain a life of consequence. Why must we heal our trauma? To be ready for growth, and to mature into our worth. By removing the rose-coloured glasses, we refuse to be colour blind. The frames soften as we heal, and the different colours we experience offer variety as we open up to accept that what was is no longer. The rosy hue is no longer a mask we hide behind and we learn to accept all the colours that life has to offer.

It's time to smell the roses and redefine the trauma that lives in us by not allowing the pain to define us. Trauma offers us a choice: to grow with maturity or to regress and remain stagnant. People suffering through trauma often say, "Give me strength," or "Give me courage." I prefer the word *allow*. Allow me strength, allow me courage, and allow me to be humble. Allow me to accept what has happened and open my heart to the path in front of me. Life isn't a given, it's a privilege, and we need to be thankful for the opportunity. *Allow* is more in line with *surrender*, and I want to surrender to life and allow for things to happen in unexpected ways. When I surrender, I stop trying to control how things happen. This enables them to happen more easily and often in unexpected ways. Things are no longer happening *to* me, but *for* me. The truth is, we cannot control everything, but we can control our perspective regarding the things that are out of our control.

It wasn't for nothing, the trauma that I have been through.

I still struggle in the darkness, but I know I was created for a purpose and so I allow myself to follow and to love. For this I know I am blessed. The tears have to fall because they fall for a reason. The wetness from those tears validates the reason. Tears are your strength, not your weakness. Does it get easier? No! It does not get easier, but it does become possible. Even in the worst storm, there is still beauty to be seen. In our worst pain, we can find peace…and a smile.

My mother rushes to me and the cat leaps out of the crib. I am blue, but upon her touch, she hears me gasp for air. Then I start crying. Relief washes over her as she knows my screams are a good sign. "We are fucking outta here," she promises.

"If I had got my hands on the fucking cat, Elisha, I would have killed it! It was a really fast cat." My mother's anger is still there years later, as she recalls the episode. She was a new, first-time mother at the time, but her instinct to check on me after I slept too long were spot on. She saved my life.

"I remember coming home after work that day. Your mother is a beautiful woman but seeing her face when I walked through the door, I knew something was very wrong," my father tells me. He talks about finding my mother sitting at the kitchen table crying and the guilt he felt for her brokenness. He knew how much she had compromised by agreeing to live with my aunt and uncle. But almost losing me was the last straw for my very hurt, angry, and scared mother.

"I felt like such a schmuck for betraying her trust. I was a dog and a coward for hurting her. I got her drunk on our honeymoon to try to soften the blow of the fact that I'd bought the house with my brother behind her back," my father explains, sharing how it all began. But, after he saw how infuriated my mother was because my safety had been threatened, my father took action. Within three months, my dad had packed up everything they owned and moved us to Prince George.

"We moved while your aunt and uncle were on their honeymoon," my mother giggles as she finishes her tale of triumph.

*Having girlfriends takes work,
but it's worth the effort*

Most Much More
17. *Prince Rupert, 2012*

I have just finished playing a game in the rain, as per usual in this small town. When I first moved to Prince Rupert, I didn't know a single soul. My husband at the time knew a guy who ran a softball team and asked if he was looking for any female players. I eventually joined the B division. I am standing with my new team off to the side watching another game take place. To the right of me are the bleachers and the left of me, a dugout. I'm taking a sip of my cooler when my attention is caught by a louder than normal voice.

"Just wait a second. I have to pee!"

Within a second, a woman with ginger hair cut in a bob emerges from the dugout with haste. I notice her very white skin, light brown freckles, and strawberry blonde locks that glitter when she moves. She is wearing a black waterproof jacket, leggings, and a bright pink undershirt. She has the biggest tits I've ever seen. My trance is broken though the minute I see her start pulling down her pants near the dugout. *Oh my God. Is she peeing right there?* Without hesitating, she crouches down and starts fire hosing the dirt while a smoke hangs from her lips. She lets out the loudest sigh of relief. "Awww. Feels so good!" she yells.

I cannot believe my eyes. There are at least thirty people around the ballpark, but she doesn't even fucking flinch. I start to giggle in admiration. A teammate looks behind to see what I am smiling at. "Oh, that's just Jenny!"

I give him a look that implies my shock. I wonder, *does she do this often?*

"That is Jenny being her normal self," he shrugs.

If this is her being normal, then what is her abnormal self?

It is always interesting to live someone else's life for a moment, learn a different perspective, and reflect on their knowledge. I have a small group of girls I call friends, women I find common ground with, whether in laughter, talent, or the way we take our tea. Our energies vibe with one another, and we support each other in our individual pursuits of happiness. I categorize these women based on their personalities. Who is best for the job of revenge? Who will help me see reason? Who will let me be angry and be angry with me? Who will see my need for acceptance and will guide me back to myself? Or give me the reassurance to stand strong amongst the pebbles in the sand and to protect my space?

I see friendships like a huge apple tree. One bad apple won't kill the tree as long as it lets it drop to the ground and doesn't hold on. You have to let go of the rotten ones. The apples that remain on my tree are strong and healthy, and the roots represent our history. These are the people who have kept me sane and cradled my heart in their own way from the moment I took a bite.

I met Rea in Vancouver for a hair show and convention in 2014. We were sitting a few tables away from each other in a restaurant, but I noticed her bright smile and beautiful blonde hair with its natural brown root shadow. She noticed me too, wondering who was the quiet one with the purple hair. She waved enthusiastically at me. "Hey, you, with the purple hair!" she shouted.

When we talk about that first meeting now, Rea tells me that she fell in love with my soul and the aura that surrounded me. She said it was powerful. "Ya see, I knew you were special. I saw something in you, babe."

Both of us are hairstylists by trade; tattoos cover our bodies in a colourful canvas, and we don't hide our wild daring. Rea is unstoppable, and she reminds me of a pinup girl. Her quick wit and eccentric attitude win me over every time. She makes me feel whole and alive and inspires me to express myself in the most authentic way. She loves that I am a passionate writer, sharing my story to help others, and it's inspired her to do the same. Rea has given me the gift of expression. This is my favourite quality about her. Deep down, she knows what I want and how I think. She never fails to encourage me to go after what I want. She is the sweetest person you'll ever meet, a happy, colourful cupcake. At the same time, she protects me fiercely. Rea defends my heart and soul against anything that might take away from it. Over the years she has given me advice, helping me construct boundaries when it comes to the people I love. I adore that part of her character; she gives me gumption.

Laurie lifts her fist to me because I said something that went against my character. "Boob punch, bitch!" I steady myself for the impact. This loser and I have been together since birth. I got a couple years on her, but we have been inseparable since we were babies. We absolutely do not take ourselves seriously at all. We're always the loudest ones in a room, kicking up a fuss, laughing, or tripping on something. Laurie keeps me as steady as the current in a river. I know I can lean on her and she'll hold me strong so that I never fall. "Pick your hard!" she always reminds me. "Healing is hard, but living in pain is harder." We have matching colourful tattoos along our forearms. I hate colour, and I was thankful as fuck she didn't make me put a watercolour panda on myself. Instead, she made the sacrifice of getting a rose. She designed it all and the colour in the design is breathtaking.

I used to *hate* being hugged. It made me feel stuck and forced onto people, and I usually recoiled; however, one hug from Laurie healed my internal pain and trauma associated with this physical union. She learned it from her father, my uncle. On a hard day, when it seems like nothing can fix it, my uncle's embrace is a life force; you feel yourself melting into him, and it gives you the energy to fight a little longer. There's instant relief and a sense of safety. There is no judgement, it's just absolute love. Laurie's hugs are exactly the same. They make me feel whole, more whole than ever before. I only allow her to hold me this way.

"What was your first impression of me?" I ask my girlfriend Rebecca.

"That chick is fucking cool, and holy damn, she's hot!" I busted out laughing when she shared this with me. I had no idea these were her initial thoughts about me. "When I met you, I said to myself, *she is going to be my best friend and a sister.*" Rebecca told me I was honest, fucking hilarious, and down to earth, and she knew she needed me in her life. I taught Rebecca that while sexy is fun, real beauty comes from within. I give her the confidence she needs whether I'm helping her with her baseball swing or teaching her how to give a great blow job. In return, Rebecca gives me a space to rest so I can restore my energy. She sees me struggling to balance always showing up for others and my need to disappear sometimes. In the fall of 2021, I was playing in an all-women's softball tournament, and my teammates and friends were asking where I was. Rebecca knew and told everyone right away. "She is napping, and we need to give her space for a bit!" Many on the team poked fun while others rolled their eyes, but Rebecca and her brother went to find me to make sure I was ok. They found me curled up in my jeep. We had only just met a few months before, but they didn't hesitate to adopt me into their lives as a sister and a part of their family. Rebecca gives me the room to cry and has sat with me and my tears. I still cry, but the difference is I don't cry alone anymore. Rebecca makes sure of that.

Iris first saw me from a distance on the ballfield. She remained distant when she heard about my second separation from Bradley. I was quiet and dodged the questions, but she noticed my calm energy, open in some ways but guarded in others. When she found out I was a hairstylist, it was her golden ticket for our sisterhood to begin. Iris struggled with post-partum depression after the birth of her third child, but she felt instantly at ease sitting in my small, home-based salon. Before we knew it, we'd been talking for four hours. Iris is always the voice of reason; when I try to control the present out of pain or dwell on the past, she pushes harshly against the spiraling effect of my thoughts. Literally, I cannot bullshit her; I have fucking tried. Iris will not let me dwell because when I do, I disappear into a dark pit, hopeless and lost. "Talk to me! Every time you do it alone, you go into the biggest state of wallowing," she tells me.

By the time I published my first book, I was losing so many women from my life, women I really thought would stay with me as I embraced this new identity. Iris knows some of these women, so not wanting to discuss it with her, I wallowed. Instead of opening my heart to Iris about my concerns, I bottled it up and then royally fucked up her haircut. That's when I knew I was not doing well. Two days after the appointment, I followed up with her and she came back to me. I was on my knees in tears screaming, "I can't fucking lose you!" I was so grief stricken, I didn't know who I was. I cried and cried. I felt weak and so very ashamed over what I did to her hair. Iris grabbed me by the face with her hands and looked into my tear-stained eyes.

"You will never fucking lose me. Ever! None of these women are my friends and bitches be jelly!" she said. The last part made me giggle. What she said next made me laugh out loud.

"Now fix my hair!"

For a while I lost each of these wonderful apples due to my pain. Rea and I grew apart after my trip to Mexico with Bradley. I didn't understand at that time, but when Bradley passed, I saw the pain in her eyes.

"I was relieved, my friend," she told me, as the tears stung her eyes. She told me she was happy that the man I love is no longer here to hurt me. She couldn't bear witnessing the abuse and had to step back. It was then and there I saw everything: what was being done to me was in fact also being done to her. When she saw my fragile, broken self, she felt it all herself. It was destroying her to see me this way. What greater love is there than this? She had to walk away to heal, but she never gave up on me, not for a second. While we were apart, she thought of me, prayed, and hoped I would return to her embrace. And I did! In fact, I hired her to be my personal assistant. Now, she travels with me on book tours and to conventions, picking out my outfits, dazzling me with her smile, and acting as my own personal therapist at times.

"This is what you were meant to do, my friend. Be the voice for those who may not have one. Be the understanding and courageous person who brings them through their pain," Rea told me, giving me the motivation to keep going on this journey no matter how scared I am at times. "Strut what the good Lord fucking gave you sister. Well, the doctors and the Lord," she added with a laugh.

Though we have since created many lovely memories together, when we were children, I took advantage of Laurie's heart. I just constantly took from her, biting down into her very apple core and leaving nothing but the scraps. When she finally told me she'd had enough and asked me why I was always taking from her, I had to answer honestly: "Because I am selfish." I knew there could be no more excuses and hung my head in shame, confessing what I had known to be the truth all along. She knew about the abuse I'd suffered, but in that moment neither she nor I would use it as an excuse. I had to take accountability for taking the love she gave freely and abusing her in return. I broke her trust, and it took her years to feel safe enough to trust me again.

One day, I was in the salon with Laurie and her mother, my aunt whose hair I had just finished cutting and styling. My aunt went to the bathroom as Laurie and I continued our conversation. Laurie went to sit down on the little rolling stool I use for cutting hair and before I know it, her legs kicked up in the air and she landed with a crash, breaking my fake lavender plant. All we heard were the sounds of breaking glass, the thud, and my burst of laughter. I was on my knees crying, holding my stomach, as she laid there in pain. "Help me up, bitch!" Laurie wailed. Seeing her lying there, helpless on the floor like a dead whale, made me laugh even harder. I was starting to try to help her to stand when my aunt yelled through the bathroom door, "I cannot leave you two together for two seconds!" That was it for me as I held my stomach over my cousin's stiff body. "Laurie is a bull in a china shop. You cannot take that girl anywhere," Laurie's mother exclaimed, shaking her head over her daughter's pathetic display.

Laurie admitted to me this is her favourite story about us so far, but not for the reasons I would have thought. "It was like we were kids again, thick as thieves, not a care in the world," she told me. Once I was free of Bradley and all the distractions of pain, I could finally connect as Laurie's equal. The flowerpot incident was the turning point, when complete and full trust was restored.

Rebecca came into my life after Bradley passed away, and it took me time to let her in. I was still in so much pain, I felt fragile, and she struggled to bring me out of my shell. She tried many times to get me to come on trips with her family, but I always turned her down. Finally, she decided to challenge me.

"Do you run away because it's new and uncertain? How long are you going to run from what's new and hide from what's uncertain?" she asked me one day. I realized I wasn't able to live my life without Bradley because I honestly just didn't know how. The last decade of my life had been invested in him and his life. For fuck's sake, I hadn't been able to let go since I was fifteen and Rebecca knew this.

"You need to have different to know different," she told me. Her words echo in my heart and mind daily because she made me realize that I was running from myself. I was hiding from the possibility of a life without Bradley. I was hiding from my new identity. Rebecca's insight helped me see the sun rise over the horizon.

I avoided seeing Iris for two months after Bradley's death. I knew I had to be ready to hear what we both needed to say out loud. Our relationship had grown distant due to the distraction of Bradley's addiction. We had many conversations about my life and how I could be free of this man. Iris knew everything: the abuse, the stress, the loss of my identity, how I didn't want to fight for my life anymore. I was fading away.

When he died, I went to her. There she was, waiting for me at the end of her driveway. I ran into her arms and fell apart completely. I don't think Iris had ever heard such sounds come from me before. I wailed in pain, feeling the long suppressed sharp aches in my heart. Iris knew I was letting out all my hurt because I was finally free of this man. Death brought me peace. Hand in hand, we slowly walked up the driveway to Iris's beautiful country home. I could not help but notice the clean-shaven, tanned, shirtless man working on the shed to the right side of the house.

"Dear God," I sighed. I hadn't seen a man in months. I also forgot what it was like to be attracted to one as my sight had been blocked for a long time. He leaned in towards me for a hug, and I didn't mind! He gathered me into him. I could still feel the warmth of the sun on his skin, and it melted my cold, trembling body. I took a deep breath in and inhaled the smell of wood chips and pine. My knees buckled a bit, but he held me up. Realizing he was trying to pull away, I desperately squeezed tighter. Iris started giggling.

"Goddamn! Is this what I've been missing all along?" I asked Iris as I finally let go of Jeff who was now laughing too.

"You can borrow him anytime you want!" Iris laughed.

At those words, I raised my eyebrows and pulled Iris's husband Jeff back towards me. He felt so good for my soul, and she didn't mind one single bit. A small sacrifice to bring some life back into me. Shortly after, we took a drive together, and I held her hand in mine. She confessed what had been unsaid for years. "I can't wait to see the version of you that no one else has ever seen." Iris's voice was strong initially, but it cracked as she finally confessed the truth. "I am more relieved that you are free because it was Bradley's time." Iris's tears poured down her cheeks. She waited so long to say those heavy words, and now she had, it was like a weight had been lifted off her heart. Iris was grateful for Bradley's death because she saw the peace it gave me. I was free of his disease once and for all.

I once accused Jenny of cheating with Bradley when he left me in 2019. She had always shared her indiscretions with men with me over the years, and when I was in pain, I used them against her. It was a low blow. I broke her heart, but she was more heartbroken when she heard of Bradley's passing over social media. We had not been in contact for two years, but the moment he died, the silence was broken. To this very day, I struggle to forgive myself. She, of course, doesn't blink an eye and forgave me ages ago.

"God! Get over it already. I did!" she barked at me one day, making me laugh through the tears that usually fall when the subject comes up. There isn't a day that goes by when I don't wish I could take back what I said and did. Sometimes I beg to go back in time so I can erase the pain I caused her, knowing it made her feel so betrayed and alone; however, then I wouldn't see her as the miracle in my life that she now is. She also taught me the true meaning of forgiveness. "How can I not forgive you? You are my equal," she told me. I collapsed in her arms when I heard her say those words.

These are the women who taught me my "more." They gave me a way to really live my life in the most extraordinary way, with the wind in my hair and acting like a child, constantly at play everywhere I go like a magic unicorn with a long, purple mane. They taught me that I'd rather be at the bottom of a mountain looking up than at the top looking down. I can still go to that mountain top as often as I want and deserve, but I always listen for my girls to call me back down; their voices are louder than any horn. They didn't all know me as a child, but each of them embraces the little girl inside me and protects her very soul. They know when to be tough with me and use the hard words.

"I am not going to try and convince you of anything. You already know your worth."

"Pick your battle! Most of this is just shit. How are you going to learn and grow without experiencing the shit?"

"Some people are just beautifully wrapped boxes of shit, my friend." (That one made me laugh.)

When I am in a panic and running around screaming at them, "I am really scared and unprepared! I can't be an author of a fucking book!" they all chuckle and carefully slide my book across the table and ask, "Can you sign my book?"

They all remind me of my purpose and to be careful who I share my good news with. This helps me to find the right people, the ones who will be genuinely happy for me. When some of the content of my first book caused tensions to rise, reassurance would be knocking on my door within the very hour. "You are trading a little bit of discomfort for the ability to help hundreds if not thousands of people, potentially saving lives with your story."

What is a soulmate? Many assume it should be their romantic partner, the person they will spend their lives with. For me, it is a best friend but MORE. It's a person who knows me better than anyone else. Someone who makes me a better person not because they make it happen, but because they inspire me to be better. It's a person I will carry with me forever even after I die. It's someone who will accept all of me, even during times of hardship. And no matter what, no matter how much time passes, or what events transpire, the love is always there. That to me is a mate to my soul, and I have that with each of these women. The little things are the constant reminder that our love is beautiful; sometimes it's tough, sometimes we can all be a bit stubborn, but we always come together, like giddy little girls who can make fun out of anything.

I have done a great job of pretending, making myself into someone else for so long, but I can't pretend with these women. Nor can I hide from them. I seriously tried to out of shame. I have been to hell and back, wearing a mask to disguise myself to the world. For years, I willingly stayed in relationships with people who betrayed my trust and accepted being treated in a way I do not deserve. My girls ripped the mask off my face and stomped it into the ground along with all the other rotten apples. They remind me of who I am and guide me back to my purpose.

Life is precious; it is a blessing, but the greatest blessing is being able to share your love with people who love you back. Five years ago, I was not treating these women well. I have learned my lesson. I will never throw away these loves of my life again. I know deep in my heart that because of them, I am not alone in this. They push me up that mountain, shouldering the burden of my fear. They help me reach my dreams, my ambitions, and my purpose, but I know they'll all be patiently waiting for me to come back down to share a serving of warm, humble apple pie with them.

Oh great! We have to pick up this chick for our team? I hope she is good, but this bitch better not think she's taking my spot. These were Jenny's thoughts when she found out I was joining her team. I had travelled an hour and a half from Prince Rupert to Terrace to play a game I love. It was my first all women's tournament, fittingly called "Queens." Not knowing anyone, I had rented a room by myself for the weekend. I was nervous but also excited. I wanted to do well. That actually is an understatement. I am by far the most competitive person you'll ever meet. I will make everything a competition when playing this sport. If you are good, I will pick you out of the crowd and have my own silent battle with you, noting how many swings you've taken, if you've struck out, dropped the ball, made a sick drive catch. I will do everything in my power to one up you. I would like to admit that over the years I have changed and toned the competitor inside me down. But that is straight up bullshit. The crazy bit is I don't actually give a fuck if the team I am playing for wins, as long as *I* feel like a winner. It's not about winning for me, it's about how I play, and I want to play better than everyone else.

I have just gotten myself tucked into bed when I think about the red-headed woman I saw relieving herself behind the dugout the previous weekend. I start laughing to myself as I recall the sight of her dropping her drawers and peeing. *I wonder if she's playing this weekend,* I think to myself.

Suddenly I hear someone knocking at my door. *Bang bang bang!* I jump at the sound, looking at the door. *It's probably some drunk fuck who forgot his key and is at the wrong room*, I think to myself. "Who is it?" I ask. I hear some laughter and women's voices on the other side of the locked door.

"It's Jenny and Bev," a soft voice responds, followed by more laughter. *I don't know any Jenny and Bev. What the hell? Who are these drunk bitches?*

"I think you have the wrong room," I reply.

"Nope! Elisha, you are playing on our team this weekend. My brother invited you. We met on the field last week."

I open the door, and the short-haired ginger busts her way in. *Wait a second!? Oh my god. It's the same woman who was pissing in the dirt. She is on my team?!* The other woman trails in behind her. She has dark brown hair, soft round cheeks, and two bold purple highlights framing her face. Bright teal feathers from her earrings pop out along her cheekbone and jaw. She is the most colourful person I have ever seen with her purple leggings, black baseball cap, bright purple rain jacket, and the teal accents in her makeup. Bev presents her hand to me, and I take it with a smile. I turn to find Jenny sprawled out on my bed, her shoes kicked off, rolling around back and forth in the covers. Her unorthodox behaviour surprises me.

"You got a nice room here!" she says with a big smile.

"We cornered you in your hotel room that night. That is when I started to really like you and said to myself, *I need this girl in my life,*" Jenny confesses with a laugh as we reminisce about that evening when all three of us ended up climbing into the queen-sized bed. Bev was in the middle because she was the smallest, and Jenny and I enjoyed crop dusting her all night.

When I ask Jenny to name her favourite memory of us, she tells me, "I don't have one favourite memory; they are all my favourites. Even the bad ones! Anytime I get to see you and talk with you is always my favourite time." The distance between us never feels far. We leave off right where we started. Jenny was my very first girl friend, the first person outside my family who I could trust with my soul knowing she would accept me without judgement. I wouldn't allow women in my life until she came along, blazing a trail, full steam ahead. I wasn't given a choice. God knew I needed someone like that. I think what bonds Jenny and me together is that, as Virgos, we are born to give more love than we will ever see in return. But between us, the love is always equal.

    I'm forever grateful that Bev and Jenny welcomed me into their friendship. I realize that I was put in their lives to show them what unconditional love is, and they came into my life to show me what self-love is. Those can be hard pills to swallow together: unconditional love and self-love. Both those loves come from pain. These ladies understand pain, the kind of pain that sticks around. They both brought me into their world, and our personalities just clicked together. In a conversation about when we first met, Bev once told me, "You could be you, and we liked that."

Death gives life meaning

Dragons and Red Coats
18. *Prince George, home base, 2022*

Once upon a time, there lived a mother, daughter, and son in a beautiful house. The three loved picking flowers in the meadow while holding hands, skipping along the yellow brick path to never-impossible land. Their days were filled with sunshine and rainbows, their smiles and laughter never-ending; however, once a month, the children would be terrorized by *a dragon*. It lurked, waiting in the deep, dark depths of its cave. It was a fierce demon, a possessed creature, who appeared once a month to feed on their innocence.

"Where is Mom?" the daughter asks.

"Shhh! She isn't here," replies the older brother.

"I want Mom!" screams the daughter. Her brother rushes to her side and with his hand covers her mouth.

"Stop! Stop! You will wake the dragon," he whispers urgently, but in his panic, he clamps his hand on her mouth too tightly, making it difficult for her to breathe. The sister starts to fight him and together they create a ruckus that escalates into an argument.

Thump! Thump! They hear the footsteps of the beast. The cave door swings open with a crash. A purple monster with bloodshot eyes, a bird's nest of tangled hair, and long sharp claws comes into view, the drool dripping down its snout. It begins searching, smelling for the things that disturbed her peace. The dragon is bleeding inside her womb, another reminder of the never-ending circle of life and cycle of agony. She spots the semen demon trying to cover the crotch goblin's mouth. A deep roar of thunder comes from somewhere inside her belly. She blasts fire at will in hopes of burning everything in her view to a crisp.

Both children run to escape the flames. The brother manages to get away, but yells over his shoulder, "The Red Coats are coming!" The dragon decides to deal with him later and grabs his sister. The dragon takes a deep breath in, so that the fire within will be extra hot and will burn every last molecule of her helpless body. The fire emerges. The dragon can't wait to eat this extra crispy chicken wing. The brother suddenly reappears, armed with a bucket for a shield, and courageously leaps at the dragon to save not only his sister, but also to save the dragon from herself.

Becoming a mother was never part of the plan, and for a really long time, I resented my children. I didn't even like kids, but the next thing I knew, my son and daughter were born, four years apart, and suddenly I was tied down for the rest of my life. Was I not clear on my plan? There weren't going to be any kids. I was going to become a police officer, and in my spare time, I would be a hot, sexy biker chick travelling the world. Instead, I lost my twenties, I lost my body, I lost my goddamned mind. Well, if I'm being honest, I was already losing it before they came around. I do, however, still have my vagina! Caesarean sections, baby. Woop!

I was twenty-one when my son was born. I had a hell of a time figuring out what to call him. Nothing resonated. Then one evening when I was eight months pregnant, his dad and I were driving to a family dinner and out of the blue he said, "What about Tanner?" Yes! That was it! I knew it was going to be a boy. I had prayed for it. "Please Lord, give me a boy first so he can look after me before I die." But I had also cheated and found out the sex before he was born. I didn't want to know with my second pregnancy. I wanted it to be a surprise. I didn't mind what I got next; I got my boy. As with my first birth, I planned for a Caesarean section, and during the ultrasound appointment the week before, I looked at the screen. The little butterfly imprint was as clear as day. I was having a girl! Once again, Dad jumped in and named her: Hailey. Yes, she shares her name with the bumbling chicken from the movie *Moana*, but it's spelled differently. She was a bit like a little chick when she was a baby though: a bright-eyed little bird that reacted to anything pretty and shiny without a care in the world. We nicknamed her Hayhay.

Back when I was working at Boston Pizza, becoming a police officer in the RCMP was the only thing I wanted. I poured everything into my application, and I know I would have made an excellent cop. When I failed the entrance exam for the second time, a part of me gave up. I felt hopeless and needed to move on. I didn't get the things I wanted so I made a last-minute decision to pop out some kids. I grew bitter about my choices.

The resentment came because I was unwilling to see *I* was the problem, not the kids. At the time, when I looked in the mirror, all I saw was a beaten-up body, stretch marks, and a ballooned-out ass. The body I had, the one I adored and was proud of, was no longer. The secret all mothers keep that we dare not share is we are constantly grieving—grieving our time, our sanity, our bodies, and our love. Mothers grieve the love we used to give to ourselves that gets diverted to the lives we gave birth to. It's bittersweet.

"You are such a great mother." This is a compliment I hear often now, and one I don't take lightly. For a long time, I felt just "good enough" as a mother. Honestly, I was a shitty mother before I could be a great one. I didn't have the patience for them, these babies, let alone myself. I was never steady or put together in any shape or form.

I never fully understood what rejection and abandonment felt like until I became a mother. The hatred I had for my body, with my saggy tummy and flapjack titties, controlled me. There was nothing I could do, no matter how much weight I lost or how fit I became. This devastated any love I had for myself. I struggled with feelings of selfishness and pettiness because of my focus on my own happiness. I felt ashamed. *Where did my spark for life go?* I wondered. I cried and cried. I cried when my body had no milk left. I cried over spilled milk. I cried when the children cried for me, but I couldn't reach them. I stared blankly into the bathroom mirror and cried more. The tears flowed nonstop from that stranger who broke into a million tiny pieces with just a glance. I couldn't eat. I couldn't think. Breathing was a chore. *Am I dying?* I wondered. *Am I depressed? What do I have to be depressed about?*

I am told depression is a made-up story that one concocts out of self pity. "Grow up and be glad you have two beautiful children to be thankful for." This is what I was told. But why did I feel so vacant? When my left breast was drained of milk, the right was fully loaded and ready. I felt like a cow waiting to be milked. Flaked out on the couch, I was a beached whale, sucked dry of all fluids, waiting until I was summoned again by the cries of a child. I wore so many fucking hats, I felt endlessly obligated. I was the maid, the cow, the chef, the wife…spread my legs for some afternoon delight? Sure, honey. Let me just dry my tears first.

What is it like being depressed? For me, it was like a switch turned off in my brain and I couldn't remember what happiness felt like. I tried to do all the things that I was told would make me better. Sometimes I truly believed they would, but they didn't; they only made it worse. Sometimes I was scared to even try.

One morning, when yet again, I didn't see the sun rise, my toddler son came running to the side of my bed carrying his baby sister. He brought her to me because he knew I wouldn't go to her. As I attached her tiny lips to my breast, my son crawled next to us and started petting her little head. I saw her eyes watching him and a smile appear on her face. Tanner started to sing to her, and Hailey cooed at him. Then it dawned on me: Tanner was singing to his sister just as I sang to him when he was a baby. That is what he remembered: the comfort that my voice brought to him. I caressed his cheek and smiled for the first time in what felt like forever. This small moment of joy was my better. These two beautiful babies were more than alright and to them, I was their better, their joy.

I finished feeding Hailey and placed her in her roller seat. I grabbed Tanner a snack and put on the cartoons. It was time to face the mirror, the same one I had been avoiding for so long. First, I looked down and closed my eyes. I vowed that the very second I lifted my head, I was going to change. Going forward, I would find joy every single day by searching for my purpose. How would I find my purpose? That answer lay in my willingness to change my thinking. At that moment, I believed I could change my life.

Are you ready, Elisha? I heard the voice inside me whisper. *Open your eyes, my love!*

The first change I saw in the mirror was my hair: it became purple, long, and vibrant—a symbol of power. Next? Ink. I wanted ink to mark my story, my journey, and my pain. I wanted something to show I had been to battle, I had been at war with myself, but I was not defeated. Finally, I wanted to wake up before anyone else and watch the sunrise in silence. I wanted to hold a hot cup of tea and sing to God before my day began. The sound of my voice brought me solace and joy. It brought me closer to God. I realized I had to first fill my cup so that I could share this joy and love with those who need it.

"Mom, can you stop taking a bite out of my sandwich?" my son requested. I have made their lunches since they started school and without fail, I have always taken a bite from their made-with-love sandwiches.

"Like, why do you do that? It's so annoying," my daughter said. Her brother nodded in agreement. My back was turned to them, and a devilish smile crossed my face.

"Oh? Is it annoying?" I asked sweetly.

"Yes!" they responded in unison.

"Does it piss you off?" I asked, sitting down at the table with them and showing concern.

"Yes!" they barked.

I looked down at my hands before I yelled, "Good, you bastard farts! All these years you annoyed the fuck out of me, pissed me off, and made me cry. Now it's my fucking turn, bitches!" I yelled, startling them both.

"You're the worst mother," my son chuckled, shaking his head and grabbing his lunch.

"Seriously, Mom. You need help letting go!" my daughter added, giving me a look of mock disgust.

"If you two don't quit whining, I'll give you something to

whine about!" I yelled, before taking them to high school. My children know I'd never raise a hand to them and that this is just my way of putting them in their place. They always smile and giggle at my pathetic attempts to force their obedience.

I swear around my teenagers every day. It's fantastic! They know the cues and what to listen for. "I will fucking kill you!" means stop pushing me. "I will end you," with my hands on my hips indicates I am serious. My eyes really say it all. We all know the look mothers have, the look of death. It's a look that makes them crumble when they see it. When I give Tanner and Hailey that look, they call it "dragon mode." There is no turning back when the dragon comes out. I lose it entirely. There's no discipline or self control anymore. They know they've pushed Mom over the edge.

Over the years the dragon comes out to play less and less because of the sense of humour I have developed with my kids now they're growing into young adults. I think that's the key: creative fun, good humour, and laughter. The dragon only comes out when the line in the sand has been pissed on.

For any mother, letting her child go out into the world is like being crucified. They are innocent, vulnerable, and still so small in our eyes, but you have to let them go. Yes, it is dangerous, but better for them to lose a part of themselves out their discovering who they are, than stay with me and never find themselves. It's hard, but I have to stand back and let them find their way. They know I will always be here to catch them when they fall.

Life has already thrown Tanner and Hailey some terrible experiences. They have been struck not just once by tragedy, but three times. The first was losing Bradley, the man they had called "Father," since they were little. The second beating was finding out that he had been a drug addict and had died from an overdose.

The third crisis, and the thing that crippled my poor children, was seeing their mother in such pain and hearing about the abuse I'd suffered because of his addiction. At a young age they learned the deep pain of sorrow and grief. They were grieving me. I was never the same and they witnessed that take effect immediately. I refused to hide the truth and bore the responsibility of healing them and mending their hearts. They did the same for me in their own way.

I was triggered during a movie one evening and the tears started to fall. I felt ashamed as a mother, and my guilt started to get to me. Hailey, who was cuddled up next to me, decided she had had enough of my sucky baby shit and said something that changed my life forever. "Mom, did you ever stop to think that torturing yourself over what you did in the past keeps it alive for me?" Her head stayed perfectly still on my chest knowing I was hurting and crying. She said it as if she was talking about the weather. It was just so smooth and causal. "For my honesty, Mom, what makes our family depressed is when *you're* depressed," she said.

What the actual fuck!? Did my daughter just mind fuck me? She was so nonchalant, but it was like she had lit a fire bolt under my ass. She was telling me to wake up and smell the roses. Damn!

Hailey - 1; Mom - 0.

Tanner's very first high school fight was over me. Tanner had warned the boy not to speak about me, but that kid called me a whore, and it was the last straw for Tanner. I got called into the principal's office for a meeting (the very same principal who suspended me for fighting all those years ago. History really does repeat itself!) As we were leaving, I asked Tanner one question: "Did you finish it?"

"Yes," he replied instantly, but tears welled up in his eyes. "No one gets to talk about you, Mom. Not you. Not ever!" he vowed, as he wiped his eyes clear of the water trickling down. I took him shopping and out for lunch that day but warned him that it will get harder.

"Everyone now knows your weakness," I told him. Tanner gave me a puzzled look. I pointed to myself. I was trying to teach him in that space to control his anger and emotions. "You can't go around punching kids in the face because they call me names," I said, hoping to knock some sense into him.

"Yes, I can!" he replied, stubbornly. I remember thinking, *this child is just like me. No one can control him; you can tell him what to do, but he will choose to find out the hard way, just like his mother!*

He is stubborn, but Tanner also has a wonderful sense of humour. I remember one time we were at the grocery store. We were at the checkout, and as usual, I had forgotten something important.

"Shit! Tanner, go to aisle three and grab me some tampons. I forgot," I whispered. He gave me the dirtiest look of disapproval.

"Fuck no, bruh!" he exclaimed. I was not in the mood. After a long day of work, the dragon was on the brink of appearing. I gave him the death glare.

"As your maker, I command you!" I hissed. He marched off in a huff. Within minutes, I heard Tanner shouting at me.

"Hey Mom?!" he shouted. I cringed. "Do you need the tampons for when you've been shot or…"

I felt my face go red as he emerged from aisle three with a shit-eating grin on his face. There was a line up of people waiting to check out and they all started laughing. A lady was in tears she was laughing so hard. I snapped the box of tampons out of my son's hands as I silently mouth the words, "I wish I had swallowed you that night." He threw an arm over my shoulder.

"Aww. Isn't it a beautiful day?!" Tanner exclaimed, meeting the stares of the other customers, enjoying the attention. "You're in good hands now, Mommy. The Red Coats will be tucked and snuggled in extra thick cotton tonight," he said loud enough for everyone to hear. Hailey started to laugh.

"Tanner!" I gasped but found myself smiling and giggling at my clown of a son who loves entertaining the crowd.

Yes. The term "Red Coats" came from my son. When I am extra moody, he knows it must mean I am on "shark week." Tanner can sense it and will run away screaming, "The Red Coats are coming! The Red Coats are coming! Run for your lives!" It's ridiculous; however, with his signature sense of humour, he does manage to make a rough situation entertaining.

Do you know what I think the greatest word to ever hear is? *Mom*. It means no one will ever replace you. You are their whole world and all the shit that comes with it. Early mornings are filled with little hands and bodies that crawl into your bed. Then in a blink, you're pulling their feet, ripping off the blankets, and pouring water on them to wake them for school. From their first word as a baby to them cursing you out because they can't get their way as a helpless teen in a fit of rage, it's all part of being a mother.

You wipe away their tears, soothe their heartaches, and bear their pain as if it were your own. You wish you could take it all away, but you know it's necessary. They have to suffer so that life slams some resilience into their soft, baby skin. It's the only way they'll develop the strong armour they'll need for their future adult selves. Children forgive freely and easily, but as they grow, they learn forgiveness doesn't mean the pain never existed. Life's trials break their trust, and they are left to decide if they will prevail or live their life as a victim.

They lost a loved one early on in their lives. I've had to teach them that death is not the worst thing that can happen to someone. It's quite the opposite. In some cases, it sets a person free from their suffering. Death also gives life meaning. If we don't die, what are we living for? Deep loss requires a deeper examination of a person's purpose.

What is my legacy to Tanner and Hailey? Time—uninterrupted, focused, one-on-one time. They know they are my whole world, and that will never change. We have a bond in love that has been forged by sacrifice. When I became their mother, a part of me died. I lost the person I was before them, but I have no regrets. That person had to die for me to become who I am now: their mother. I *am* a good mother, and they love me for it.

"Mom! You left Dillion out again," my daughter squawks, unimpressed. *Shit! I've left my black silicone dildo out again?! Oopsie. My bad.*

I am a good mother, but I never said I was perfect.

Suddenly, I am freezing cold and soaking wet. My son hovers over me out of breath and staring at me. His body is between me and his sister. The fear in my daughter's eyes shocks me. In shame, I run away immediately to the bathroom. In the mirror, I see a wet mess of a woman. Purple stains my shirt and long strands of hair fall past my shoulders. I collapse to my knees, put my hands over my face, and cry in defeat. All I can see is her, Hailey, and her face. "What have I done?" I cry out loud to myself. Then I hear a knock on the door and my son comes in with the same bucket he used to put out the fire.

"Are you done? Or do you need another cool down?" he asks in a sharp tone, as he stands over me with a sly smile spreading across his face. He sees my tears and gives his sister, who is still fearful of the dragon, the signal that the coast is clear, and she can come in. "Mom! You told us we are allowed to get angry, but we are not allowed to take it out on anyone or anything," Tanner reminds me.

"Yea bitch!" Hailey joins in. We all start laughing at the situation. I can't believe my son had to throw a bucket of cold water on me to calm me down. I find it ironic that these teenagers both cause my "cray cray" (my daughter's slang for crazy) and keep it in check. It's a constant push and pull and anyone who is a mother understands this. We really do feel like we hate these bastards sometimes, but love prevails every single time.

"You both piss me the fuck off!" I scream and then mumble under my breath. "I really dislike you."

"Does dragon mommy need a tea with her bath or a bottle of wine?" my son asks with a smirk.

"Go fuck yourself, Tanner!" I yell after him as he goes to make the tea.

"Extra honey for the cray cray!" Hailey yells after him. I don't drink the tea because Hayhay has a vengeful streak and spits in it often. She is evil and sneaky that way. After years and years of her brother torturing her, she has found ways to pay him back. The most entertainment I get is watching Hailey plot out her retaliation plans for her older brother. Whether she is throwing him down in a surprise judo hold, shocking him with her seven years of experience, or locking him out of the car until he dances in a way that satisfies her, I always find it hilarious and never stop her. I taught both my children since they were little: If you can dish it out, then you can take it. Hailey took this to heart. She in turn taught me the true meaning of vengeance!

How do we unconditionally love our kids? Accept the chaos and find the joy in the simple pleasures.

*Pain is worth
a lifetime of glory*

I and the Father
19. *Fraser Lake, 2021*

The definition of love lies somewhere between ignorant and stupid, I think to myself as I walk along a dried-up dirt path. I look down at my hiking boots and the imprints they are leaving in the crusty earth and realize I forgot how to love myself long ago. I don't remember what that feels like. I know I can love others. I proved that with Bradley, but in the end, it has only caused me trouble. Love has been an inconvenience for me.

"Isn't that the fucking truth?!" I yell out loud to no one in particular. I reach around the side of my hiking bag to grab my water. "Ayms!" I call to my sheltie. He comes trotting over, and I bend down cupping my hand for him to drink from. He is too fancy to drink straight from the bottle. I swear my dog is a total priss. He is pretty, almost like a cat. He avoids puddles, and prances around like a pony with attitude, and whines when he doesn't like something. When I stand up, I register that I've been casting my eyes down for most of my hike toward a break in the tree line. There, I see a small meadow with tall, dry grass as high as my shoulders swaying in the light breeze. As the wind pushes the dry straw, it creates patterns that are like a current, like something you'd see in a stadium of people waving their arms up and down in a synchronized pattern. Hundreds of parachute-like structures lift off, ten times the size of dandelion puffs. These pappus are made up of brush-like bristles, and they oscillate in a design of their own. I catch myself drifting away from the path and into the tiny field. A memory of my Oma hits me as I lightly touch the fluffy balls, careful not to disturb their enchantment.

"Oma, why are you picking those?" I ask her. "They are dead looking and ugly." I am a little girl again, trailing behind her and my father who is carrying a gun to shoot some grouse, which I assume are just weird looking chickens. They taste like chicken, except sweeter. Oma is picking everything that is dried up: straw, bead-like pods on a stem, and these ugly puffy things (which I later learned were pussy willows). I don't get it. These things aren't beautiful, not like the orchids my mother loves. They don't smell nice, like the lilies that can fill a room with their scent. To me, my Oma is collecting bundles of withered, brittle, rotten weeds.

"Beauty is in the eye of the beholder," she answers.

Now, here I am, standing in the middle of a dried-up field touching the same "ugly" puffs as she did. It's only taken me twenty-five years to finally appreciate her words. I am struck that it's at a time when I am feeling so disillusioned that this memory of my Oma appears to comfort me. She was right. It is the most beautiful thing I have ever seen. And I realize now that she wasn't just talking about the puffs sitting on a stem all those years ago; she was teaching her granddaughter a vital lesson about love.

Where do I begin to explain my relationship with God? It's kind of like a love-hate situation. I'm prone to playing the blame game for my unhappiness, but in the flick of a switch, I find myself thanking God for my happiness. My relationship with God used to be pretty one sided and lonely. That was when I trusted him without understanding the faith part. I felt like I was in a never-ending cycle of doubt and God was testing me constantly.

"Trust me with all your heart," he commands. How can I when my heart is broken? My mind tells me I am batshit crazy for believing in this so-called God. I don't even know if it's a man or a woman.

"I am all things," he tells me.

Maybe God is a fucking llama and spits down from the heavens onto his children who piss him off. I bet that is what rain is, God spitting on me! There's a lot of spit because I defy him often.

"But look at what you're asking of me?" I shout in defiance. I often wonder what God thinks of me when I throw raging hissy fits like a child (*his* child, I have been told many times over). Why can't God be simple and stop asking me to do the impossible?

"Because I am the God of possibilities," he responds.

"Aw, come on, man! Give me something more than your word," I whisper tearfully, hoping he doesn't hear me through the banging of my head on my kitchen table. It doesn't matter. God hears everything, including my non-stop internal dialogue.

"How do you describe your relationship with God?" a close friend once asked me. Internally, I thought, *complicated as fuck*. God heard that. How I actually answered was more true to his spirit as I feel it inside me.

"He isn't just important to me. God is a *part* of me. Just like a father is to his daughter," I said. Curiosity got the better of my intelligent friend. She's wise beyond her years and has been successful in all that she's worked for. She couldn't understand how I could believe in something without proof of its existence. She wanted a better answer than "faith."

"I have studied, trained, and fought for everything I have. *I* did this. I created the life I wanted from what already exists in front of me. Without the examples of these things, how could I have the life I worked for?" she inquired reasonably. She has been hard working and disciplined in everything: her studies, her schooling, and her life plan. She counted all these things as the examples that existed and guided her success and happiness. And she did it without God in her life. My friend is an atheist. She believes that all religions are forms of delusion that people succumb to. So, for fun I entertain her.

"Does it really matter if it makes someone better? It's no different than someone believing no matter how their life is going or what pain they are in, if they go to the gym, it will bring them relief. They believe when everything and everyone else has failed them, the gym will always be there. To me, the gym is a form of God," I mused. In effect, I was agreeing with her statement regarding self-inflicted delusions. "But what happens when something changes or the quality of life you worked so hard for deteriorates? Say it just doesn't exist anymore, or if it does, it's not the same. Covid-19 wiped out a lot of things and changed the quality of life for hundreds of thousands of people," I continued. "The point is that without *hope*, life is chaos, and you risk losing a part of yourself. It can be so destructive. One of the greatest philosophers that ever lived is proof of God's existence," I told her. Her eyebrows raised at the mention of some sort of historical reference.

I was speaking her language now as I knew she responded to facts. "His name is Jesus. He was sent to instruct, guide, and speak the truth for us to follow. Or as you would put it, to give us an example of the quality of life we should all aspire to," I said.

Jesus was a real person. He existed. There is proof. Accounts of Jesus's brutal crucifixion and death exist outside the Bible. There was a paper trail even back then! Besides the gospels and letters of Paul, there are other sources for the existence of Jesus. The historian Flavius Josephus mentions him in the *Antiquities of the Jews*, which dates to 93–94 CE. The Roman historian Tacitus also mentions Jesus in the *Annals*, which date to 116 CE[1].

We believe in Hitler and the concentration camps, do we not? There is evidence proving this person and these places existed. What about Elvis and his blue suede shoes? He has a whole museum for all his shit. The Church of the Holy Sepulchre in Jerusalem was built to enclose the site of both the crucifixion and the tomb of Jesus. Many will never see any of these things, but we all believe they are real. And yet, people demand more proof of God's existence, opting to not live honourably until there is more substantial evidence.

"I could sit here and teach you the lessons of Jesus and give you all the evidence your heart desires. But the truth is, there is no hope without faith, faith in fucking something! I put my trust in Jesus, the one who doesn't want slaves. The one who wants *friends*. The one who wants people to change by knowing about him," I told my friend, as I wrapped up the conversation. I knew it would just be going around in circles forever. After all, it's not my job to convince her or anyone else for that matter. So, I ended it with a question.

---

1 https://www.theguardian.com/world/2017/apr/14/what-is-the-historical-evidence-that-jesus-christ-lived-and-died

"What is the difference between an atheist and someone who believes in a form of God?" I asked. "An atheist has no hope for something greater than themselves. Take away all the education, books, governments, rules, medicine, gym membership, you name it. If it was all gone with the snap of a finger, what would you place your hope in then?"

God moves me. He leads me in what to say when the pain and anxiety starts to stir inside me and I'm unsure of what he wants from me. "God, I don't want to talk about this, and I don't want people to know that I struggle," I tell him. But he reminds me that it's not about me; it never was, and it never will be. I cannot save anyone. I was never meant to. In the past, I used to put up a front and hide my pain. It only kept me captive to my problems and the result was a false impression of someone who wasn't affected by anything. God's true power comes in moments of weakness. My pain glorifies his strength. His true love is reflected in my frailty. I can declare that I have failed, hurt others, taken from so many and fallen so short, but he continues to welcome me, telling me, "Come as you are, Elisha!"

Sometimes praying to God is coming to him and not knowing what to say. Sometimes a prayer is not saying anything at all. Many times, my tears and crying took the place of praying. God knows what my tears mean. God knows I don't swear *at* him; I just swear in his presence sometimes because I am really angry and frustrated. For some people there is no rock bottom; their life is bottomless. At times, I felt bottomless and empty. Sobriety is your greatest defense, but for many, the opposite keeps them alive. It kept me alive when the pain was too great. My drug of choice: sex with broken and unhealed men. Many times, this offered me a sort of haven where I felt encouraged and free of judgement. The reality was that it made me high and allowed me to disappear and avoid the torment of flashbacks to my trauma. I filled my cup with distractions rather than seeking peace. I didn't want peace. I was sick and my whole system was on the verge of collapse. The addict in me was trying to sell me on the same shit it got me hooked on in the first place. It was a never-ending cycle of pain that only resulted in a double dose of nightmares when the dopamine disintegrated. I knew if I kept going, I would rot from the inside out until I caved in completely and died, either figuratively by changing into an embittered person, or literally.

"If you say you love me and want a life with me by your side, Elisha, then let's put that to the test!" announces the almighty.

"You may just find yourself washed up on the shores of a new beginning, with a newfound ability to make this young, new love grow."

The greatest gift you will ever give yourself is the acceptance of the place of death in your life. So many people are afraid to die that they barely live. Because if you're afraid to die, you're afraid to live. Every moment is a dying one. Any moment could be the end of your life as who you used to be and the next, the birth of yourself as you now choose to be. The secret of life is to die. Die often and don't let death be a one-time thing! In every moment, you will see yourself born again and recreated anew as the next version of who you are. To continually evolve toward the best version of yourself is the whole purpose of life.

A moment of pain is worth a lifetime of glory. I endured the pain of altering my tattoo of the word "Whore." I may have approved of that stamp long ago, but it was time for it to die. I had the tattoo artist black it out and now the words "Queen" and "In Between" can be read on my lower back.

We must look at the mountains ahead of us and yet also acknowledge the ones that are behind us. They too were painful to climb but effort is a part of life. Over the years, I have heard many people say, "I tried to make it work." Isn't that the problem right there? Whether facing inner battles, relationships, or addictions, failure is inevitable. "Try." What does that mean? Attempting to do something or putting in some effort? Sure. Ok. Maybe that works when you are taking your first steps. But not after years and years staying stuck as the same individual you've been for the last ten years. There shouldn't be any more "try." "I tried to make it work" doesn't work.

How about pain? We *try* to argue it away. Good luck with that. Pain is the fundamental truth. Shit, ok that's rough, but hear me out. Pain can lead to hopelessness, so much so that some of us live in denial of the pain we are in. But the pain is fundamental! We have to accept the pain because pain is our greatest teacher! We have to take it, experience it. It is only through facing the pain that we can truly heal. And healing is the only path to love, which is the only thing more fundamental than pain.

Suffering causes our focus to turn inward, to face the parts of ourselves we might otherwise ignore. This is where God has cradled me; he helped me transform my suffering into something positive. It allowed me to develop into a better version of myself. He didn't just do this *with* me; he did it *for* me. Jesus suffered terribly dying on the cross, but his suffering was for the good of all humanity. The pain that Jesus Christ endured resulted in our salvation and eternal life. I believe the crucifixion, though painful, was a demonstration of God's love. His suffering resulted in our glory. My suffering, my pain, became my glory.

I have been bullied my entire life about my choice to walk alongside God. His path was set before me and how I choose to love is a reflection of his son, Jesus. Matthew 22:14 states, "Many are called but few are chosen." I decided to answer the call.

God chose me, although I often tell him he made a mistake. I'm the fucking weirdest person you'll ever meet with my purple hair and my crazy tattoos; however, I stand before him, commanded to do his work. In return, he has granted me the gift of creativity. I truly believe God's gift to us is our talent, but what we do with that talent is our gift back to God.

False leaders of Christ have attempted many times to stomp out my voice, or take credit for my growth in God, saying only men can inherit God's spirit and words to lead others. Let me be absolutely clear about something: men are no greater than women in God's eyes. Men and women are equal in the eyes of God. Read your Bible. No *man* led me to God. *God* led me to God. No *man* taught me the word of God. My father's spirit in his son Jesus guides me to trust in him to give me the foundation, like the frame for a house. God though is always there to help with the rest of the construction, to patch, repair, and guide the plans. No man has convinced or enticed me to adopt God into my life. In fact, if this story tells you anything it's that men have done quite the opposite.

Sometimes the end of one journey is the beginning of another. There is beauty in discovering love for a stranger, even if that stranger is you. My hope is for spiritual revolution. It's at the core of my beliefs, my morals, and my way of living. The key word here is "*my*." God doesn't fucking care if I don't believe in him. He believes in *me*. To believe in something greater than yourself, reconstruction of the spirit is imperative. Trust in God requires an internal change, a different way of thinking.

Some people say that nature is their god, or they choose to put their faith in the stars, in words, or in other people. The problem there is that those things will fail you. Mother nature will send a flash flood through your house, clouds will block out the stars, words without action are pointless, and people? Don't get me started. Wait. It gets better. *You* will fail you!

Everything changed for me when I realized I was willing to lose anyone *except* myself. God has cultivated peace in me by demonstrating the compassion of silence. Because it is in silence that I hear God, see God, and feel God when I need him the most. Miracles are real and that is how God shows all he is. The things I have prayed for have materialized, maybe not in the way I expected it, but in a way that he approved of. I am the most grateful for the abundance he has bestowed upon me with respect to my growing businesses. I started with one small business, and now I own and operate three. I am blessed with the opportunity God has given me to be a public speaker and influencer. It means I can share my experiences to help others.

To me, God's biggest miracle is the fact that nothing is impossible. I had no idea I could be a great storyteller, and now I have found my purpose as a writer. I am finally complete. I catch myself crying in happiness for all God has done for me, for the wholeness I feel, for the visions I now see, and for the power in my voice as I stand to claim what is my destiny: to proclaim the glory of God and to see that my life is of great significance to him.

I don't love God because my life has been all sunshine and roses. I love God because he pulled me out of the trenches. I love God because he's taken every wrong that I've done in my life or every wrong that's been done to me and turned them into good. I simply cannot live a life that does not acknowledge him. Because of him, my life has meaning, my children are blessed, food is nourishing, wealth is overflowing, decisions are guided, and love? It's as timeless and endless as the ocean.

Ayms's whining brings me back to reality; he makes it clear he has waited long enough and will continue without me if he must. We both follow the long, narrow path nestled in the dense forest. I see a break ahead and soon a deep valley comes into view. I can barely see the water at the bottom but know it's there because I can hear it. Ayms smells something exciting and quickens his pace. I start walking faster to catch up with him. He leads me off the path and down towards the valley side. As I rush to catch up to him, I push my way through the thick brush, some of the branches slapping my face along the way. He is a smaller dog and would make a great snack for a bear. I lose sight of him and start to panic until I hear the sound of splashing nearby. I follow the sound, and a stream of water nestled in a rock gully comes into view. To my surprise, Ayms is in the water. I start to laugh as it's so out of character for him. This is the dog who avoids puddles, remember.

 I move towards him, and I see he has found a deep pool to swim in. I am hot and sweaty and could use a cool down. I look at him briefly for consent before getting naked as quickly as I can. The water is perfect, not too hot nor too cold, not too deep nor too shallow. It's as if it is meant for us. I feel the cool water begin to infiltrate every crevice of my body, washing away the dirt, sweat, and dead skin, and leaving me with a silky, clean canvas. I continue to submerge my body slowly into the water, feeling the coolness flush over my chin before it reaches my nose. I take a deep breath before I immerse myself entirely.

 I realize I have been worried for so long that I've forgotten how to just *be*. Be happy. Be still. Be beautiful. Now here in this place, naked in a pool of the cleanest water I will ever experience, I realize it's time to stop holding onto the pain and the nightmare it has become. It's time to wake up and accept the pain with all its glory. I needed to be lost in order to be found again.

There, in that valley, surrounded by nature, I baptize myself in God's presence (with a furry, four-legged creature as a witness), and I let go of my anger.

"I and the Father are one." John 10:30

Life is too short for shitty sex and bad relationships

Long Haul
20. *Elisha Rose Beauty & Style Salon, 2022*

"Why did you get married?" I ask my client who is clearly heartbroken. Her husband has been unfaithful for a while now but unfortunately, I feel as though she is still in denial about that fact. I know that every time she finds out her husband is cheating, she wants her hair made over because she believes if she creates a new identity, he will change or finally notice her.

"Because I love him," she sniffles, blinking faster so the tears won't fall. I watch her for a moment in silence as I grab another foil and weave out a highlight around her hairline to blend the grey, slapping on a thick, gooey glop of bleach.

"You still love him?" I ask.

"Yes!" she immediately replies. Now I have her right where I want her.

"Really?! Tell me. What do you love about him?" I ask.

Just as I suspected, she can't answer that question.

The biggest mistake I have seen people make in life is in their interpretation of love. Many people seem to believe that love is finding the right person when actually, love is *becoming* the right person. You want to become the type of person you would spend the rest of your life with. True love is based on choice, not need. Do you *need* your husband? Or do you *choose* your wife? Choice matters more than need. I hear so many people say, "I don't like being alone." That sounds like need to me. Sleeping in the same bed with someone doesn't make you close to them. Living in the same house also doesn't make you close. The only thing that makes you feel close to someone is when you can be open, seen, heard, and understood in your most vulnerable, darkest moments. If you love someone, and it's genuine love, you see their hidden soul. You get a glimpse of the light they want to give.

The truest act of love is to encourage that light to shine as brightly as possible and to discourage anything that gets in the way of it. A person who truly loves you doesn't strive at all costs never to upset you. If you love someone and they are doing something stupid or self-destructive and you can see it, it's imperative to say, "This isn't ok, and what you are doing is hurtful."

Life is too short for shitty sex and bad relationships so find someone who will fuck you well and put a smile on your face. The key to great sex is a connection that blooms into love. I think love is being stupid together. Being stupid together makes you laugh and will put the biggest smile on your face. You experience abundant joy when you find a weirdness in someone else that is compatible with yours. It's like you get to be your childlike self with your guard down; you feel safe. Finding your person is finding someone who will accept your authentic self with all the goofiness that comes with it. The rest always falls into place.

The truth is, once you get into a good relationship, you'll be insecure at times, but you will be able to manage that with the other person. There will still be fears and in most cases more fears will arise because you're breaking down those walls—the walls inside you that have protected you but no longer need to. I always tell people, the walls that are there to protect you are the same walls blocking your blessings. The other person will protect you and work through those fears with you. It's not about the absence of insecurities but the ability for them to finally be present and recognized. Why must your insecurities be present? Because when they are, it means your true self is coming forward.

The relationships that involve true love and have a true connection will be scary. It will feel as if you are losing yourself. Love is a heart attack, and most times, it's complicated. Love is the best and worst of everything. Being in a healthy relationship is weird. It's almost as if you're waiting for the other shoe to drop. You question everything at a higher standard and level because this person is so kind, honest, and genuine. You can finally be yourself. The other person's energy will match yours, and you can trust that they do love and support you.

When I look back, I realize that the more I found myself telling my past partners what to do, how to think, and who to be, the less attracted I was to them. The type of man that I am seeking is one with a sense of leadership who will make a stand in a powerful way and help inspire that in me. I, Elisha desire this. Why? Because it helps me to embrace my feminine energy, which is vital to my survival and more precious than anything this world can give me. When a man acts like a leader, it makes me feel safe because he places me first. All those wimpy, unhealthy, unhealed, and toxic men who took from me? They put me in last place. What is the difference between a healthy partner and a toxic one? A toxic partner will want to be served whereas a healthy partner will want to be of service. A toxic individual will never see your worth unless you are serving them, but a healthy person will see your value and worth and want to expand on it by being of service to it.

I am a leader myself, so I need a man who will out lead me. He needs to be bigger, stronger, fitter, and more successful in order to inspire me. Otherwise, what is he going to offer me? Why else would I follow his lead?

I wasn't always this way. If you've read this far, you know my experiences with men have not been great. I needed a final slap of reality, one last major wake-up call. It started with me venting to friends about my feelings for a man I started dating and building with after Bradley passed. What a fool I was. I simply replaced one bad relationship with another. Once again, I was in a relationship characterized by abuse, drinking, and chaos. And there I was, yet again, trying to fix it all. The thing is, it was not my problem to fix, so instead, I became the enabler. I struggled to walk away and close the door because I knew I would weld it shut for good. That was what scared me the most: entering new territory without the addictions, saying goodbye and choosing my peace. I had tried to get away, but I was still being seduced by his words. I felt trapped like a dog begging for scraps. I talked to my friend and tried to convince her that maybe, just maybe, he was the right guy after all.

"Elisha?! Haven't you already been there and done that?" My friend's raised voice stopped me in my tracks. "You don't understand this love because if you did, you wouldn't be repeating the same pattern over and over again!"

This hit me in the gut hard. She was right on all accounts. I've always been taken advantage of because I allow it. I'm always chasing the next man to give me the false high, the illusion of love when really, it's just an attachment to cope with.

"The right man will find you when the time is right, when you are ready," she said. I started to feel defensive. *How dare she say that to me? What the fuck?* However, I realized in my heart what was said was the truth. I was not ready because if I was, I would have welded the door shut, gone head-to-head with my addiction, and fought at all costs to defeat the pain by seeking peace within me.

"You deserve to be treated like a queen, like you are the last woman on earth. One day it will happen, but you need to be ready," she said.

Thank God for her insight. Those words stuck to me like sticky candy and echoed louder than ever in my heart. *When the time is right and when I am ready...* it couldn't be truer. I am loved, by *myself*. But this door that needed to be shut, locked, and welded closed kept me believing that I lacked that love. All because poor, cry baby Elisha wasn't loved by a *man*. Boo Hoo! Cry me a river and go suck on a grape juice box. I finally decided to grow up and pull on my big girl panties, the ones made of cotton with little red hearts on them. I kicked the victimhood right in the mother fucking head because I was not a victim anymore. It was time to stop holding myself back from my worth. I knew who I was and what I deserved, and I fought for that in everything I was doing, but I was limiting myself to scum when it came to men. That didn't make any sense at all.

Hello! Light bulb moment! I have chased after every man because I didn't trust in myself: my hard work, my time, and my dedication to all I am. The worst part is I controlled what I allowed them to see. I'd keep them interested until I stopped pretending and they realized it had all been an act.

Now I prefer to just be myself. Nothing but the facts. "Come as you are." I offer myself openly and freely and under no circumstance will I be changing for anyone. It's the only way to be. I choose to make a stand: here I am. Take it or fuck off. Most men don't run from an amazing woman; they run from the parts of themselves they're unwilling to change to be worthy of her. This is very immature behaviour.

You know what chaps my puss? Most people don't want to hear this. No relationship is perfect; they all require a lot of tolerance. Disappointments, pains, and irritations are inevitable. Loving is recognizing there will be flaws, weakness, and moments of doubt in that person just like there are in you. The key is to be able to see beyond the arguments, misunderstandings, and mistakes so that you can embrace their imperfections. There is beauty in the effort to stay united. Loving is a choice to fight, to forgive, to stay, and to build something strong. It's a decision to deepen love, strengthen bonds, have meaningful conversations, and to build so each person can grow together.

Being a real man doesn't mean figuring out how to love a hundred different women. A real man will find one woman and love her a hundred different ways. People who go to a buffet can still be nourished by that one thing that's good for their soul and gives them everything they need. But instead, it seems many zero in on the less nutritious offerings and then stuff their faces at the dessert table. What do these people offer your soul? What do they do for you? Do they bring you peace? What do they bring to your heart? Life is already a war; it's hard enough. Why make it harder on yourself? The most masculine men and feminine women have the courage to love. The men and women who are insecure or hollow just want to be worshipped. The power of loving is different than the need to be loved. You have to be rich and mature within yourself to understand where that power draws from. Worship who you are and carry that through you in how you treat others.

It's my belief that men love more authentically than women. Why do I say this? I think women are in love with the process. They fall in love with the dating process, the courting, etc. But when a man falls in love, it's not a happy experience. *Fuck. I love this bitch.* That's what men think, because his two jobs are to provide and protect. The *I love you* translates to *I will die for you*, and she becomes his responsibility. A man isn't designed to fall in love with the process. He falls for the truth of what is to be.

But women?! Dear God, when did we become so weak minded? I've heard it all. "But I love him!" they say, when there is absolutely nothing redeemable about the guy. Go shit in your hand. What is there to love? Or women who play games, tease, and cheat. The saddest thing to me is a woman who plays hard to get and loses. Guess what, sweetheart. Looks are the first to go! "All men want is pussy!" Bitch, please. Did you ever stop to think that maybe the reason you think this is because that is all you're handing out? I mean, in that case, hell yeah, most men will take it! If you make it easy, that is all a man will see. If you want to be valued, then stop acting cheap. Stop using what's between your legs and give more. Show some intelligence, integrity, and class and see what comes across your path.

We've all felt those butterflies when we first meet someone. Here is what I think about this crap. That is the body's warning system telling you, "This feels familiar." Red flag! That is your body telling you something very crucial: this individual is going to open up old wounds. It is imperative that you heal your wounds otherwise you risk repeating all your old mistakes. Finding someone who will dredge up those old problems is like an over-the-counter medication that will result in another toxic relationship between two unhealthy and unhealed people, both attached to one another's pain and blind to any real connection.

I cry now more than ever before. I am experiencing the loss of my old self as I give birth to the new me. I tell her, "My love, my sweet, beautiful soul, time to wake up, my love." I have the power to walk away from any man who isn't loving me the right way. I allow the space for my heart to heal. Forgiveness isn't a feeling. It's a choice. More importantly, when I say I forgive you and walk away, I am sending a powerful message: I am taking the time and space to heal. The space I give to myself allows them all to gain clarity. Or not. Until then, they can watch me win from the side lines.

Perhaps someone must make us upset before we ask the hard questions and confront the turmoil of love. Is pain more powerful than love? I don't know, but I do know that if we stop asking questions, we'll never find the answers. I also know I can only accept love if it is given freely. The love I have for myself is unconditional, and I know I'll always have it. I have no desire to reshape myself to someone else's ideal. I embrace my individuality. I want to be uncommon. I do not like being easily classified, and I will not be controlled or tamed. This is the way I want to live my life. Is what I seek, seeking me? Love is so many things, but the one thing it is not is unsure.

I stop foiling, grab my little grey stool, and sit down right in front of her. It was time to wake her the fuck up.

"I don't doubt for a second the intent you have to love your husband. But how can you understand love for him, or anyone for that matter, if you have none for yourself?" I ask.

Tears start to pool in her eyes. I grab a box of tissues and hand it to her as I start to share my story and truth with her. I confess that I thought I was in love with a man for a very long time too, but I realized that I was actually in love with the *idea* of him, the possibility he represented. I can see myself in her, the old me: lost, broken, alone—so alone that I convinced myself that I still loved the person who was destroying my soul. That person had no right to be a part of my life.

"Most people think that getting married is about passion, because it's *romantic!*" I say, singing "romantic" to her as she giggles back. "I asked you why you got married. You said, 'love.' And how is that working out for you?" I ask gently. Again, she is unable to answer my question.

I never saw this client again. I know in my heart that was a good thing. It meant she either stopped colouring her hair or she fired me for such a blunt, first-appointment conversation! Nah, I had her smiling and laughing by the end of it all. Before she left, she thanked me for explaining to her the part she was missing the most: *her* love.

Greatness is measured by our response to adversity

Don't Run Away, Walk ON!
21. *In the middle of nowhere, 2023*

I am driving along a road I don't recognize. It's not just the road that is unfamiliar; it's the landscape too. There are no trees, nothing green, just a long stretch of highway that goes on for miles. I am so sweaty from the thick air. I feel my pores exploding from the heat, and I am as dry as a prune. I feel shriveled up and sticky at the same time. The piece of shit clunker I'm driving smells of rotten eggs and burnt oil. It wobbles off centre when I go over sixty kilometres.

I hate my life, I think to myself as my hair gets progressively more damp from the perspiration. I gave up on my appearance months ago. I'm wearing a sheer, white, cropped t-shirt that's rocking a couple of food stains. It barely covers my flapjack titties that are flying free from the constraints of a bra. My I-don't-give-a-fuck attitude is complemented by my grey sweatpants, which have holes in the knees and the crotch. I reach for the window button to give myself some sort of relief. This old, rust-covered car didn't come with AC. The window jams and won't go down. I scream so loud my hand jerks the wheel. I struggle to regain control as the cheap rust bucket swerves off the road. I slam my foot down on the brake and bring it to a halt.

I look up and see nothing but a reddish dust cloud and smoke coming from the hood. Frustrated, I punch the centre of the steering wheel. I cry out the last of my anger in defeat. Hot and sweaty tears burn my eyes and cheeks as they fall. I have nothing left in me to give. I want to quit officially, but I lack the courage to drive off the cliff. I collapse forward into the horn, which, surprise, makes no sound. I cry harder than ever before. I can't even beep for help. I hate all that I am. I can't stand the sight or even the existence of myself. I have all but ten dollars to my name, no colour to my soul, and feel completely alone.

Knock! Knock!

I wonder, *Am I imagining this sound?*

Knock! Knock!

Again, I hear the sound. *I must be dying*, I think to myself. *This is my fate: a sweaty pile of crap disintegrating into a state of decay.*

Knock! Knock! Knock!

I notice three knocks instead of two this time. Bleary-eyed, I look up at the window. I don't anticipate seeing anything. I am sure I am just hearing things. But when the dust settles, I see a crisp, white suit and a satin, lavender top underneath it. Shimmering in the sun is the longest, most delicate, gold necklace I have ever seen. It catches my attention like a fish gleaming in the water. I wipe the tears from my eyes, which are stinging from the sweat. *I am seeing things and losing my mind*, I think to myself. *I need water.* As soon as I think it, the thirst hits me, and I am desperate for cool liquid.

KNOCK!

One very loud and powerful knock sounds on the window. I immediately feel afraid. I look up again through the window and see the hand that is making the sound turn towards me. A coil of rose gold with tiny, sparkling diamonds wraps around the long stem of an index finger like tinsel. I instantly recognize that ring means something, but I don't know what it means to me. Her almond-shaped nails are perfectly manicured with an ombre polish that fades from lavender into white tips. My eye is drawn to her hand where I can see a heart tattoo with ten lines that connects to the shape flowing away from it. I can't move an inch. It's as if someone has frozen me in place. I am perfectly still.

"Elisha, my love! Please let me in," she says. Her voice echoes softly through the thick glass window as I wonder, *how does she know my name?*

I am no fussy hussy. I do not give a fuck what I look like. If I don't want to wear makeup while attending to clients, I just don't. But I can also slap on a full face of makeup in ten minutes. I can't believe I used to spend an hour and a half doing my face. Not anymore. I am in love with who I am. I'll show up not wearing underwear if I want to. I love how my body wiggles and jiggles. All those years pretending to be someone else just robbed me of my joy. Trying to live up to what others expected me to be made me lose my self-worth. I've had short hair, and I've had long hair. I used to wear tons of makeup: all black and no colour. No one would recognize me. I couldn't recognize myself. In the past, it was more important to me to have a flat ass with zero curves. This is what I was told was ideal for most of my life. I was led to believe that curves meant you were fat, and it was time to starve yourself.

Now I realize that my body is naturally an hourglass figure, and I embrace it. In fact, I want to invest in it. I want to feel confident in my body. And that means both embracing what's natural and making changes where I want. Can I get a hell ya to Botox and fillers? I know what you're thinking. First, I tell you to love yourself, and next, I tell you to pump your face full of fake shit. Am I being fake? No. I'm merely advocating for investing in yourself no matter what it looks like to the outside world. I have opted for artificial tits, fuller lips by way of fillers, fewer wrinkles thanks to Botox, and long, purple hair. I purposely made these choices for myself. It's about how I want to be seen in this life. I will never explain why. Instead, I say nothing. I allow people to see me for me and they can express their opinions or judgements how they see fit. The right people will always choose to see more.

One hot day in July, I was standing outside the concession of my hometown baseball park where I volunteer my time whenever I can. I wiped the sweat off my brow with my t-shirt, which was covered in grease stains and smelled of deep fryer. I breathed in the fresh air, closed my eyes, and felt thankful for being there. When I opened them, I saw a woman walking towards me. We know one another well and have shared our stories and tears over the years, fighting for the lives we deserve. I greeted her with a warm, love-filled smile.

"You are so beautiful!" she exclaimed. I decided to accept the compliment so as not to insult her. I humbly bowed my head down and blushed.

"Aside from all this…," she began, as she waved her hand over my body from head to toe, "…you are beautiful down to your soul, and that makes you irresistible." I giggled back and accepted her words because they are the truth. I embraced her body in a tight hug and thanked her for the compliment. In the end, it doesn't matter what we do to our bodies. The point is, never do anything that will corrupt your soul because that is where the real beauty comes from. My friend reminded me of that and inspired me to live up to it.

Sometimes we create a vision of the perfect life, and decide we'll only be happy if we get it. What kind of sick, fucked up way of thinking is that? Here's the punch line for you: once you get the house, a fancy car, two kids, and buy your wife a new pair of tits or whatever the fuck it is, you will not necessarily be happy because you are living according to your ego. Money can't buy happiness. Sure. Alright. But it *helps*. Money has allowed me the freedom to live my life the way I want. I wanted to make over my body. I wanted more time to devote to writing. I took some financial risks for these things. Instead of owning one small business, I now own three. I believed in myself and invested the money that I worked for back into myself, and it's paid dividends.

What is the definition of power? The ability to direct or influence another's behaviour or a chain of events. I believe in the power of authentic apologies. Simply saying sorry doesn't fly with me and over the years I have learned it takes regret, remorse, and resolution. I have seen people refuse to apologize because they believe it would mean giving away their power. The truth is, you're actually taking it back. When I want to make amends for hurting someone I care about, I am saying, "I am not afraid to be vulnerable in front of you." How are authentic apologies and power linked? It takes so much strength to admit when you are wrong.

It's hard to see clearly when tragedy strikes and the darkness hovers; however, greatness is measured by our response to adversity. It's imperative to face forward and leave the pain, trauma, and suffering you have endured behind. If you find yourself struggling after suffering a loss, it could be because you're still stuck there, in the past. I have learned that you are your own worst enemy until you make peace with your past. Did you know the right thing to do and the hardest thing to do are usually the same thing? Nothing that has meaning is going to be easy, but peace takes root the moment you begin to grow from your experience.

    I want to understand joy, but I realize that I have to appreciate the meaning of happiness to discover joy. What is happiness? Well, I will tell you what it is not. Happiness is not found in travel or possessions. Happiness isn't worn or bought. Happiness isn't found in another, although part of your happiness can lay there. I believe that happiness involves a spiritual awakening within oneself when one experiences love, grace, and gratitude. Love is the most powerful force in the universe. It breaks all rules and laws, overpowers any army or government. I have lost family, friends, and a part of my future, but I am still willing to forgive. That is real love.

    A lot of the time, people believe certain things will make them happy, but they keep it to themselves. They don't put it out there. Talk about it. Say it. Shout it from the roof tops, because when you do, it will become a reality. I see a vision of happiness and joy in my mind and have the courage to speak about it. I don't shy away from my vision, nor do I stay silent. Not anymore. I see opportunities and I see the potential I have. I have attracted the beauty and wealth I desire. Over the past five years, I have manifested everything I wanted. But I had to know what it was that I wanted in order to be able to aim for it. I started over with my family, relationships, career, and education. I identified the bad habits and addictions that were dragging me down, and I challenged those choices. I developed a vision and focused on it with the attitude that nothing is impossible. Little by little, I moved towards my vision. Did you know that all the pleasure is in the moving forward part? Just like sex. You know where you're going to end up but there are so many exciting and new ways of getting there. When you set up a goal that is on the edge of conceivability, but you move towards it anyway, you will be stronger.

Dipen Parmar said, "The magic you are looking for is in the work you are avoiding." I fell in love with this quote, but I'm not advocating for being hard on yourself; it's not fucking motivating. I've watched members of my family endure shame because of some perceived failure. Either they are stressed about money or overwhelmed with regret over past choices. "What if I had done things differently?" they ask themselves.

"But you didn't," I tell them. "So, beating yourself up about where you are now doesn't make any sense. It will just drown you and take you deeper into the gutter."

Sometimes, I celebrate my losses more than my wins because I feel like I am still winning. To me, if I get what I want, that is direction; but, if I don't get what I want, that is *protection*. I didn't get to be a police officer. I didn't actually want to have kids. But now, I have a career that is beyond anything I could have dreamed of. It fills my soul and ignites my passion. And I know now that I was meant to be a mother. There have been many lonely moments in my life, but I have pushed through. I have not given in to failure. When it was hard and I was overwhelmed, I felt afraid. I walked alone and often felt invisible. I had no answers and couldn't see a way through, but I kept going. What is done is done, and what is gone is gone. Always move on. Don't run away but walk the fuck on. This is why the rearview mirror in your car is smaller. You are meant to take a glimpse to see how far you've come, but not to focus on it.

Stop waiting around for something or someone to save you. Be your own hero. It is about your life and your vision. Surrender to your greater self. Even in the most terrifying times and during the hardest and most stressful things, you will radiate. That, my dear reader, builds unstoppable character. You are impenetrable. Uncomfortable situations will not be easy, but don't shy away. Greatness isn't attained by never failing; it's acquired by never giving up on your vision.

How do you start? By making it a priority and removing distractions. I tell the people who are not worth my time, "I am busy." What am I really saying? I have no time to waste on you. Outgrowing people who are bringing you down shows you are healing. You're able to make space for healthier and more enriching friendships. I've thought a lot about losing friendships over the years, and I realize that the older I get, the more accepting of myself I become, and I just have less need for validation. When it comes to friendships now, it's more about quality than quantity for me. I have fewer friendships, but they are more meaningful.

I know people talk. How can they not? Everyone wants to question the unknown and what they see as unfamiliar. If everyone around me was supporting me, then I wouldn't be striving so hard to expand my level of success and reach beyond the stars. I chose the road less travelled. I stopped waiting for the light at the end of the tunnel and lit that bitch up myself. The adversity I faced was the spark to my mother fucking fire.

I hate it when people say, "We are all in the same boat." The fuck we are! We are in the same shit storm. Some of us are in yachts, some are in canoes, others are in rafts with a slow leak, and some of us are fucking drowning. Let's be fucking nice to each other. I'm more interested in how someone treats me than what other people think about them. I get questioned all the time about this. People ask, "How are you friends with so-and-so?" Because they treat me really well. I may not like the way they drink, play ball, or dress, but none of that matters to me. I care about how someone makes me feel.

You cannot change your life by doing the same thing you've always done. You must change something. If you always do what you always did, you'll always get what you always got. Become the author of your life. I did. It started by placing "I am" in front of my name and being truthful. But there is more. I want to show people more of my life when I became my true self and how I secured more wealth, joy, abundance, power, peace, and love. I want to pass on all my knowledge for the greater good. I want to leave my mark and finish my story with one last ride.

Dream big because dreams are free. Those who dream small are afraid of disappointment, but I say take the risk. Seriously take it and if you fail, accept the pain, and try again. Remember to have an attitude of gratitude. I understand where this gift comes from. It's not mine; it was given to me by the grace of God. I use what I have been given to help others because I know that on my last day, I can't take any of it with me. I choose to leave it here. I choose to influence people.

Isn't *that* the definition of power?

I place my hand carefully on the car door handle and hear it creak open. The scorching heat hits me like a wave, and the skin on my face is instantly on fire. The sun is beating down, and there isn't a cloud in the sky nor a hint of a breeze. Suddenly, I feel something cool touch my cheek; it brings me relief. I see that I have been handed an ice-cold bottle of water. I snatch it up in desperation. I chug the entire contents within seconds and gasp for air when I pull the bottle away from my mouth. My body starts to rejuvenate as my brain reconnects. For a brief moment, I have clarity. The sun is no longing blazing down. I am in the shade. Did a cloud finally grace me with its presence? No, it's *her!* This mysterious woman has moved her body in front of the sun to shield me. Before I have time to blink, she holds out her hand to me. She doesn't say a single word, but I know in my heart to grab hold. She carefully leads me to a white car. I have never seen hair so long and perfectly shaped into soft waves. They bounce gently along the curve of her back, shiny and vibrant. The colour is something else; it's rare and majestic. For some reason, I feel safe with her.

Her car is not ordinary either. A kind of holographic, rose-coloured shimmer reflects off the white paint. As we approach, I see a bright light also bounces off the tires—rose-gold rims radiate a special glow. It is the most beautiful car I have ever seen. She opens the passenger door and guides me carefully inside to the white leather seats with her left hand, as a gentleman would escort a lady. Before she lets go, I see the tiniest rose gold band on her left ring finger; it has three small pink diamonds in the center of it and two baguette diamonds on each side. The ring itself is so little, but I feel its significance. I can tell this miniature jewel that encircles the tattoo of a rose on this finger is of great importance.

After closing my door, she moves delicately but with purpose and direction. She puts one foot in front of the other elegantly as she strides along the front of the car. There isn't a single speck of dust or dirt on her. Next to her, I feel immediately ashamed. I don't belong here. Her white seats are now covered in my filth. I feel unworthy of all her kindness.

I watch her place her hands on the steering wheel and press the ignition button. The power she holds puts me in a trance and cold tears start to restore my dry cheeks. I am lighter. I decide to be brave and look at her for the first time. She meets my gaze with a look of delight. I see her cheeks dimple and her glowing skin light up. I want to look away so badly. I feel my eyes start to slowly turn downward in defeat. But then something happens. She does something I haven't done in a lifetime. She flexes the muscles at the sides of her mouth and generates a smile. I sense joy. She is smiling at me, and I see that I am her joy. Words don't need to be said. With that smile, she is communicating to me that I am of great importance. I am important to *her*. But what comes next changes my life forever.

"It's time, my love, to let *me* drive!" she says with all the love in her heart as she takes that same bejeweled finger and tucks a purple strand of hair behind her ear.

*End the silence
by pursuing yourself*

EPILOGUE

This was my story, emphasis on *was*. It was a story that held me back from reaching my life's full potential. It was a story I told others about how hard or bad I had it. It was the same story I told myself: that I wasn't meant to be happy, successful, wealthy, or sexy and that I didn't deserve a man to share it all with. I told that story with a pen, filling pages and pages of my journals. But with this book, it is different. I realize now that the story I had put down in my journals had actually been written by other people, and it was time to let go of those pages. It was time to take control and write my own story. The most empowering thing I have done is to simply be *me* and let others be *themselves*. Let them be wrong. Let them misunderstand. Let them judge. I now recognize I cannot control the actions of others, but I do have the power to choose my response.

There is so much in life that is unnatural, but a feeling between two people can be the most natural thing. I thought the ocean was the bluest thing in the world, but I was wrong. His eyes stare at me and I am incapacitated. I lose all feeling and strength in the depth of calm I find in those deep blue circles that embrace me. If I ever doubted that there was a God, I am faced with the proof that is before me. How else did such a beautiful man come into existence? When those eyes lock on mine,

I can't help but fall into a trance. His gaze lifts my soul as his hands cradle my jawline and he pulls my face towards him.

It's not what he does for me that makes me love him—dare I say love? Has my heart opened to love? This will be the first time I have ever loved a man and not his potential. It's the first time that I am focusing on him as he is now, and not what he might possibly become. He leans over ever so carefully, as if my lips were made of glass. I close my eyes so I can drink in his scent—a mix of orange, vanilla, and cinnamon from the cologne that he's just applied to his skin. I am falling in love with his kindness and his strength that protects me from the rain and the hot sun. His love is my safe haven. I have never been cared for so completely by a man before.

"You, just as you are, are enough," he tells me. He knows he doesn't need to save me. He just needs to stand by me. He even takes my crying in stride. "I love you, my beautifully cascading waterfall of emotion," he tells me as he brushes my tears away. He is there to hold me and to kiss me, and the warmth in his kiss immediately comforts me. I trust him with my life. He has my heart, and my whole being. He worships the ground I walk on, but I kiss his feet with every step. My lips are still attached to his when they start to form a smile. I gently pull back. Our eyes lock. "What are you thinking, my love?" he asks.

In the beginning, I never thought anyone would take my writing seriously. Why should they? I never took any part of myself seriously. I now realize how common that feeling is, to not ever feel like you are enough or that you are seen for who you are. I started writing because I was being held captive by the life I had lived. When I started writing, it was so freeing. I suddenly felt as if I had found my voice, my purpose. I had power.

Anyone who has ever had a taste of that knows how intoxicating it is. At the same time, it takes courage to live my life out in the open, to lay bare my weaknesses for all to see. But regardless of the outcome, I know my worth. I chose not to conceal the most important thing I have: the truth. And by telling the truth, I have given myself peace. I have proven to myself that I can have any kind of life I want. I can persevere through anything and achieve what I want. In fact, I am entitled to it. If I refuse to set limits, they don't exist.

I'd never have found true love if I hadn't embraced my true self first. If you don't know what to pursue in life, pursue yourself. Pursue becoming the healthiest, happiest, most healed, present, and confident version of yourself. Then the right path will reveal itself.

What am I thinking? I ask myself, as I look away from him with pools of water brewing in my eyes. My smile spreads bigger than ever before. I can't believe how much joy and peace I have. I look at the last man I will ever kiss and answer his question.

"I am now complete."

ACKNOWLEDGEMENTS

I am beyond blessed to have the support of so many wonderful people who brought my career as a writer and motivational speaker to life. There will never be enough words to convey my gratitude.

- To Alison, my beautiful editor, I wouldn't be the writer I am today without your strength. You have created the space I needed to heal. You have helped me write unforgettable words of powerful meaning. I couldn't have done it without you.

- To Petya, my incredible designer, thank you for listening to every word and idea throughout our collaboration on both books. You make me look good.

- To Megan and Ira, the TSPA team who helped create Elisha Rose, thank you for hearing me. I am so grateful to have both of you in my corner every step of the way as a writer, author, speaker, and influencer. You have helped me become the woman I am today.

- To Mackenzie, my social media manager, you have captured my heart. Your influence and knowledge have helped me become the kind of inspirational leader I have always dreamed of being. A huge thanks to you.

- To Lisa, my friend, you have opened so many doors for me and given me endless opportunities within the indigenous community. Thank you for believing in my work.

- To Lindsay, my friend and travel agent, without your consistent efforts and the attention you pay to every detail, I would be lost. Thank you.

- To my clients, thank you for your ongoing support. You are the reason I continue to get behind the chair.

- To Ayms, my fur baby, whenever I cried, no matter where you were or what you were doing, you would find me and sit with me. Thank you for joining me on a month-long adventure away from any human soul and for carrying me, protecting me, and keeping me alive.

- To my immediate family, I love each and every one of you. Thank you for accepting me as I am through all the hardships and triumphs.

- To my girls, you know who you are. Thank you for giving me my greatest lesson in life: always remember to eat the slice of humble apple pie.

- To Kalyn, Jena, and Chelsey, thank you for all the laughs, sweat, and tears. You ladies keep my blood pumping.

- To my children, Tanner, Hailey, and Remi, know that everything I am and have become is because of you. You keep my heart beating.

- To Marshall, thank you for being my best friend, my soulmate, and the last man I will ever kiss.

www.ingramcontent.com/pod-product-compliance
Lightning Source LLC
LaVergne TN
LVHW072021060526
838200LV00009B/225